ECONOMICS OF THE BRITISH BOOKTRADE, 1605–1939

Bibliographical note:

This title was originally to be published in the Publishing Pathways series by Oxford Polytechnic Press. Unfortunately, as a consequence of radical reorganisation of the Publishing programme at Oxford Polytechnic, the Press can no longer operate as originally devised and this book, which had already been prepared for publication by the Press, now forms the first volume in an occasional series to accompany the journal Publishing History. Other titles in the Oxford Polytechnic Press Publishing Pathways series are listed at the back of this volume.

PUBLISHING HISTORY
OCCASIONAL SERIES
1

Economics of the British Booktrade 1605-1939

EDITED BY
ROBIN MYERS
AND
MICHAEL HARRIS

CHADWYCK-HEALEY
CAMBRIDGE/ALEXANDRIA, VA
1985

First published 1985

Chadwyck-Healey Ltd
Cambridge Place
Cambridge CB2 1NR
U.K.

Chadwyck-Healey Inc.
1021 Prince Street
Alexandria, VA 22314
U.S.A.

ISBN 0 85964 169 4

House Editors (Oxford Polytechnic Press): Kate Annis, Dawn Ashmore, Christine Evenden, Caroline Hersey, Sarah Hornsby, Nancy Miles
Text set by: Jennifer Watts
Production: Robin Adams

Contents

Illustrations		vii
Preface		ix
Notes on Contributors		xi
List of Conference Members		xii
Acknowledgements		xiii
Robin Myers	The Financial Records of the Stationers' Company, 1605-1811	1
John Hetet	The Wardens' Accounts of the Stationers' Company, 1663-79	32
Frank Melton	Robert and Sir Francis Gosling: Eighteenth-Century Bankers & Stationers	60
Michael Turner	The Personnel of the Stationers' Company, 1800-30: Work in Progress	78
John Hewish	The Patent Office as Publisher, 1853-60	103
Mirjam Foot	Some Bookbinders' Price Lists of the Seventeenth & Eighteenth Centuries	124

Michael Harris	Moses Pitt & Insolvency in the London Booktrade in the late-Seventeenth Century	176
James Barnes	Depression & Innovation in the British and American Booktrade, 1819-1939	209

Illustrations

1 From Check Book 1738-1743: 'Received out of the Poors Box to pay the fees of Wood Street Counter for the Delivery of John Vousden, a poor member of this Company, £1.10s.' 4

2 From Journal Book of Money Disbursed 1650-1698: showing haphazard marginal crosses which indicate separation of Corporation Stock accounts 8

3 From The Poor Book 1608-1676: showing payments to Clerk, Beadle and Clerk's assistant: 'To the Clerk of this company for Ingrossing and Entring this Account £1. To the Beadle for giving notice for the Pensioners to attend £1. To the clerks man 2s.6d.' 10

4 Typical entry showing auditing of accounts: from English Stock Disbursements 1667-1777 16

5 Unidentified memorandum on flyleaf of Books in the Treasurer's Warehouse 1663-1723: 'Quere. Whether any Composition money was ever Charged to acct which was received of severall persons who compounded with the Company for stolen & Counterfeit Impressions of School Books and Almanacks...' 19

6 The title-page of the octavo Livery List of the Stationers' Company issued in 1810 81

7 The head of the List in the 1810 issue showing the Master, Wardens and Assistants of the Company 82

8 The first page of the List of Liverymen in 1810 84

9 An extract from Apprentices Bound, Turned Over, Free and Cloathed 1810-65 88

10 An example of the Company's apprenticeship records found in the Memo Books showing details of each apprentice 92

11 An extract from the Beadle's Book 94

12 A page from the Treasurer's Abstract of Wills giving details of the deceased, the executors and the transfer of shares 96

13 List of binding prices 'Imprinted at London 1619.' 139

14 List of binding prices 'Printed at London 1646.' 146

15 List of binding prices 'LONDON: Printed, and are to be Sold by John Whitlock near Stationers-Hall. 1695.' 157

16 Detail from John Ogilby and William Morgan: 'A New and Accurate Map of the City of London', 1676, showing the location of Pitt's shop at the junction of Pater-Noster-Row and Paul's Alley (i 35) 179

17 Plan 'Taken between 1734 and 1738' and printed in John Thomas Smith: Antiquities of Westminster, 1807. It shows the main area of Pitt's Westminster developments 184

18 Detail from John Kip: 'A Prospect of the City of London, Westminster and St James's Park', c. 1710-20, showing the house extended for Chief Justice Jefferies (with the steps into the Park) and other properties built by Pitt 196

Preface

The sixth annual conference on booktrade history, held under the auspices of the University of London Extra-Mural Department, took place on 22 and 23 November 1984, in the Department's rooms at 32 Tavistock Square. It was a larger conference than before, both in size of audience (nearly fifty) and in number of papers given (eight instead of the customary six). It provided, even more than usual, we thought, a stimulating mixture of hard work and socialising, for both speakers and audience. The theme of the economics of the booktrade had been chosen originally so that J.J. Barnes could make a contribution to the 1984 conference during his sabbatical leave in England. But in the event his was almost the only paper not to be based in some way on the Stationers' Company records; as such it made a relaxing finale to the concentrated mental diet of the first one-and-a-half days. The inclusion of two extra papers was also something of a happy accident. Mirjam Foot offered us her paper on some early bookbinders' price lists which we could not refuse, as the saying goes, while Frank Melton happened to come to Stationers' Hall in July in search of Gosling material for his forthcoming book on the bank's origins. This also seemed an opportunity not to be missed to include a paper on the man who became the Company's banker in a symposium by then so largely given over to Stationers' Company research.

Once more we are indebted to Tom Colverson, Tony Watts, Bob Woodings and Keith Vaughan for preparing the text and organising the publication of our proceedings by Chadwyck-Healey. Alas, the Oxford Polytechnic Press, as originally constituted, has been phased out with the replacement of the Diploma in Book Publishing course by the new Publishing degree programme. But fortunately Chadwyck-Healey have undertaken to continue publication under the new title of Publishing History Occasional Series, which will be companion to the journal Publishing History. The next conference will be held on 23 and 24 November 1985. The theme will be bibliophily and the proceedings will be published as Publishing History Occasional Series no. 2. Speakers will include Mirjam Foot, Michael Harris, Brian North Lee, Anthony Lister, Murray McLaggan, Robin Myers and Katherine Swift.

Robin Myers
Michael Harris

London
January 1985

Notes on Contributors

ROBIN MYERS is Honorary Archivist of the Stationers' Company. She is the moving force behind past conference papers and has written extensively on areas of booktrade history.

JOHN HETET was editor of the Early Imperial Project based on the Alexander Turnbull Library, New Zealand. He is currently working in Cambridge on a study of Dissenters and the London booktrade in post-Restoration England.

FRANK MELTON is Associate Professor of History at the University of North Carolina. His book entitled Sir Robert Clayton and the Origins of English Deposit Banking, 1658-1685 will be published by CUP in 1987.

MICHAEL TURNER is Head of Conservation at the Bodleian Library, Oxford, where he also lectures on the History of Printing. He is editor of Publishing History and is now working on a study of the membership of the London booktrade between 1800 and 1830.

JOHN HEWISH, a graduate of Lincoln College, Oxford, is at present working in the Patent Office, a part of the British Library. He has written and translated a variety of scientific and literary works.

MIRJAM FOOT is Assistant Keeper at the British Library with special responsibility for the bookbinding collections. She has published extensively on this subject, her major study being of the bindings in the Henry Davis Gift.

MICHAEL HARRIS is Lecturer in History at London University's Extra-Mural Department. As well as acting as joint-editor of these conference papers, he has written and lectured widely on areas of booktrade and newspaper history.

JAMES BARNES is Hadley Professor of History at Wabash College, Indiana. He has written widely on Anglo-American bookselling and publishing. His most recent study examines the 1930s' translations of Hitler's Mein Kampf.

List of Conference Members

Sarah Adair

Klitos Andreas, University of Leeds

Jean Archibald, British Library

Nicolas Barker, British Library

Patience Barnes

Charles Benson, Trinity College, Dublin

Gerald Bentley

Michael Bywater, Institute of Chartered Accountants

Fiona Campbell, bookbinder and bookseller

Tom Colverson

Andrew S. Cook, India Office Library

Michael Crump, British Library

Nest E.M. Davies

J.A. Edwards, Librarian, University of Reading

David Foxon

Peter Hames, Worshipful Company of Stationers

David Hall, University Library, Cambridge

C.M. Hartley

A.W. Huish

Barry C. Johnson, British Library

Anna Kasket, Trinity College, Cambridge

C.L. Lee

Dr Anthony Lister

Laurie Maguie

Giles Mandelbrote, St John's College, Oxford

Ian Maxted, Library of West Country Studies, Exeter

E.M. Mitchell

Charles Parry

Margaret Payne, National Book League

Michael Perkin, University Library, Liverpool

Julie S. Peters

Esther Potter

James Raven, Clare College, Cambridge

Christopher Rivington, Worshipful Company of Stationers

Laura Roe

Alison Shell, St Hilda's College, Oxford

Peter Stockham, bookseller

Katherine Swift, St Anne's College, Oxford

Keith Vaughan, Oxford Polytechnic

Tony Watts, Oxford Polytechnic

Eva Weininger

R.B. Woodings, Oxford Polytechnic

Guests

Kate Annis

Caroline Hersey

Acknowledgements

Illustrations for 'The Financial Records of the Stationers' Company, 1605-1811' and for 'The Personnel of the Stationers' Company, 1800-30' are reproduced by permission of the Worshipful Company of Stationers and Newspaper Makers and of the Curators of the Bodleian Library; illustrations for 'Some Bookbinders' Price Lists...' are reproduced by permission of the Society of Antiquaries of London (list dated 1619) and of The British Library; illustrations for 'Moses Pitt & Insolvency in the London Booktrade...' are reproduced by permission of the Guildhall Library, City of London.

Grateful acknowledgement is also made to the R.R. Bowker Company for permission to reprint James Barnes's 'Depression and Innovation in the British and American Book Trade, 1819-1939', which was first published in <u>Books and Society in History</u> (© 1983 Xerox Corporation).

The Financial Records of the Stationers' Company, 1605–1811

Robin Myers

'The foreigner', J.B. Priestley wrote, 'hears us whispering together in public places and concludes that we are exchanging trade figures or doleful news, and not the little jokes he would not understand if he heard them'.[1] My subject is just trade figures and doleful news about the haphazard way that the Stationers' Company kept its financial books between 1605 and 1811, with little in the way of jokes to lighten it.

'A tradesman's books are his repeating clock', wrote Daniel Defoe in the Complete Tradesman, 'which upon all occasions tell him how he goes on'.[2] Not so those of the Stationers' Company in the period under review: its books bore little relation either to the recommendations of experts and teachers of book-keeping or to what was ordered by the Court from time to time, as a comparison of Appendixes I and IV will readily reveal.

'The company faced in every possible direction', Michael Treadwell wrote to me when I first mooted this paper, 'since it bought, sold, loaned, borrowed, ran a joint stock company etc etc, so that it presents as wide a range of evidence as you could want and any one of a number of angles to exploit'.[3] Cyprian Blagden's classic paper on the management of the English Stock in Stuart times provided a masterly exploitation of one such angle.[4] He used the Stock book and other financial records to tabulate the Stock's income and expenditure in order to show how the payment of a large dividend outweighed all considerations of solvency and trading common sense. Blagden was accustomed to making such deductions from balance sheets and accounts in his daily life as a director of Longman, and he had a monumental grasp of the Company's complex history. Another angle was exploited by John Hetet in his paper on evidence of the Company's policy in search and seizure drawn from the Wardens' Accounts in the crucial years 1663-79 leading up to the Exclusion Crisis of 1679.[5]

Instead of trying to exploit yet another angle I shall describe the range of the Company's financial books, showing how they interlock and overlap, how they supplement the non-financial records and are supplemented by them. I have chosen to start at 1605 chiefly because the setting up of the English Stock two years earlier revolutionised the Company's affairs and ought to have revolutionised its method of book-keeping; it made the Stationers, alone amongst livery companies, into a trading organisation needing to keep efficient profit and loss accounts.

The earliest financial records are contained in a single all-purpose volume, known as Register A and labelled on the spine 'Wardens' Accounts'. It is kept on the shelves among the later entry books and generally considered to be a mainly non-financial book. The accounts in this volume were admirably dealt with by Blagden in his paper on 'the Accounts of the Wardens of the Stationers' Company, 1557-96',[6] and this was based, in its turn, on Edward Arber's introduction to the early registers.[7] By the middle of the nineteenth century (to turn to the other end of the period under review) the Company had moved into the contemporary world, was using cash books, journals and ledgers and was having its books balanced and audited by professionals, in a way that continued everywhere until the advent of the computer.

What I here present is very much work in progress and merely purports to offer a few lines for further investigation. The start of my study was an attempt, for another purpose, to put the records in order as they stood on the shelves of the newly-set-up muniment room, which was formerly the Musicians' Company's robing room. The room is large enough to accommodate all the records previously scattered through the building, some in a small muniment room behind the hall, others in a book-case in the library, the rest in the damp silver vaults under the hall. Not only did they inevitably get jumbled up in the move, but an examination of existing indexes and catalogues showed that they had always been arranged somewhat haphazardly and that, in any case, there was too much overlap of the contents of the volumes for any arrangement which accorded with the ideals of logic and immutable order to be possible.

The muniment room contains some four hundred and fifty bound volumes of records as well as boxes of supplementary material. The pre-1800 records consist of some one hundred and sixty volumes, of which only about thirty-five can be positively identified as financial, being labelled 'accounts', 'disbursements', 'account of books delivered', and the like, and comprising columns of figures inside. It is impossible to exclude certain categories of record not wholly (or at all) financial, if a complete picture is to emerge of the way the Company's books were kept.

There are two broad areas of Stationers' Company finance, that of the corporation, or Company as a whole, and that of the English Stock. A joint-stock company trading in books in the English language, its shareholders or partners were all members of the Company. Not only did the Stock operate from Stationers' Hall and keep its book stocks in the warehouse on the premises, but it owned most of the corporation's real estate during the time that concerns us, and even, until 1771, the corporation's very hall.

'Inextricably mixed as usual', Blagden comments from time to time, and he put it in a nutshell when he wrote 'The borderline between Company affairs and Stock affairs, between Company income and Stock income, between Company property and Stock property, was always wavy and at times indistinguishable even to the officials involved'.[8] Yet it is essential to distinguish between the two if any sense is to be made of the records. The Court itself tried to do so on several occasions. On 2 July 1658 it appointed 'a committee...to view the accounts of the corporation and Stock, to set the same even, to ascertain for the time to come the distinct charge of either'.[9]

The earliest extant financial record, if we leave Register A out of it, is the Book for Entraunce of Fines (1605-40), which itemises fees paid for membership and fines for misdemeanours such as binding more than the permitted number of apprentices, as well as fines for non-service of office. It is rather crudely bound in limp vellum and the way it is entered up indicates something more than a waste book or book of first entry, but less than a ledger or book of third entry, suggesting that it was made up after meetings as a temporary record. There is almost no other book devoted entirely to corporation finances. It is followed, after a gap of eight years, by a series of three 'check' books spanning the years 1648-1805. Greg described these as 'similar to...a bank "pass book"'[10] and I hesitated before disagreeing with such an authority; but they are certainly nothing of the kind and are more nearly approximate to memorandum or waste books of fees, fines and payments to the poor. They are more hastily written than the Book of Fines and arranged according to Court, as General Purposes, Pension and Stock. They are the record, made by the Clerk, of payments made during the progress of each Court. Unlike the Book of Fines the check books include certain charitable disbursements such as the following for 21 July 1711: 'Received out of the Poors Box to pay the fees of Wood Street Counter for the Delivery of John Vousden, a poor member of this

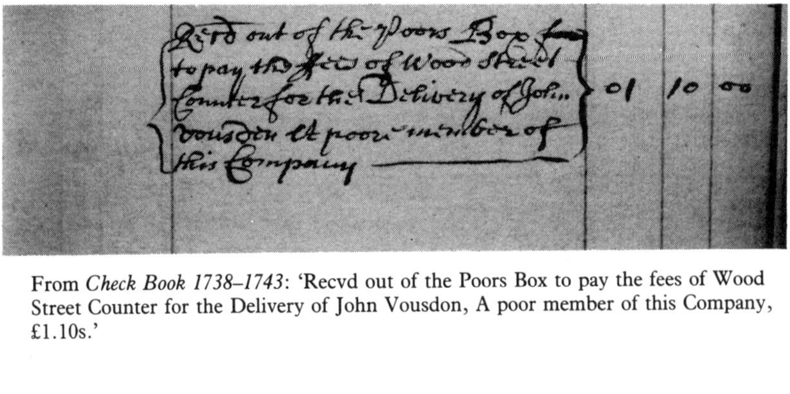
Recd out of the Poors Box for
to pay the fees of Wood Street
Counter for the Delivery of John
Vousden the poor member of
this Company — 01 10 00

From *Check Book 1738–1743*: 'Recvd out of the Poors Box to pay the fees of Wood Street Counter for the Delivery of John Vousdon, A poor member of this Company, £1.10s.'

Company, £1.10s.'

The Renter-Wardens' Accounts of dues of 4d per quarter paid by the freemen at Quarterly Courts, were entered in Quarterage Books, (1646-1800). Greg found them 'done up in brown paper parcels and placed in the loft'[11] in the 1920s and there they apparently remained until 1940 when Graham Pollard tried to warn Sidney Hodgson, the Company's first archivist, of the danger they were in during the Blitz. He replied to a letter of Pollard's on 22 October 1940:

> When you wrote some days ago asking if I would go to Stationers' Hall to find certain items which you said ought to be taken care of, I went to the Hall and to the place you mentioned, but I found nothing which corresponded with your description. And now, alas, a great tragedy has happened - an incendiary bomb dropped through the roof just in the lobby between the Hall & the Court Room & has done considerable damage.[12]

The importance of the Quarterage Books was that they 'noted the addresses of the members of the Company each quarter, and these books were important for tracing the careers of journeymen and other freemen who were never admitted to the livery', as Pollard put it, 'These details were not available from any other source.'[13] They were the only serious archival casualty of the Second World War, and the many rulings in the Court Books concerning the way these Renter Wardens' accounts were to be kept and audited make their loss all the more tantalising for those who came on the scene in later years.

The sole surviving book of second entry, or journal, is the Journal Book of Money Disbursed (1656-98), but we find occasional references to other journals in the Books in the Treasurer's Warehouse where, in 28 July 1713 we read of 'money as per journal', for example. The Journal Book exemplifies, among other things, the difficulty in 'setting even' the corporation and Stock accounts. The end of the volume is given to Stock disbursements from 1679-98, but the larger part contains a mixture of Stock and corporation entries. There are marginal crosses against certain entries, probably indicating posting marks, but from February 1691-2 onwards, the marginal marks are set against corporation items only which makes it almost impossible to work out a rhyme or reason for the marks.

Blagden did not fully document the sources from which he skilfully unravelled the legal and financial tangle of ownership of the hall, but it is to be assumed that he used the Court Books, the Wardens' Accounts, the Journal Book and the supplementary loose bills from the Company's builder Robert Wapshot and other workmen. From this data it would seem he discovered that the cost of rebuilding the hall after the Great Fire was shared between corporation and Stock, although the land the hall stood on belonged to the Stock. It was leased for ninety-nine years at ten pounds per annum to the corporation, who also bore the costs of maintenance and alterations, that is to say they had it on a full repairing lease. Always short of money, they looked round, then as now, for ways of defraying their costs and let the hall to companies which had no hall of their own, as they still do, and for celebrations such as St Cecilia's Day, weddings, funerals and the like.[14]

In 1690 the Court sought to double its income from lettings by building a new kitchen 'on the company's void ground' and converting the old kitchen into warehouses which, it was estimated, would bring in thirty pounds per annum. There had been complaints that the existing kitchens, 'being under the hall, the smoak and steam of the victuals' wafted up and spoilt the festivities'.[15] In 1734 the corporation made a profitable deal with the managers of the charitable corporation lottery by letting the hall for three months, 'they making good all damages'.[16]

When the corporation at last came into possession of its own hall in 1771 the Court ordered a financial survey to be made of all the corporation and Stock property. It was the first of its kind, despite the order of 28 February 1678 for a 'book of Rents [of the Stock] and when due'. William Leybourn, the Company's surveyor, had made an exhaustive set of plans of the Company's property after the Fire, but this was not a financial document. The Particular and Rental of Estates Belonging to the Company of Stationers (1773) is thorough, methodical and beautiful. Red-ruled throughout, with fine calligraphic headings and initials, it sets out details of tenancies, names of tenants, terms of leases, fire insurance, land tax and repairs. We learn from it that the warehouses under the hall, which replaced the old kitchen, still belonged to the Stock, whereas the houses and warehouses round the hall were corporation property. It was the first successful attempt to disentangle corporation and Stock possessions. There is no evidence to suggest that the efforts of 1691 were ever carried out: in that year the Court ordered the setting up of a committee 'to consider some effectual ways of checking all accounts relating to the company and their Stock'.[17] Their findings were approved and the Court ordered that: 'the Upper Warden...to keep a book, and every court enter therein, on one side all receipts and payments on the corporation account, and on the other side all receipts and payments on the stock account to be a check and charge to the under warden and treasurer'.[18] In the event, only the haphazard marginal crosses in the Journal Book of Money Disbursed indicate any such separation.

The three volumes of Wardens' Accounts (1663-1837) provide the fullest single record of the corporation's income and expenditure, but they also include Stock finances. The Wardens' Accounts are the most imposing looking of all the financial books in the muniment room, being massive folios bound in reverse calf and they lack the tell-tale doodles and memos which so often denote that they were entered up by an apprentice.

These accounts were the responsibility of the Under Warden but were copied up fair by some underling. The accounts for the gild years ending 30 June 1694 and 4 July 1696, but not the intervening year ending 30 June 1695, are in the hand of Nicholas Hooper, Beadle from 1692-1703, whose writing is as distinctive as it is indecipherable. Further identification of hands should tell us a good deal more about the way the accounts were kept and the relative importance that the Court assigned to each of them.

There survive two volumes of duplicate Wardens' Accounts, one for the years 1663-9, the other for 1756-9, the first a slim vellum-bound

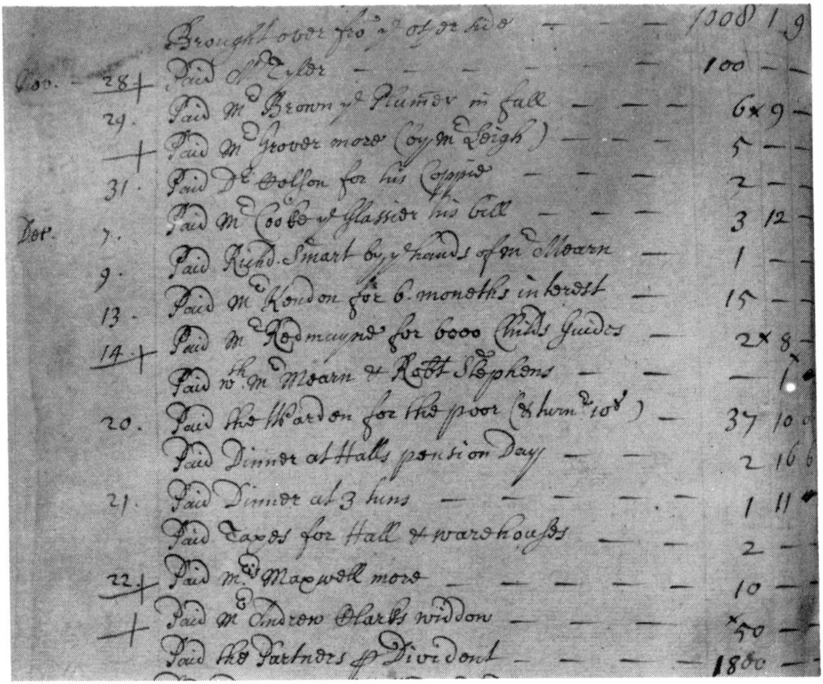

From *Journal Book of Money Disbursed 1650–1698*: showing haphazard marginal crosses which indicate separation of Corporation Stock accounts.

folio, the second a quarto in contemporary marbled wrappers. They are neatly written, with decorative initials, and they are audited. Defoe, writing in the 1720s, advised the 'keeping of a duplicate or pocket ledger in case of fire; especially in the City of London... because so many accidents frequently happen in London, more than in other places, I mean by FIRE'.[19] Duplicate books, kept either as a fire precaution or for secrecy, were not uncommon at this date and the earlier volume, 1663-9, leads one to surmise that it was kept at the instigation of the careful George Tokefield, elected Clerk in 1663, who took the Company's records into the safe keeping of his house in the suburbs during the Great Fire.

I now turn to the charitable side of the Company's finances which ought to be easier, though it is not, to separate into the components of corporation and Stock. The original letters patent setting up the Stock in 1603 stipulated that two hundred pounds per annum of the Stock's profits were to go to the poor of the Company. The Stock Keepers and Court were soon interpreting this as meaning ex-dividend profit; Blagden's examination of the stock accounts revealed that the Court went to the length of borrowing money at interest to pay the dividend, leaving poor payment to be made when the Treasurer had cash in hand. We might expect that the charity accounts would be carelessly kept but for once we would be wrong. Although charitable payments of various kinds are recorded in several books, in Stock and Wardens' accounts, and in the check books, there are also methodical registers of pensioners and the amounts paid to them. The corporation's charitable donations were made from bequests and legacies from individual members of the Company who often specified the kind of alms they wanted to be given. These were entered in a small folio, in account book binding (diced calf), which is labelled 'C2 Wills'. It contains extracts from wills where legacies are left to the Company, (1593-1623), as well as two much later wills, those of James Figgins (1884) and of C.E. Layton (1908).

There were two sorts of alms, one the regular or extraordinary sums doled out at the Pension Courts, the other loans to the penniless to tide them over hard times. The first was recorded in methodical registers of Pensioners, with the amounts given and the Courts at which payments were made. The first of these registers is the <u>Poor Book</u>, whose wrap-around vellum binding proclaims its account book purpose. It is inscribed on the top cover, 'liber computi pro pauperibus'. Professor Craig Ferguson transcribed the list of Pensioners (1608-76) together with those to 1700 in the companion volume,[20] but he omitted such items as the following for October 7th, 1671, which show the book's financial nature: 'To the Clerk of this company for Ingrossing and Entring this Account £1. To the Beadle for giving notice for the Pensioners to attend £1. To the

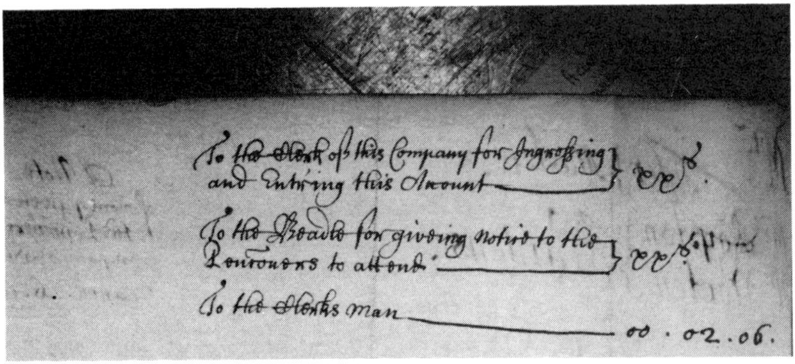

From *The Poor Book 1608–1676*: showing payments to Clerk, Beadle and Clerk's assistant: 'To the Clerk of this company for Ingrossing and Entring this Account £1. To the Beadle for giving notice for the Pensioners to attend £1. To the clerks man 2s.6d.'

clerks man 2s.6d'. This provides evidence of the clerk fulfilling his legal role as an attorney while the Beadle was concerned with the care of the Pensioners themselves. The Beadle continued to look after the care of the Pensioners in this way for more than 350 years until the last man to hold the office, Dudley Ward, retired in December 1984. The Poor Book was followed by an increasingly methodical series of Pension Lists, starting in 1733 and continuing well into the present century. In these later books the Pensioners were listed according to the charity that they were paid under, doled out at Pension Courts which were held quarterly in theory, but rarely in practice.

The interest-free loan made to a member of the Company who had temporarily fallen on hard times or was without enough capital to set up on his own was a different kind of charity paid out from one of five loans bequests. 'This aiding of the enterprising but penniless freeman', Blagden observed, referring to sixteenth- and seventeenth-century custom, 'was a common practice in the London companies.'[21] The borrower generally entered into a conditioned bond, without any penalty for non-repayment, and these bonds are written on blank leaves of the Book of Bequests (1623-75) and, with some overlap, in twelve scattered pages of the disbound Bonds for Moneye Lent (1671-88).

These bonds are meticulously penned legal contracts, signed by two witnesses, the Clerk generally being one. The system of charitable loans was much abused in the mid-seventeenth century when some booksellers retained loans for years on end, thereby blocking the way for the genuinely needy. In 1653 a committee was appointed to look into the matter and to report. Nothing happened and the abuse continued. In 1830 the Charity Commissioners found that all five loan benefactions had 'for a long time been absorbed in the general funds of the Company instead of being used for loans to young Stationers'.[22] Twenty-five years later these bequests went to found the Stationers' School, but that is a story outside the scope of this paper.

Quite a lot can be inferred about the domestic power struggle between Court and Freemen by looking at the relative number of volumes allotted to corporation and Stock finance respectively as they stand on the muniment room shelves. Combined finances of corporation and Stock are contained in seventeen volumes taking up three shelves, while twenty-eight volumes ranged on seven shelves are given entirely to Stock accounts. A cursory look at the contents confirms the impression given by the outward appearance that the Court always concentrated on Stock affairs; the Stock books show a fairly efficient division throughout according to type of business transacted. We see on the other hand that the corporation was constantly starved of funds and it is no wonder that the non-stock-holding freemen, mostly journeymen printers and bookbinders, broke out in open rebellion four times during our period.

At a Court of 28 February 1687-8 the Treasurer of the Stock, henceforward to be called the Warehouse Keeper, was instructed in the 'sort's of bookes to be used'. The Court was aiming to stamp out thefts from the warehouse, printers' sales of overprintings and the Treasurer's trading on the side. Five full pages of Court Book F detail what each book was to be used for. A so-called day book was to be used for noting all sales and purchases of paper 'and other things belonging to the Stock' and the Warehouse Keeper 'shall not sell or deliver any bookes belonging to the Stock (other than almanacks to the Master and Wardens for presents or New Years gifts as hath been accustomed) without present money...' The order concluded with strong words about all books having to be properly kept and produced 'upon the demand of the Master Wardens and Stock Keepers... and full satisfaction given them in any particular from time to time'.[23] The irony was that the order appears to have gone almost unheeded and, as always, practice lagged far behind theory. Curiously enough though, Blagden found that 'the fire of 1666 was rather a stimulus towards a short-lived period of better management'[24] as this order of 1678 and others of 1674 and 1703 prove. The improved efficiency was not to last; we have already seen that no 'booke for rent received and when due' was kept until the one-off survey of rentals of 1773.

We cannot equate the 'sort's of bookes' prescribed with existing books although the Books in the Treasurer's Warehouse, already in use fourteen years before the Court order of 1678, may be regarded as a kind of 'acquittance book': the dividend and Stock assignment books are 'books for business relating to the transferring of parts, fines, and forfeitures',[25] and there are several references in the 1690s to a 'Cambridge book' although there is no extant 'book for business relating to the universities' as such. The Company's arrangements with the two universities were not the same, which can explain the lack of an Oxford or a joint book. Blagden found mention of a separate paper stock ledger before 1650 and a single reference to a seventeenth-century printing book, but neither has survived.

The Stock's income and assets, including rents from property, are recorded in three tall narrow folios, the first, rough calf, labelled Books in the Treasurer's Warehouse (1663-1723), followed by two vellum-bound volumes labelled Accounts of Books Delivered (1723-74). Payments-out were recorded in the English Stock Disbursements but no comparable set of sales ledgers survives. The first profit and loss record for a single title is the Account of Dr Brady and Mr Tate's Psalms (1706-64). It began as an account of the fees paid to the compilers and as time passed it became an analysis of sales and costs. It seems curious that there was no separate almanack account before 1789: it was a momentous event indeed which drove the Court to keep track of the profit and loss of its best-seller. Thomas Carnan's infringement of the almanack patent threatened to scupper the whole Stock prosperity by overturning the rule of perpetual copyright as granted by James I. The story is well known. Carnan died in 1788 and the Stock immediately acquired his interest for £1500. There can be little doubt that this is why the Company started to keep a separate set of almanack account books within a few months of that purchase. From then on until 1869 a methodical sequence of annual accounts was kept, recording numbers of almanacks printed and sold, with details of disbursements and an analysis of profit and loss.

It comes as no surprise to find that the most regular and orderly of all the books is the uniform run of regular dividend payments made to the partners, 1644-1803 and thereafter until 1924. As well as these, there are the records, legal rather than purely financial, of the transfer of shares from one partner to another at death or, less frequently, in cases of bankruptcy or misdemeanour when a partner's share was taken from him. These transfers are to be found in the English Stock Assignments and Receipts (1679-94), the Receipts for Shares Paid out (1785-1800) and the Account of Stock Transferred (1702-43). There is only one surviving minute book of the Stock Board (1755-66), although we know that the Stock Keepers met regularly and minutes must have been taken.

The most efficient part of the Company's early book-keeping was the auditing. 'Many interesting references to auditing are supplied by the existing records of the Livery Companies', wrote Richard Brown.[26] He found that the companies had their books audited from the fifteenth century. The Stationers followed normal livery company practice in having the Company's books checked at the end of each gild year, not by external professionals as they are today, but by senior members of the Court who did the best they could to check the totals and look for irregularities. Arithmetical errors often slipped through, and if the auditors could not get the books to balance they would happily put cash from their own pockets to make up the deficiency.[27] They then signed and dated the last page to signify their satisfaction that all was well. At a General Court of 3 July 1676 there was an order for 'auditing all the Stock Keepers account since the late dreadful fire',[28] and in 1678 there were two separate orders for auditing 'all such bookes as the auditors shall have occasion for'.[29] It was at that point that a case of embezzlement came before the Court, probably not the only one in the Company's long history although the only one to come before the Court. Richard Clarke, the retiring Under Warden, was told to prepare his accounts for the gild year 1677-8 and hand them over to the Under Warden for the following year, Mr Martin. On 6 July 1678 the auditors disclosed that they had found something amiss and 'Mr Clark then being present could not answer the objections which were made by the Auditors. This Table did then think fitt and so order that Mr Clark should be fined £3 for bringing so imperfect an Account And that such fine should be full of all the deficiency in the same account'. Ten days later the Court was told that he had received '£6.13s.4d. from the Company of Clothworkers which he had not brought to account'. A committee of five Court Assistants in addition to the auditors was appointed 'to take retrospect of his accounts' and to report their findings at the next General Court. On 9 September they reported that they had completed their 'retrospecting' and had 'carefully examined ye particulars mencioned in ye same account And several Vouchers produced by Mr Clarke. And finding very considerable sumes for which no Vouchers are produced nor any Reasons given for ye same', they advised that Mr Clarke 'might not be any further questioned or troubled thereupon', so long as he paid to 'Mr Warden Martin ye sume of £55... and be discharged from any further accompting Providing nothing more shall appear to be received by him as Warden, then what he hath already brought to Account in ye same account'. He was ordered to pay 'ye money accordingly' and there the matter ended, leaving unsolved the mystery of his getting off so lightly and being elected Upper Warden for the year 1680-1.

Both the Wardens' and the Renter-Wardens' accounts were audited regularly and there are a number of Court orders for auditing throughout the seventeenth and eighteenth centuries. The committee appointed in 1658 (already referred to) was 'to meet from time to time to view the accounts of the corporation and stock', and in 1674 the Court ordered that the Under Warden was to submit his accounts on the first Monday in August each year, at the beginning of the next gild year, when the Clerk was 'to attend the auditors appointed to audit every such account. They shall be audited within one month next following, and subscribed by the said auditors.' They were to be returned the next month by the Clerk for the Court's inspection. In 1691 a committee was once more appointed 'to consider some effectual way of checking all accounts'. There was rather more concern, needless to say, about the Stock than the corporation accounts and the recommendations made included one that 'the stock keepers do meet and examine the treasurer's accounts' on alternate Wednesdays. This was put into effect and both Benjamin Tooke, Warehouse Keeper 1676-1704 and his successor, Joseph Collyer, 1702-23, signed weekly accounts in the volume of Books in the...Warehouse. This signature was a confirmation that the Warehouse Keeper accepted his responsibility for the accounts, in accordance with the accounting practice known as 'charge and discharge', of which more will be said later in this paper. The books for 1723-74 were checked fortnightly, and usually signed jointly by both Treasurer/Warehouse Keeper and a senior member of the Court. A typical eighteenth-century entry reads 'October 23d 1771. The above Account being examined the Ballance of Twelve hundred and forty four Pounds five Shillings and 7½ is allowed due from the Company to George Hawkins'. It is signed by:

Thos. Gameell Master
and by Matthew Jenour, J. Jenour) Wardens
Thos. Longman, J. Bancroft)
Lacy Hawes, R. Brooke

None of the City companies employed trained clerks during the

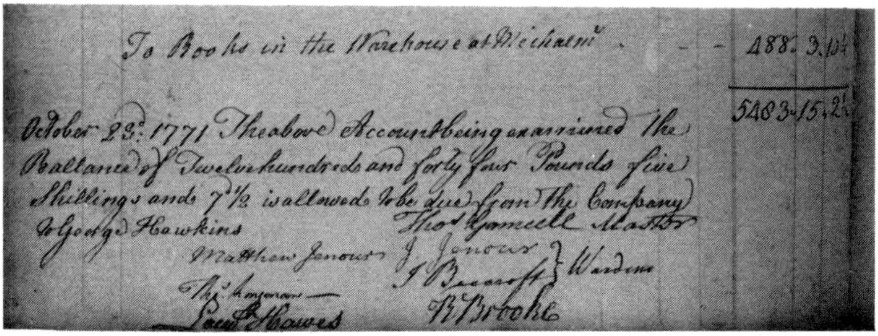

Typical entry showing auditing of accounts: from *English Stock Disbursements 1776–1777.*

seventeenth and eighteenth centuries and a glance at the financial records of other livery companies, even the biggest and richest such as the Goldsmiths and Drapers, shows that the Stationers kept their books according to the practice of the day, however haphazard they may now seem to us. Few, even of the shrewdest merchants, employed professional book-keepers so it was nothing out of the ordinary that the Stationers, though their trading company made them unique among livery companies, had their books kept as they did.

We may wonder who made use of the stream of manuals and school books on book-keeping, arithmetic and penmanship, three skills generally taught together by one master. Some of them ran into several editions and such a guide might have made a valuable addition to the Stationers' schoolbook stock, and might also have helped them to get on better with their domestic housekeeping into the bargain. The only author with any booktrade connections was John Collins (1624-83), author of an Introduction to Merchants' Accomptes (1653). He was, according to John Aubrey, 'a learned mathematical Fellow of the Royal Society, first prentice to Thomas Ailom the book binder who therafter went out of business'. Collins's later involvement with the trade was in buying books for his friends and helping them to publish their work. But his Introduction to Merchants' Accomptes was based on the knowledge of accountancy gained whilst he was a seaman and then an excise officer.[30]

R. Campbell, in the London Tradesman (1747), tells his readers that the Merchant's apprentice 'must write a fair legible Hand, and ought to be a compleat Master of Figures and Merchants' Accoumptes'.[31] Among the Stationers' records is the school exercise book of one Thomas Werret, otherwise unknown, who was learning penmanship and arithmetic in 1686. Inside crude ornamental borders he copied out arithmetical problems of inordinate tedium and complexity and then worked out the answers to the best of his ability, often making mistakes. His master, whoever he was, drew an elaborate decorative initial for each problem. One of those on the rule of three was 'If three yards of canvas cost 4 shillings and 7d how much will 199 yards cost after the same rate?' The boy did his rough working and then 'I answere that 119 yards will cost £9 1s 2 groats after the rate aforesaide'. He worked his laborious way through questions in which merchants put their money together for profit, bought cloth, tapistrie and houses as well as melting gold and silver to combine them. The manuscript, though none of the problems relates to book matters, throws a gleam of light on the training of apprentice-clerks and book-keepers.

The numerous guides to book-keeping nearly all plagiarise from their predecessors, as is to be expected. They itemise what books are to be kept and explain their use and the system of book-keeping to be adopted in each. Some writers recommend the keeping of as many as twelve books while Stephen Monteage recommends only two.[32] Frank Melton has shown that the financial success of Sir Robert Clayton was due, in great part, to the able and methodical way that his books were kept by Monteage and his recommendation of a mere two kinds of account book was based on practical experience. Debtor and Creditor Made Easie (1682) was written 'for the accommodation of merchants, lesser Trades, Retailers, handicraftsmen, and the like'. Monteage commented that: 'those learned authors have contrived a method... by waste book, journal, and ledger with several others depending thereon, as cash book, petty-charge book, invoice book etc...all orderly and commendable in their way. But my intent in this, is to reduce all these books into two books, viz wast-book and ledger...'[33] On the other hand what now seems an extravagant number of different books might not have been so for a merchant doing his business under the family roof, surrounded by his wife, children, apprentices and servants. Some might be used merely to keep the idle out of mischief.

Benjamin Booth, in the Complete System of Book Keeping (1789), gives three reasons for keeping an 'invoice book inward or bought-in book'; the first of these is that 'it gives employ for junior clerks'.[34] A merchant might keep a duplicate book for privacy or a pocket book, as Edward Hatton recommends, 'to take the minits of what business you do abroad, for the ease of your memory'.[35] Theory and practice generally diverged but any well-run business, be it merchant house or livery company, surely needed two or three different books, those of first, second and third entry. Robert Chamberlain described the book of first entry for 'buying, selling, receiving, paying, drawing, remitting, assignments, shipping etc'.[36] James Peele explained that such a 'memoriall or first book serveth for every servant of the house, to write therein all suche thynges as are by them received or delivered in the absence of the Maister or the Accompt Keper'.[37] Such waste books rarely survive because the information was posted into a book of second entry, a journal kept in a neater and more orderly style, generally with both payments in and out in date order in a single column. If only two books were used, there was no journal. The Company's Journal Book of Money Disbursed is a standard second entry book, though for disbursements only.

The ledger was the keystone of the accounting arch, being the 'great book of accounts', otherwise called the Quartern because it was to be balanced and audited quarterly. It was the 'Great Book' which was to contain 'all the concernments of a man's affair in such order that all belonging to every subject lie together in one place making distinct particular accounts'.[38] Chamberlain even stipulated that 'in the journall or leager no man must write but he that keepeth the accompts...at the top of the first page Laus Deo London in the name of God Amen in a fair large Roman hand'.[39] A feature of the ledger was that it was to be indexed with a 'calendar, otherwise called a repositor or finder, in which...ye shall sette all your debitors and creditors uppon such letters as the names have their beginning, with the number of leaves on which they stand in the leager'.[40] There is no volume labelled 'ledger' until the nineteenth century was far advanced, and not until the mid-eighteenth century was there anything which could at all correspond to Alexander Malcolm's definition of a ledger.

We do not know whose duty it was to keep the various financial books although, as we saw, some were in the hand of the Beadle. The quasi-legal books were probably kept by the Clerk or his man, but it must have been a youthful and mischievous hand that wrote on the fly-leaf of the Book of Bequests, 'For Mr Nobody'. 'Boys go apprentice while they are but boys',[41] Defoe warned his readers, and the Company's older books evidence prentice hands among the doodles and scribbles on fly-leaves, though seldom in margins where a sharp-eyed master might spot them. It was an older, more care-worn hand that wrote the unidentified memorandum on the fly-leaf of the <u>Books...in the Warehouse</u> (1663-1723): 'Quere. Whether any Composition money was ever Charged to acct which was received of severall Persons who Compounded with the Company for stolen & Counterfeit Impressions

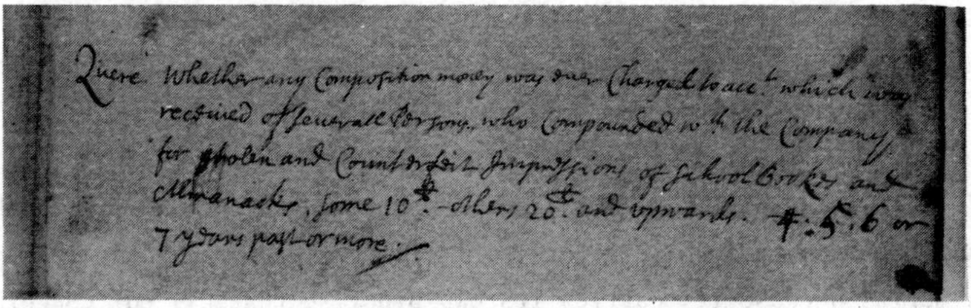
Quere. Whether any Composition money was ever Charged to acct. which was received of severall Persons who Compounded wth the Company for stolen and Counterfeit Impressions of School Books and Almanacks, some 10£. others 20£. and upwards. 4.5.6 or 7 years past or more.

Unidentified memorandum on flyleaf of *Books in the Treasurer's Warehouse 1663–1723*: 'Quere. Whether any Composition money was ever Charged to acct which was received of severall Persons with the Company for stolen and Counterfeit Impressions of School Books and Almanacks...'

of School Books and Almanacks, some £10 others £20 and upwards 4, 5, 6 or 7 years pay or more.'

The suggestion that 'an Accomptant' be received into the service of the Company 'to methodize the Stock Accounts'[42] was a very advanced step to contemplate in 1692 and it is not surprising that the members of Court could not bring themselves to act on the committee's advice for some years; in 1703 they at last ordered that 'An Accomptant be chosen to assist the Stock Keepers in keeping the account of the English and Oxford Stocks', and a few months later 'Mr William Bowyer was chosen Accomptant, at the salary of £20 a year'.[43]

But no more was heard of the matter and one searches in vain for evidence of any 'methodizing' of the accounts after 1703; no change whatever being discernible. He does not seem to have worked for long, although there is an order to the treasurer to pay him £20, 4 September 1704.

'It would be too much to say that balancing was unknown', Richard Brown wrote of this period, 'but it was extremely rare', and few heeded Robert Chamberlain, that 'when the accompts in the Leager are added up and ballanced the debtor and creditor will amount all to one sum, for if they differ but a farthing there is an error committed somewhere'.[44] Edward Hatton explained it thus: 'The ledger is that in which all Accompts meet, and are placed debtor on the left hand page and creditor on the right, so that the folios on the Right and the Left are numbered alike because one and the same account is placed on both sides.'[45] This was most easily done if the books were kept by the system that has come to be called double entry, then known as the Italian method, first taught by Fra Luca Paciolo in Florence in 1475 and introduced into England in the mid-sixteenth century. From then on nearly all writers on accountancy extolled its merits because it 'carries its own proof so that all our concernments lie before us the one to check the others'. Richard Dafforne waxed lyrical in insisting that 'It is the unfailable thread to Rosamund's Bower, and the right track to Dedalus trace; wherein if any one digresses, they are in danger (with Icarus) to perish in ignorance's lake, as many therein have been presidents.'[46]

In practice the traditional system known as 'charge and discharge' was nearly always used until the nineteenth century, although hardly any of the writers on book-keeping took account of this, and continued to insist on the superiority of a system none could master. Only the ever-practical Monteage wrote his Instructions for Rent-Gatherers' Accompts Made Easie (1683) for those of 'meaner intelligence' who were likely to use his book and profit by it. By the traditional system the accountant '"charges himself"', in Richard Brown's words, 'with the estate entrusted to him...and "discharges himself" of the monies lawfully expended or paid over to him'.[47] Needless to say the Stationers' books were kept by this ancient system throughout the period under review. To modern accountants they look so haphazard and unmethodical that it seems a marvel that the Company escaped Icarus's fate of perishing in Ignorance's lake. But, muddled and mismanaged though they might be, the Stationers' book-keeping was little different from that of their contemporaries and as the eighteenth century advanced we see a slow but steady progress towards more method and order. Change was necessarily slow with, for the most part, old men at the helm, who came and went, and none was Master for long enough (two years at longest) to see through any innovation he might introduce; while the paid officials, the Clerk, the Beadle and the Treasurer-cum-Warehouse Keeper, even when perfectly honest, had no interest in exchanging a workable system with which they were thoroughly conversant for a new-fangled one which would be less restful to operate. Their less than meticulous book-keeping worked well enough for their purposes. How could they foresee, and why should they trouble themselves with, the scholarly posterity that would have to try to puzzle it out?

Appendix I: Stationers' Company's Financial Records, 1605-1811

	Books Kept	Type of Transaction	Additional Comment
1	Wardens' Accounts, 3 vols, (1663-1837)	Account of income and expenditure of the corporation and English Stock; kept by the Under Warden and audited annually	Continued to 1907 in a further 6 vols
2	Wardens' Accounts, (1663-69) and (1756-59)	Duplicate accounts, also audited	
3	Journal Book of Money Disbursed, (1656-98)	Includes both corporation and Stock outgoings, sometimes separately itemised	
4	Book for Entraunce of Fines, (1605-40)	Receipt book for fees for bindings, turnovers, freedoms, clothings etc. and fines for non-service of office and for misdemeanours	Almost the only book devoted entirely to corporation finance
5	Check/cheque/checque/Books, 3 vols, (1648-1805)	Waste book of fees and fines as paid into Court and itemised under specific Court, as corporation, Stock or Pension	Described by Greg, Catalogue as 'similar to a bank passbook' but actually a kind of continuation of the Book of Fines, though differently arranged, as well as being a waste book
6	Book of Bequests labelled 'C2 Wills' (1593-1623) and (1884) and (1908)	Called 'extracts of wills, where legacies are left to the Company'	Not strictly a financial document, except that it contains some conditioned bonds half-way through

	Books Kept	Type of Transaction	Additional Comment
7	Bonds for Moneye Lent, (1671-88)	Conditioned bonds issued under the terms of the Nortons' and Evan Tyler's wills	Disbound
8	Liber Computi Pro Pauperibus, The Poor Book, (1608-76)	Lists the Company's pensioners, with amounts paid and date of court, according to the terms of the English Stock patent, 1603	Partially edited by W. Craig Ferguson, for The Library (1976)
9	Pension Lists, 3 vols, (1677-1811)	From 1733, itemised according to charity	Continued to 1929
10	A Particular and Rental of Estates Belonging to the Company of Stationers, (1773)	A survey of the Company's property distinguishing corporation from English Stock property	
11	English Stock: Books in the Treasurer's Warehouse, subsequent volumes labelled Account of Books Delivered, 4 vols, (1663-1774)	Includes such other capital items as Stock property and rents	
12	Rent Book, (1743-86)	English Stock receipts	
13	English Stock Disbursements, 3 vols, (1766-1803)	Payments for production and publication of Stock books, including general overheads, wages and tax	Continued to 1871
14	Dividend Books, 10 vols, (1644-1803)	Names of English Stock partners, with amounts paid	Continued to 1924

	Books Kept	Type of Transaction	Additional Comment
15	Dividend List, (1782)	Not a financial record: Treasurer or Clerk's list of partners	
16	Stock Keepers' Book, (1755-66)	Only surviving minute book of Stock Board in our period	Further books to 1924
17	English Stock assignments and receipts, (1679-94)	Itemises transfer of Stock shares to partner's widow or new partner	
18	Account of Stock Transferred, (1702-43)	Ditto	
19	Receipts for Shares Paid out, (1785-1800) with Extracts of Wills	Covers both share transfers and extracts of wills relating to share transfers	
20	Rent Book, (1743-86)	English Stock receipts	
21	Almanack Accounts, 5 vols, (1789-1800)	Profit and loss accounts	Continued annually until 1801, then 1811-69, also Journal of Almanacks, 2 vols, (1823-40)
22	Account of Dr Brady and Mr Tate's Psalms, (1706-64)	Payments made to Tate and Brady together with analysis of sales	

Appendix II: Records Known to have Existed, now Lost or Destroyed together with those which must have existed excluding incomplete sequences

	Books Kept	Type of Transaction	Additional Comment
1	Renter-Wardens' Quarterage Books 1646-1850	The only early record of Freemen's names and addresses recording quarterly dues paid at Quarterly Courts	Most of those 1851-1920 survived
2	Stock Accounts before 1650	Disappeared early on	
3	Paper Stock Ledger before 1650	Ditto	
4	Book of Seizures, (17th century)	Ditto and may not have been a financial book	See Hetet p. 49 and n. 53, p. 59
5	Printing Book, (17th century)	Blagden found a single reference in the Court Book	
6	Book of Business with Cambridge	References in Journal of Money Disbursed, (1691)	

Appendix III: Additional Financial Documents

1 Accounts, receipts, estimate for barge etc, (1672-77), catalogued by Major Hall of P.R.O. items numbered 599-609

2 Miscellaneous almanack accounts, bills for printing, paper, advertising etc. (1770-95) (in Box C catalogued by R.M.)

3 Receipts for engrossing Charter, (1684), for preaching (1681-1708) etc. Box F

4 Building and maintenance of hall, 1670s-19th century, Box G

5 Accounts etc. of George Hawkins, 1740s-1780, Box H

6 Accounts relating to the barge: the fire engine: insurance: 18th century: Box K

7 Bills and receipts etc for food, drink, candles, etc. Box L

8 Additional financial documents relationg to English Stock and Corporation finances, Boxes M & N: not yet fully catalogued

Appendix IV:

Books Recommended in the Training of Book Keepers and Clerks, 1543-1779 (with alternative names)

1 Waste book/Memorial/Book of Remembrances/cash book: described as 'forerunner to the journal' - the book of first entry

2 Journal/Daily or day book: 'forerunner to the Ledger'

3 Ledger or Leager/Great Book/Quartern: 'index to the journal'

4 Cash book/petty cash book: 'waste book for all receipts & payments of money': 'Page or Footman to the Great Cash Book'

5 Great Cash Book: for large-scale money transactions

6 Bill book/Waste book for all bills of exchange

7 Pocket Book: either for 'ease of your memory' or duplicate account book to be carried in pocket

8 Book of Factories or invoices: recommended for those using a middle man for import/export

9 Book of receipts/Acquittance Book

10 Invoice Book Inward/Bought Book

11 Invoice Book Outward/Sold or sales book

12 Book of Household Expenses

13 Letter Book/Copy Book of Letters

Stock Accounts Ordered by Court 1687

	Name	Purpose
1	Day Book	For paper and book receipts, and cash sales
2	Posting Book	Cash receipts and payments
3	Bought Book for Paper	Receipts and payment
4	Acquittance Book	For Stock receipts
5	Book for Business Relating to the Universities	All receipts and payments

	Name	Purpose
6	Book for Business Relating to the Transferring of Parts fines & forfeitures	For share transfers and fines for non-service or misdemeanours
7	Book for Rents Received and when Due	

Notes

1 J.B. Priestley, English Humour (1929).

2 Daniel Defoe, A Supplement to the Complete Tradesman, (1720), Letter 1, p. 14 (cited as Defoe).

3 Private correspondence (March 1984).

4 Cyprian Blagden, 'The English Stock of the Stationers' Company in the Time of the Stuarts', The Library, 5 XII (1957), pp. 167-225 (cited as Blagden, E.S.).

5 See pp. 32-59 in this volume.

6 Cyprian Blagden, 'The accounts of the Wardens of the Stationers' Company, 1557-96', Studies in Bibliography, Virginia, Vol. 9 (1957), pp. 69-95.

7 Edward Arber, A Transcript of the Registers of the Company of Stationers of London 1554-1640, (5 vols, 1875-94), vol. i, Introduction, pp. xiii-xliv.

8 Blagden, E.S., p. 178.

9 Court Book D, f. 36a.

10 Catalogue of Records at Stationers' Hall, reprinted from the Transactions of the Bibliographical Society, (March 1926), p. 8 (cited as Greg, Catalogue)

11 Greg, Catalogue p. 15.

12 Correspondence between Sidney Hodgson and Graham Pollard, now in the Bodleian and brought to my notice by Mrs Esther Potter who transcribed it for me.

13 Graham Pollard, The Earliest Directory of the Book Trade by Joseph Pendred (1785) (1955), p. 52.

14 The present Clerk, Captain Peter Hames, tells me it was recently let for a wedding reception for the first time in many years, but that the bride changed her mind and the reception was cancelled.

15 Court Book F, f. 146b.

16 Court Book J, f. 21a.

17 Court Book F, f. 162b ff.

18 ibid. f. 163b.

19 Defoe, Letter IV, p. 146.

20 W. Craig Ferguson, The Stationers' Company Poor Book, 1608-1700, reprinted from The Library (March 1976), pp. 37-51.

21 Cyprian Blagden, The Stationers' Company: A History 1403-1959, (196), p. 113.

22 ibid. p. 254.

23 Court Book F, ff. 163b and 164a. Thereafter the two terms were used indiscriminately until, by the middle of the eighteenth century, they had reverted to the easier 'Treasurer'.

24 Blagden, E.S., p. 185.

25 See Appendix IV.

26 Richard Brown, A History of Accounting and Accounts (1905), p. 72.

27 Michael Bywater, Librarian of the Institute of Chartered Accountants, pointed out several such examples in the Wardens' Accounts, for which I am most grateful.

28 Court Book E, f. 264b.

29 3 July 1676 Court Book D, f. 264b and 2 December 1678, Court Book D, f. 333a.

30 M.F. Bywater and B.S. Yamey, Historic Accounting Literature: A Companion Guide (1982), pp. 105-7.

31 R. Campbell, The London Tradesman (1747), p. 293.

32 Frank Melton, who has written a study of Sir Robert Clayton and his bank, gave me this information.

33 Stephen Monteage, Debtor and Creditor made Easie (1682), Preface (Bywater facsimile) (many of these early guides are neither paginated nor foliated; in which case I give chapter numbers).

34 Benjamin Booth, Complete System of Book Keeping (1789), p. 20 (Bywater facsimile).

35 Edward Hatton, The Merchant's Magazine or Tradesman's Treasury, (2nd edn. 1695), p. 58, (cited as Hatton).

36 Robert Chamberlain, The Accomptant's Guide or Merchant's Book Keeper, (1679), p. 51, (cited as Chamberlain).

37 James Peele, The Maner and Forme how to Keepe a Reconynge (1553), Chapter 3.

38 Alexander Malcolm, A Treatise of Book-Keeping... (1731), Chapter 1, p. 6.

39 Chamberlain, p. 51.

40 John Mellis, A Briefe Instruction and Maner how to Keepe Bookes of Accompts (1588), Chapter 11, 'Of the last and third principall booke, called the Leager'.

41 Defoe, Letter I, p. 6.

42 Court Book F, f. 182b.

43 Court Book G, f. 90a.

44 Chamberlain, p. 53.

45 Hatton, p. 138.

46 Richard Dafforne, The Merchants' Mirrour, (1635), Preface (Bywater facsimile).

47 Brown, p. 58.

The Wardens' Accounts of the Stationers' Company, 1663–79

John Hetet

As from 1663 the Stationers' Company began to keep a set of financial records which provide evidence of how the guild managed some of its affairs and reveal how money was raised to provide for these duties. The Accounts kept by the Wardens of the Company can be used in a number of ways and in this paper I have attempted to set the financial records in an historical context so that they might throw some more light on the problems associated with the Company's often paradoxical rôle as an agent of ecclesiastical and state censorship. I have not endeavoured to make a comprehensive financial reconstruction of the Accounts, but have instead used them in a selective manner to help answer three specific questions. Firstly, what do the Accounts tell us about the money and time spent by the Wardens in fulfilling their obligations to make regular searches of London printing houses, booksellers' shops and bindery houses? (These responsibilities are connected with the Licensing, or Printing, Act of 1662, the Stationers' Company by-laws, and the periodic directives from Whitehall and Lambeth.) Secondly, who were the printers that had their presses dismantled, removed and at times sold by the Company; and what happened to these presses and the literature that was seized by the Company? And, finally, do these Accounts in any way modify the widely accepted assertion that the Stationers' Company was more interested in protecting their control over the English Stock than in acting against the unlicensed printing and sales of controversial political and religious literature?

The Accounts alone do not provide a complete answer to these questions. But used together with the Court Books of the Stationers' Company, the relevant State Papers in the Public Record Office and passages from the Historical Manuscripts Commission Reports we can begin to discern the scattered pieces of a complex puzzle. Indeed, part of the conundrum is made up of external pressures from authorities, overriding pecuniary motives, the furtive ways in which books were printed, and the attempts to protect privileges in the Equity Court of Chancery.

The Accounts kept by Richard Royston and Samuel Mearne while they served the office of Under Warden illustrate some of these claims and provide us with two case studies of how a Warden of the Company could utilise his position for the purposes of 'search and seizure'. We must keep in mind that Royston and Mearne were important entrepreneurs in their own right and both cases depict the ways a Warden carried out his duties in the face of conflicting demands: on the one hand to be an agent of government enforcement and on the other hand to meet the diverse demands of a reading public with a taste for polemics. But before I look at the Accounts in detail it is necessary to provide a context for the records and to say something about the debate on censorship.

Regulation of the London booktrade entered a new phase with the restoration of the exiled Charles Stuart, the election of the Cavalier Parliament and the resumed authority of the anglican bishops. Although the Convention Parliament had adopted interim measures to curtail the activities of some printers it was not until the Cavalier Parliament had been elected that a concerted legislative attack was made on the press. It was clear to the governing bodies that to achieve a peaceful settlement, in a nation split by differing religious and political opinions, they would have to exert some control over the undisciplined activities of the London press. When parliament began to introduce statutory acts to regulate the booktrade they drew upon a number of laws which had been in abeyance, and in particular resorted to the provisions of the Star Chamber Decree of 1637. Along with this comprehensive though unwieldy decree, designed to correct the problems of an unrestrained number of printing presses and unlicensed publications, they were able to implement a number of common and statute laws which impinged directly upon the dissenters and their links with the London booktrade.[1]

In the vanguard of these regulatory measures was the so-called Licensing Act of 1662. It was introduced to help contain three specific problems that were believed to be a consequence of the relative press freedoms of the prior period of unrest. In the first place there was an active market for 'seditious' and 'scandalous' literature which had to be controlled; the second problem had in many ways helped create the first: the large number of illegal tradespeople - the printing trade, for example, had an estimated sixty master printers, thirty-five of whom had set up business after 1640; and finally many of those working in the trades of printing, binding and bookselling were thought to represent a disaffected cartel whose sympathies lay with some of the nonconformist and catholic communities.[2]

Along with the Licensing Act, the laws of treason and seditious libel were used to constrain and further limit the booktrade. By exercising these laws the government declared that all statements attacking the legitimacy of the monarch, the established church and parliament were now proscribed.[3] Both the new legislation and the polemical works of the government's propagandists referred to the bitter memories of the 1640s and indicated that the root cause of the 'revolution' and attendant execution of the king lay in the misuse of the pulpit and the press.[4] They held that the dissenting opinions promulgated by the sectarians, radical protestants and disaffected gentry in printed texts and manuscript libels had been instrumental in the challenge and eventual usurpation of Church and monarchical rule; and it was supposedly the London booktrade that had harnessed and dispersed these radical ideals. All those writings in which such ideas as the defence of revolution, resistance to lawful authority, Salus Populi Suprema lex, and the evils of ecclesiastical establishments were now prohibited.

Although studies have been made of the laws which were imposed upon authors, printers and booksellers, in particular the excellent studies by Pollard, Siebert and Blagden, they have not always provided a clear analysis of the political motives underlying the regulations, or the implications these laws had for those singled out for harassment, conviction and imprisonment.[5] And more needs to be said of the way in which the various enforcement agencies operated. I am thinking here of the actions of Roger L'Estrange, of Robert 'Hog' Stephens - Messenger of the Press - and in particular the Wardens of the Stationers' Company.[6]

The divergent attitudes of today's historians on the question of post-Restoration censorship are reflected in a recent discussion between Blair Worden and Christopher Hill on the evaluation of James R. Jacob's work Henry Stubbe: Radical Protestantism and the Early Enlightenment in England.[7] Worden disagrees with Jacob who considers Stubbe's ironic and ambivalent statements to be a means of evading the axe of censorship. 'It would be a mistake to reduce the issue to one of censorship, an obstacle which seems to have worried most seventeenth-century writers less, than it exercises some of their twentieth-century historians'. 'How does he know that?' is the prompt reply of Christopher Hill, who considers censorship to be a significant factor in post-Restoration England. According to Hill the lack of open criticism against censorship cannot be regarded as a testimony to its ineffectiveness: 'For anyone who wanted to say really unorthodox things the censorship posed a real problem...Stubbe had systematic thoughts which he dared not publish.' Hill has pursued an almost solitary campaign in reminding his readers that censorship hindered and embargoed the works of authors, especially those writers with a reputation for discussing controversial issues: 'Under censorship men restrained themselves from telling the whole truth as they saw it, proceeding by analogy, implication and innuendo.'[8] Clearly the problems facing the author, his printers and publishers were manifold, but what seems to have escaped consideration in the debate has been a detailed account of the mechanics of censorship in post-Restoration England. It is only by understanding how the legislative acts were supported, by considering the alternative forms of control exerted on the press, and by looking at the search and seizure work of the Stationers' Company, amongst others, that we begin to appreciate the scale of the problem of censorship.

There are evident inconsistencies in the way the law was applied and supported. Indeed, one bibliographer has suggested to students of the press not to take the numerous enactments concerning censorship too seriously. He qualifies this a little later by stating 'that while little attention was paid to the letter of the regulations, save in the period immediately following a new order, their spirit was on the whole fairly well observed'.[9] But is this qualification supported by the available evidence? A year after the introduction of the Licensing Act of 1662 Roger L'Estrange complained that 'the Effectual Regulation of the Press is not at all the Stationers' Interest, so is it strongly to be suspected that it is as little their Aym: for not One Person has been Fin'd, and but one Prosecuted...'[10] Whereas l'Estrange actively worked against London's nonconformist printers and booksellers, the Stationers' Company, as the Wardens' Accounts show for this year, only hounded printers of pirated primers. The haphazard way in which these guardians of the press exercised their authority can be shown to have depended primarily upon economic interests.

The Stationers' Company policy on matters such as search and seizure was determined by the Master, the two Wardens and the Court of Assistants; the King's periodic nomination of so-called 'loyal' members to the Court suggests an attempt to influence the way in which Company affairs were handled. Promotion to the Court of Assistants was at the same time a form of payment for services rendered and it entitled the member to a share in the profitable English Stock. Such promotions by royal *mandamus* skirted the long established, and slow, route to the top of the Company. After

1662 many of the King's appointees rose to positions of greater power and influence in the guild.[11] It was thought that with supposedly reliable and sympathetic Wardens at the helm the company would display an interest in censorship.

There are basically two methods by which books can be censored. The first applies before the publishing of a text and is known as censura prœvia. Licensing, the bête noire of Milton's tract Areopagitica, falls into this category. The second means of censorship, censura repressiva, occurs after the printing or publishing of a text when some authority suppresses the work and endeavours to search and seize all copies. The laws which had been introduced to control printing in the seventeenth century operated along one or both of these lines. Despite the see-saw of political power and the shifting criteria upon which literature was banned, all authorities had found it expedient to adopt some form of censorship as a necessary protective and prohibitive measure.

The latter form of censorship is readily reflected in the financial records kept by the Wardens of the Stationers' Company. Such entries as: 'Item, Paid 4 Messengers for Searching for Darby, & taking downe his Presses' £3.17s.6d. and 'Item paid...upon the taking downe Mr Redmaines Presse and seizing of the sheetes of the Leviathan' 4 shillings, testify to the Wardens' fulfilling duties which were laid down in the fourteenth clause of 'An Act for preventing the frequent Abuses in printing seditious treasonable and unlicensed Bookes and Pamphlets and for regulating of Printing and Printing Presses.' This section of the 1662 Act states that:

> the Master and Wardens of the said Company of Stationers or any one of them shall have power and authority with a Constable... to search all Houses and Shops where they shall knowe or upon some probable reason suspect any Books or Papers to be printed bound or stitched especially Printing Houses Booksellers Shops and Warehouses and Bookbinders Houses and Shops and to view there what is imprinting binding or stitching and to examine whether the same be licensed.[12]

Failure to produce the necessary licence would lead to the seizure of the text and the arrest of the erring person. The seized book or part of the book was to be taken either to the Archbishop of

Canterbury, the Bishop of London or to one of the Secretaries of State who would determine any further course of action.

However, the problem of inducing the Stationers' Company to carry out these duties became apparent to those attempting to regulate the booktrade. Indeed the clearest exposition on the evident reluctance of the Master and Wardens to search and seize unlicensed literature is contained in Sir Roger L'Estrange's Considerations and Proposals in Order to the Regulation of the Press. According to L'Estrange:

> they are both Parties and Judges; for diverse of them have brought up Servants to the Mystery of Printing which they still retein in Dependence: Others again are both Printers and Stationers, Themselves; so that they are Entrusted (effectually) to search for their own Copies; to Destroy their own Interests; to Prosecute their own Agents, and to Punish Themselves...[13]

By 1667 L'Estrange was arguing that the booktrade had developed a number of interwoven financial interests which meant that certain members of the Stationers' Company did not observe their duties and were encouraging unlawful printing.[14] By giving the Company the responsibilities of searching for unlicensed literature fellow members could be forewarned of imminent searches and a matter which required prompt attention could be frustrated by delaying the search. The Accounts for 1669-70 support L'Estrange's assertion when 5s.2d. was paid out 'in Forewarning the Printers to Print nothing about General Monke but what the Secretaries of State should License'.

It was Cyprian Blagden's work on the sixteenth-century Wardens' Accounts that alerted me to the possibilities of charting specific activities of the Company through their financial records. In his study of the Accounts from 19 July 1557 to 15 July 1596 he was able to conclude that the two most important items of expenditure were those of legal actions and Search Dinners.[15] These costs were a direct consequence of the Company's attempts to suppress treasonable and recusant literature and prevent the pirating of works belonging to the English Stock. Furthermore the Accounts showed 'that they cost the Company a great deal of time and a certain amount of money.

There were lawyers' fees and police expenses, there were journeys to Whitehall, Fulham and Greenwich (and further afield): there were "sweeteners", in money and in kind; there was the cost of drafting ordinances and decrees'.[16] And according to Blagden 'Search Dinners' showed 'more quickly than anything else the amount of time - otherwise unrewarded - put in by the senior members of the Company on Company business'.[17]

The later seventeenth-century Accounts show that the costs of legal consultation and court hearings had become an important part of the yearly payments. In bringing indictments against unlicensed printers in the London Quarter Sessions and in mounting Equity Court proceedings against rival patentees the Wardens had to dig deep into the Company's pockets. Although Search Dinners are no longer a readily identifiable feature of these Accounts, nevertheless the guild continued to spend a great deal of time in London's taverns both during and after Company business. We are also given reasonably detailed entries of the searches mounted by the Wardens to track down unlicensed and pirated publications. The successful seizure of an illegal tract, the confiscation of a supernumerary press, or a court hearing which favoured the Company was often a good reason for celebrations in a local tavern. But it is the overall variety of the entries which make up the yearly receipts ('charges') and payments ('discharges') of the Wardens' Accounts that are their most noticeable first impression. As Cyprian Blagden has stated 'No year can be called typical'.[18]

The receipts, for example, have entries such as: the sale of old books from the Wardens' room (£113.6s., 1663-4), the repayment of loans (£500 from the city, 1664-5), bequests from former members (£300, 1669-70), the sale of Company property (£325, 1670-1), the sale of confiscated printing material (£32.17s., 1676-7) and the sale of damasked sheets (£5.2s.6d., 1678-9). But there are also standard charges which we find for every year: fees paid to the clerk for the registration of licensed publications - usually 6d. for a pamphlet or a book; 2s.6d. for each apprentice presented;

the admission of free men at 3s.4d. per man; £20 fine for each yeoman elected to the livery; and the quarterly payments gathered by the Renter-Wardens from Freemen of the Company.

Likewise, the yearly record of payments follows a similar pattern; there are the odd entries such as Warden Robert White's expenses in 'goeing to Cambridg at Cambridg coming home againe and for Coach hire' £19.16s.5d. (1669-70), 'one hundred Dutch penns given to L'Estrange at 2s.' (1670-1), payments to informers about illegal presses (Thomas Rookes printing house, 1671-2) or purchasing a copy of L'Estrange's Proposals (1678-9). But as with the receipts there are payments which occur with annual regularity and these can be conveniently categorised into the following: expenditure on dinners and tavern meetings, retaining fees and wages, repairs to Company property and rebuilding, legal expenses, pensions, sermons, rates and taxes, loans made to stationers, and the search and seizure of illegal presses and unlicensed literature.

From 1663 to 1679 the amount of money which made up the yearly receipts and payments was variable (see Table 1). When Richard Royston was Under Warden in 1666-7 and 1667-8 receipts were £179.2s.6d. and £90.3s.6d., while payments were £189.10s. and £103.18s.8d. The Fire of 1666 had a particularly destructive impact on the businesses of some members of the Company. As Pepys discovered, his own bookseller, Joshua Kirton, was 'utterly undone, and made 2 or 3000l. worse then nothing, from being worth 7 or 8000l.'[19] The devastation had encompassed most of the great booksellers and a shortage of books was predicted: 'especially Latin books and foreign books; and among others, the polyglottes and new Bible, which he [Mr Kirton's "kinsman"] believes will be presently worth 40l apiece.'[20] This meant that Royston's ability to obtain money from members was greatly limited and is in part reflected by his consecutive yearly balances which were debts of £10 and £15. In contrast Samuel Mearne's term of office, 1672-3 and 1673-4, was much more successful with receipts of £1158.7s.2d. and £1268.12s.11d. and payments of £1152.16s.6d. and £1211.8s.4d.

If we go through the Accounts looking at those entries which relate to the Company's attempts to regulate the London press we discover that they fall within one of three headings: consultations, searches, and seizures. First there are the costs of consultations with the Secretaries of State, the Bishops, the Lord Mayor, the Surveyor of the Press and lawyers. These consultations at Lambeth, Whitehall or in one of London's taverns often took place before and after a search mounted by the Wardens. If a search was successful and a printer, press or publication was taken the Company was obliged to take the printer to one of the Secretaries of State. The seized literature was supposed to be conveyed to either Whitehall or Lambeth. The discovered press and printing materials were often removed or dismantled at a later date. These meetings and subsequent duties cost the Company in travel and cartage charges, plus there were the fees of lawyers. The second distinctive form of entry was connected with a search; the detail given in the accounts varies from the succinct: 'Item spent about a Search' 17s.6d. to the more informative: 'Dec 2 [1672] Item spent on a Search for ye Rehearsall transposed [sic]' £1.5s.

A successful search resulted in the confiscation of the discovered publication or press. This third type of entry appears in the accounts as, for example, 'June [1673] Item spent and given when Mr Rookes 2 presses were taken away' £1.16s.6d. And a little later in the same month the Warden records 'Item paid ye Joiner for taking downe Oakes & Rookes's Presses' 10s.

To illustrate these points let us consider the careers and accounts of Richard Royston and Samuel Mearne.

On 11 May 1663 Richard Royston was elected to the Court of Assistants following a royal letter commanding that the King's bookseller be promoted to a position of influence.[21] Earlier in the year Royston had been one of the jurors who found the printer John Twyn guilty of high treason and Simon Dover, Thomas Brewster and Nathan Brookes guilty of printing, publishing and selling the seditious books, <u>The Speeches and prayers of some of the Late King's</u>

Judges and A Phenix, or The Solemn League and Covenant.[22] Royston's promotion into the senior ranks of the Company was in recognition of his loyal services. In 1660 he had been appointed the King's bookseller as acknowledgement for his publishing efforts during the Commonwealth period and in particular for the popular propagandist work Eikon Basilike.[23] Royston's election to the Court was also part of Charles Stuart's political strategy to place suitable sympathisers into the various City corporations. This coincided with attempts made to purge the companies of certain nonconformists by imposing the Oath of Allegiance and Supremacy (1661).[24]

Royston used his position in the Company to seize the imperfect sheets of Richard Alleine's Vindiciæ Pietatis, or A Vindication of Godliness. The text was particularly popular and according to Calamy although it was refused a licence 'greedily brought up and read by sober people'. The seized sheets were placed in the King's kitchen to be used as wastepaper. It was here that Royston managed to purchase the impression. He had them bound and put on sale again. However, his enterprising act was exposed and he was reprimanded by the Privy Council for selling the nonconformist tract.[25]

None the less in July 1666 Royston was elected Under Warden and during his term of office he appears to have displayed a distinct lack of zeal towards the duties of searching for unlicensed literature and presses. In 1666 the only entries in the Accounts that relate to these matters are: 'Item Paid 10 searches about Primmers and Almanacks' £7.13s.3d., and the second entry was a meeting at Lambeth with the bishops concerning printers. We don't know what went on at this meeting but it is conceivable that the established church was voicing its concern over the renewed publishing activities of nonconformists. For on 5 February 1667 Royston informed the Court of Assistants that one of the printers associated with nonconformist works, John Darby, was 'printing and desposing divers Books belonging to ye English Stock'.[26] Later in the year Warden Royston 'paid 4 Messengers for searching for Darby and takeing downe his Presses, p^{d} 6 Porters, Carmen, Normans Men and other Expences 03: 07: 06'. By 4 June 1667 the Company was preparing an indictment against Darby for the London Quarter Sessions.[27]

But the action against Darby was the exception rather than the rule. The only other action of note was on 17 December 1667 when Royston informed the Court that Gilbert Sheldon, Archbishop of Canterbury, wanted the whole impression of the Protestant Almanack to be stopped and that the publisher of the almanack, Nathaniel Ponder, be notified of the Archbishop's command.[28]

We do not have to look far to begin to appreciate some of the reasons why Royston appears to have been relatively inactive. Amongst the State Papers Domestic at the Public Record Office is an undated document entitled 'Questions for ye Master & Wardens' which can be dated as 1667 on internal evidence.[29] There are seven questions in all and beneath them are the answers which reflect Royston's intransigence. Not only had Royston failed to move against Francis Smith who was attempting to get Andrew Marvell's The Second, and Third Advice to a Painter printed, but he had forewarned John Crook to remove his copies of Fiat Lux prior to a search by the Warden of the bookseller's house. Moreover, the wife of the printer Thomas Milbourne said she could prove that Royston had 'sold some of ye Bookes concerning ye Firing of ye Citty, wch He had seized himself'.[30] The practice of selling seized books was an attractive one, for many a Company member had discovered that unlicensed and controversial works fetched premium prices. When Edmond Hickeringill discussed the question of restraint of the press much later he concluded that:

> For as in other Trades, things that are rare, dear and hard to come by, are the readiest Commodity; so also in the Booksellers Trade, no Books vend so nimbly as those that are sold (by Stealth as it were) and want Imprimaturs. This Restraint by Licensers will not prevent the flying Pamphlets and Reputation-Wounders; we may well say, it will not because by Experience 'tis found it never did.[31]

I would like to pause briefly to consider the question of books printed and sold by stealth. In the Wardens' Accounts we come across titles which were well known because of their controversial content: The Poor Whores Petition (1668), Rehearsal Transprosed (1672), The Womans Petition Against Coffee (1674), Naked Truth (1675), Mr Smirke; or, The Divine in Mode (1676) and Leviathan (1651 [sic]).[32] All these texts were printed when both Mearne and Royston held Company offices. Although action was initiated against the publications and their printers the attempt to suppress them was not always successful. Hobbes's Leviathan, for example, is mentioned in the Accounts on the 6 October 1670 when sheets of the work were seized at the printing house of John Redmayne. The book had been shrouded in controversy following publication in 1651; and at the Restoration the House of Commons ordered a committee to consider whether the Leviathan was amongst those texts that were either atheistic, blasphemous, or profane.[33] It is evident that the text was both 'rare and dear' by 1668 as the first edition was being sold at between three and four times the original price of eight shillings. Hobbes's attack on the clergy's jure divino principles of authority had led to the work being proscribed. According to Pepys it was said to be 'a book the Bishops will not let be printed again'.[34] Although Hobbes had his admirers it was clear that any publisher wishing to print the Leviathan would have to run the gauntlet of official censorship. We capture a glimpse of the difficulties facing the author from the authorities in his letter to Secretary of State, Joseph Williamson:

> I send the book containing the words concerning heresy which you mislike, and which may be left out without trouble, but I see no cause of exception against them, and desire they may stand unless the rest of the book cannot be licensed whilst they stand.[35]

However there were members of the Stationers' Company willing to adopt a less compromising stance.

While Hobbes was having his problems with the censors Andrew Crooke had surreptitiously engaged John Williams to employ John Redmayne to print the Leviathan.[36] On 6 October 1670 the Wardens' Accounts record that 10s.1d. was spent on 'takeing downe Mr Redmaines Presse and seizing of the sheetes of the Leviathan'. It is interesting to note that when the Court of Assistants met they were concerned with not only Redmayne's printing of the Leviathan, but also with his printing of Fabulæ Æsopi.[37] Despite Redmayne's loss of his texts, a duodecimo edition of Fabulæ Æsopi was on sale and boldly proclaimed 'Ex officina Johannis Redmayne'. Perhaps one of the two different editions of Leviathan falsely dated 1651 had, likewise, escaped suppression in 1670.[38] The next mention of Leviathan in the Accounts was on 24 March 1674 when Samuel Mearne paid William Bailey 'Thirty shill. for Damasking forty five Reams of the Leviathan'. The charges to the Wardens' Accounts were recovered in the following year from the 'publisher' John Williams who paid Warden Roycroft £2.13s.6d. But our story of the text's chequered history does not end here. In 1675, when Andrew Crooke made an assignment of books to John Wright, the Court of Assistants 'ordered that Hobbes Leviathan be not entred' in the Company Register.[39]

The example illustrates one of the many ways in which Company members endeavoured to circumvent the regulations by concealing their responsibility. Apart from the widespread use of anonymous imprints and the stratagems of shared printing, booksellers favoured the employment of intermediaries, often binders and their wives, to collate and distribute the texts. Often this allowed very respectable booksellers to finance and yet avoid direct association with a controversial text.[40]

With the aid of the Accounts we can trace in part a text's path from printing, via seizure to damasking and at times back to the market place. Another text which was seized by the Stationers' Company but was shortly after once again available for sale was Henry Danvers's A Treatise of Baptism. Following the seizure of a press at Shoreditch in January 1674 the Wardens Robert White and Samuel Mearne seized 1,500 copies of Danvers's book. Indictments were exhibited against the printer John Darby and the treatise was given to the Bishop of London. Mearne had apparently declared that the bookseller Francis Smith, who had commissioned the work, would never have them back. Meanwhile William Downing in St Bartholomew's Close, a neighbour of the indicted John Darby, had reprinted the text for Thomas Sawbridge and Randall Taylor. Although Smith complained to Mearne of this flagrant infringement of his rights the Warden 'put him off with excuses and threats'.[41] Furthermore when the texts were completed the imprint still carried Smith's name and sign although his own impression remained in the custody of the Bishop.

Because of the evident inability of the Company to attend to the duties of censorship L'Estrange, with the King's mandate, began to meet with the Court of Assistants to negotiate a set of by-laws to help discipline Company members. On 5 September 1670 the Surveyor of the Press tendered a paper to the Court entitled 'The Particulars of his Majesties commands towards the regulations of the Presse'.[42] It contained three provisions. First that all members of the Company be bound by a recognizance to the King not to print, publish, bind or stitch up any unlicensed item. Secondly that any printer transgressing the former would not be allowed to practise his trade for three years. And finally transgressors with an interest in the English Stock would have the profit of his Stock sequestered for one year. This was the beginning of a long struggle over the question of Company by-laws in which an interesting confrontation developed between the representatives Roger L'Estrange and Samuel Mearne. L'Estrange on the one hand represented the interests of State authority, and later took up the cause of the patentee Captain John Seymour, while on the other hand Samuel Mearne was ensuring that the Company did not lose any of its privileges. The Wardens' Accounts show that the Company was obtaining regular advice from London's foremost lawyers during the eight-year debate over the by-laws. Further light was to be thrown on the underlying interests of the two parties between 1676-7 when the Lords Libels Committee met to investigate the growth of libellous publications.[43]

Samuel Mearne during his period of office as Under Warden, from July 1672 to July 1674, established a reputation for the trouble he took to seize unlicensed presses and suppress libellous publications. A document in the Stationers' Company Hall states that:

> In Anno 1672 & 1673 Mr. Mearne being then one of the Wardens of the Company of Stacon^{rs} expended in searches & disbursed in buying severall Printing Materialls of deceased Print^{rs} neer the sume of 1000^{l} in hopes to reduce the number of printers according to the Act of Parliam^{t}.[44]

But this was as much a piece of astute self-promotion as it was a public appearance of loyalty to the dictates of authority. For beneath the appearances was a shrewd businessman willing to capitalise on the opportunities that came his way.

Promotion had come quickly to Mearne after the Restoration. In June 1660 he became the King's bookbinder. Two years later the Secretary of State Nicholas wrote to the Stationers' Company recommending that Mearne be made a partner in the English Stock and 'that they will have especiall regard to him'.[45] Mearne appears to have kept a low profile in the Company until 1668 when he started to direct his attention towards London's unlicensed presses. On the 14 April 1668 the Bishop of London, Humphrey Henchman, informed the Stationers' Company of his concern at the number and activities of 'supernumarie master printers'.[46] Not long after this Mearne detected an illegal press in Southwark. Along with the Messenger of the Press, John Wickham, he had entered the home of the widow Elizabeth Poole and discovered, in the room let to Elizabeth Calvert, cases of type, a printing press, and reams of an unlicensed book. Later in the month Mearne claimed from the Secretaries of State £24.0s.6d. for his successful seizure.[47] At the first meeting of the Court of Assistants in May Mearne informed the Company that he had removed the press and cases of type lodged in Calvert's room to Wickham's chamber in Whitehall. Three days later as encouragement for his detective work the Secretaries of State granted Mearne the private press.[48]

Charles was obviously pleased by this display of loyalty for on 27 May 1668 he requested that Samuel Mearne, Roger Norton (the King's printer in Hebrew, Greek and Latin) and Thomas Roycroft (the King's printer in Oriental languages) be admitted to the Court of Assistants.

Indeed the King's letter to the Company declared that Mearne and colleagues 'having contributed much to suppress licentious practices in the Mystery of Printing; we expect that your Company henceforth will be accountable for scandalous abuses of the Press'.[49] But how loyal were in fact the King's appointees and in particular Samuel Mearne?

Not long after the deposit at Whitehall of Calvert's printing materials and seized publications, attempts were made by both Mearne and Richard Royston to take possession of the unlicensed text. According to Wickham, Mearne was the first to approach the Messenger and pleaded 'that there was no hurt in it and that Mrs Calvert must have it again'. But the suspicious Wickham remained steadfast in his resolve not to give up the reams. However, when Warden Royston approached the Messenger and stated that he had a general warrant from Secretary Morrice to seize unlicensed publications, the Messenger allowed the text to be removed. It appears that the text was once again in the market place as John Wickham was facing charges of disloyalty later in the year. Furthermore Wickham's petition defending himself from the charges named the culprit as Royston.[50] Not surprisingly Royston was reprimanded by the Privy Council as he acknowledged that he had 'bought unlicensed books'.[51] But the connection of Royston and Mearne with unlicensed publications did not stop. They were, however, more cautious in being directly connected with controversial publications as they played their twofold game: on the one hand posing as loyal supporters of State censorship while on the other supporting their associates in the surreptitious printing and sales of libellous and unlicensed literature.

I think that it is necessary to appreciate the range of economic interests and relationships between individuals in the book trade, especially amongst those who were supposed to be regulating the press, if we are to make correct inferences from the Wardens' Accounts. This will help to explain some of the inconsistencies between the seizure of illegal literature and the continued sale of these works.

Samuel Mearne, unlike Royston, managed to steer clear of accusations of improper conduct until 1676 when L'Estrange accused him of participating in the sales of unlicensed books. Moreover, according to the Surveyor of the Press Mearne was giving support to the Sawbridge brothers and the notorious Randall Taylor, all of whom were heavily involved in the publication of libellous texts.[52] However against the weight of this evidence we must acknowledge that Mearne carried out more searches, dismantled more presses and expended more money in buying the presses of deceased printers than any other previous warden. There are, I believe, at least two reasons for these activities. Firstly, Mearne had somehow to appease the authorities, in particular L'Estrange, who was attempting to pin the Company to a comprehensive set of by-laws. On 27 January 1672 L'Estrange had also proposed that the Company 'Keep a Distinct Book, or Register of all Offences, comitted by any of their members, against his Mat^y Church or State.' The Company appear to have followed the wishes of the Surveyor in this particular case for in 1681 the former Company clerk, John Lilly, handed into the Court two books of 'seizures of seditious & unlycenced Bookes'.[53] The second reason was that he (Mearne) wanted to stop further encroachments being made by rival patentees into the English Stock. One way to achieve these aims was to seize those unlicensed presses connected with their competitors. The rival patent holder Captain John Seymour, for example, had established a number of private presses to print various Greek and Latin titles, almanacks and psalters. The King had granted Captain Seymour the privilege of printing a number of classical texts in 1669 which was in direct conflict with an earlier grant to Roger Norton and the Stationers' Company.[54] The Company contested Seymour's monopoly in the Court of Chancery and the time and money expended by the guild can be followed in the Wardens' Accounts. But this was not the only course of action open to the Company.

It became clear to the Company that the activities of Seymour's private printers could be hampered by using their powers of search and seizure on the grounds that these printers were engaged in the publication of unlicensed literature. Indeed many of the printers who were to lose their presses were printing books under Seymour's patent. Thomas Rookes, for example, became the subject of Warden Mearne's searches in 1673. The printer was discovered printing psalters and almanacks. By June 1673 the Company had removed two of Rookes's presses at Uxbridge and one from his home in Ludgate. Along with the presses the Wardens had seized 8000 copies of 'Psalterium Carolinum' and 1000 almanacks.[55] In September 1673 Rookes petitioned the Privy Council claiming damages against the Company. However, the Company had already obtained a copy of the petition from a member of the Court and had sought out the best possible legal advice. The Council decided in the Company's favour and ordered the damasking of the psalter. This led Rookes to bring specific charges against certain Company members amongst whom were Randall Taylor and George Sawbridge. In their defence the Company pleaded that these men were only observing the fourteenth clause of the Printing Act 1662.[56] (See above, pp. 36-7.)

Another person whom Mearne mentions in the Accounts was the unlicensed printer Robert Battersby. In January 1673 Battersby was amongst the fourteen illegal printers summoned to the Table of the Stationers' Company 'to give an Account uppon what Tearmes they keep their seuerall printing-houses'.[56] Battersby informed the Table, at which sat Samuel Mearne, that he had entered the trade as a partner to the printer Henry Lloyd, but after several years working and living at Lloyd's home the printers decided to divide the printing stock and go their separate ways. Battersby appears to have had problems getting sufficient work and in order to avoid mounting debt he undertook to print a pirated edition of Richard Allestree's popular text <u>The Ladies Calling</u>.[57] However, the Bishop of London, Humphrey Henchman, interrupted the printing when he requested the Company to act against the printer of the pirated text. On 18 August 1673 a letter from the Bishop was read to the Court of Assistants in which accusations were carried against

Battersby. He was called before the Court where he confessed to printing 'the foure last sheetes' of the work.[58] On the following day the Wardens' Accounts record that Mearne had 'spent and given about taking downe Battersbyes Press' £1.10s.8d. Although Battersby refused to name the promoter of the pirated work it appears that the Company Beadle, Randall Taylor, may have been behind the publication. Prior to the Company's search of the printing house Taylor made an effort to warn Battersby to remove all controversial and pirated works.[59]

I stated earlier that Mearne, during his wardenship, began to buy up the presses and printing materials of deceased printers. The Accounts show that on 2 June 1673 Mearne spent £138 buying the presses and printing equipment of Edward Oakes. This was a half-hearted attempt by the Company to reduce the number of presses outside guild control. We know from the receipts in the Wardens' Accounts where Oakes's equipment went:

For Oakes's Printing Materialls	of Mr Jos: Leigh for Mettall	017	
	of Mr Andrew Clark	016	
	of Mr Lillycropp for a Presse	005	
	of Mr Ratcliff & Mr Thompson ꝑ bond	053	
	of Mrs Purslow by bond	048	04

There is a certain ambivalence underlying the sale of Oakes's materials because Peter Lillycrop, Thomas Ratcliffe and Nathaniel Thompson were all to be linked with the printing of libellous texts. Furthermore when the Accounts for 1673-4 were audited in March 1675 it was recorded that George Sawbridge owed £48.4s. 'for Oakes Materialls that were sold to Mrs Purslowe'. Presumably Sawbridge, described by John Dunton as 'the greatest bookseller that has been in England for many years', had helped enlarge the stock of the Purslowe printing house while his friend and colleague Samuel Mearne had provided the bookseller with extended credit. It was often asserted by printers that the booksellers were using their financial influence to make them (printers) dependent creatures. Thus Sawbridge's investment may have been a means of obtaining cheaper printing rates.[60]

Perhaps the strongest evidence of Mearne's double dealing came from two of the King's Messengers. On 23 October 1673 Gammon and

Blundel seized at the house of Randall Taylor 'three porters' loads of Dyer's sermons'. Although Taylor was arrested Mearne immediately interceded and put up bail for the publisher. According to the witnesses at the Lords Libels Committee hearing Mearne 'threatened the messengers, and dissuaded Taylor from paying them their fees'. Moreover Mearne later removed 1000 copies of Dyer's Sermons which he sold to Richard Royston who sold them to Robert White.[61] William Dyer's publications were immensely popular in Restoration England and although he avoided direct political comment he did criticise some of the practices of the clergy, judges and lawyers. Ironically in the preface to Christ's Voice to London the dissenting Dyer had protested that 'as soon as my books came forth, several men made a prize of them, by printing them without my knowledge, with many gross mistakes and abuses'.[62] Indeed it appears that Elizabeth Calvert's early attempts to publish Dyer had been usurped by the more powerful interests of Royston, Mearne, Taylor and Sawbridge.

My survey of the Wardens' Accounts has been necessarily selective. I believe, however, that these documents do provide a suitable starting point for helping us to understand some of the complex and entangled issues at the heart of the London book trade; in particular some of the motives that lay behind entries to the search and seizure of presses and literature. By exploiting their privileged positions the Wardens of the Stationers' Company were furthering their own interests. They seized unlicensed books so that they and their associates could sell and publish them at enhanced rates. Indeed the expedient practices of the Company was a constant source of comment for both the authorities, who saw their designs subverted, and the author who saw his text corrupted. In 1679 Thomas Hobbes was sufficiently disillusioned with the Company to voice his annoyance in a letter to his friend John Aubrey:

> I have been told that my Booke of the Civill Warr is come abroad, and am sorry for it especially because I could not get his Majestye to licence it, not because it is ill printed or has a foolish Title set to it. For I

believe that any ingenious man may understand the wickednesse of that time, notwithstanding the errors of the presse...The priviledge of Stationers is (in my opinion) a very great hinderance to ye advancement of all humane learning.[63]

Table 1: Receipts and payments of the Warden's Accounts, 1663-4 to 1679-80

Date	Under Warden	'Charges' Receipts			'Discharges' Payments			Balance			
		£	s	d	£	s	d	£	s	d	
1663-4	L. Fawne	1406	08	11	1372	16	00	+33	12	11	
1664-5	R. Tyler	879	05	02	792	18	05	+86	06	09	(1)
1665-6	R. Smith	314	15	08	295	16	03	+18	19	05	
1666-7	R. Royston	179	02	06	189	10	00	-10	07	06	
1667-8	R. Royston	90	03	08	103	18	08	-13	15	00	
1668-9	T. Hunt	800	15	04	799	05	08	+1	09	08	
1669-70	R. White	897	17	11	830	02	08	+67	15	03	
1670-1	A. Roper	1040	18	10	1029	09	00	+11	09	10	
1671-2	R. Norton	601	14	00	601	03	10	+00	10	02	
1672-3	S. Mearne	1158	07	02	1152	16	06	+5	10	08	
1673-4	S. Mearne	1268	12	11	1211	08	04	+57	04	07	
1674-5	T. Roycroft	477	00	06	443	03	06	+33	17	00	(2)
1675-6	J. Maycock	487	10	10	471	02	00	+16	08	02	
1676-7	R. Clarke	817	07	06	781	04	05	+36	03	01	
1677-8	T. Vere	1219	15	02	1152	06	11	+66	08	03	
1678-9	J. Martin	862	08	01	789	15	08	+72	12	05	
1679-80	T. Newcombe	588	04	03	361	13	08	+226	10	07	

It should be noted that there are often discrepancies between the figures given in the accounts and what one gets by adding up the receipts and payments for the various periods. I carried out spot checks for the accounts and found that the sums did not always tally:

(1) the figures given at the end of the account are 'Charge: £853.18s.06d.' and discharge: £792.18s.05d.' and a balance of £61.00s.01d.;

(2) the figures at the end of the account are 'charge: £476.19s.06d.' and 'discharge: £444.07s.01d.', and a balance of £32.12s.05d.

Notes

1 See for example 'AN ACT for Safety and Preservation of His Majesties Person and Government against Treasonable and Seditious practices and attempts' (13 Car II, St I, Cap. 1) 1661, and 'AN ACT against Tumults and Disorders, upon pretence of preparing or presenting public Peticons, or other Addresses to his Majesty or the Parliament' (13 Car II, St I, Cap. 5) 1661.

2 The list of London printers is to be found in Lambeth Palace Library, Gibsoniani MS 941 f. 62. For an account of the disaffected in the booktrade see Roger L'Estrange's Truth and Loyalty Vindicated (1662), and his Considerations and Proposals in Order to the Regulation of the Press (1663) (hereafter cited as Considerations).

3 See the introduction to An Exact Narrative of the Tryal and Condemnation of John Twyn (1664).

4 Both 'AN ACT for Safety and Preservation of His Majesties Person' 1661 and 'AN ACT for preventing frequent abuses in printing seditious treasonable and unlicensed Bookes and Pamphlets' 1662 expound the causal link between the press, the pulpit and the troubles of the 1640s. According to the author of An Exact Narrative of the Tryal and Condemnation of John Twyn (1664) part of the plan was 'to publish the designs of the living in the words of the dead; and the most conducing to their Project of destroying the Present King, to persuade the Multitude into a good Opinion of the Murder of the Last'. On sig. A3.

5 Alfred W. Pollard, 'Some notes on the history of copyright in England, 1662-1774', The Library, 3, 2 (1922), pp. 97-114. Cyprian Blagden, The Stationers' Company: A History 1403-1959 (1960). Frank Siebert, Freedom of the Press in England, 1476-1776 (Urbana, 1952).

6 There are two exceptions to this claim: George Kitchin's invaluable study Sir Roger L'Estrange (1913) and Leona Rostenberg's study of Robert Stephens in Literary, Political, Scientific, Religious and Legal Publishing in England 1551-1700 (2 vols, New York, 1965). Nonetheless both works could be updated in the light of new evidence.

7 Blair Worden, 'Radicalism between the lines', Times Literary Supplement (5 August 1983), p. 837. Christopher Hill, 'Henry Stubbe', Times Literary Supplement (30 September 1983), p. 1044.

8 Christopher Hill, The Experience of Defeat (1984), p. 21.

9 Ronald McKerrow, *An Introduction to Bibliography* (Oxford, 1927), p. 141.

10 *Considerations*, p. 25.

11 For some of the promotions see Stationers' Company Hall Court Book (hereafter cited as SCH) D, f. 81. 11 May 1663 and F. 140. 2 June 1668. Richard Royston was Under Warden from July 1666 to July 1668. He was Upper Warden from July 1671 to July 1672 and was Master from 1673 to 1675. Samuel Mearne was Under Warden from July 1672 to July 1674 and Upper Warden between July 1676 and July 1677. He was Master in 1679 and in 1681 for a year.

12 *The Statutes of the Realm* (9 vols, 1810-22), vol. v (1819), p. 432.

13 *Considerations*, p. 24.

14 *Calendar of State Papers Domestic* (1666-7), p. 430.

15 Cyprian Blagden, 'The accounts of the Wardens of the Stationers' Company', *Studies in Bibliography*, 9 (1957), p. 76.

16 ibid. p. 77.

17 ibid.

18 Cyprian Blagden, *The Stationers' Company: A History 1403-1959* (1960), p. 181.

19 R.C. Latham and W. Matthews, eds, *The Diary of Samuel Pepys* (11 vols, 1970-83), vol. vii, 5 October 1666, p. 309.

20 ibid. pp. 309-10.

21 SCH Court Book D, f. 81. 11 May 1663.

22 *A Complete Collection of State Trials...Compiled by T.B. Howell* (21 vols, 1809-14), vol. vi, col. 519.

23 H.R. Plomer, *A Dictionary of the Booksellers and Printers who were at work in England, Scotland, and Ireland from 1641 to 1667* (1907), p. 158.

24 See Douglas R. Lacey's chapter 'Electioneering and Lobbying Activities', in *Dissent and Parliamentary Politics in England, 1661-1689* (New Brunswick, 1969), pp. 99-120.

25 C.H. Timperley, *Encyclopaedia of Literary and Typographic Anecdotes* (1842), p. 543; E. Calamy, *The Nonconformist's Memorial* (2 vols, 1775), vol. ii, p. 346.

26 SCH Court Book D, f. 127^{v}, 5 February 1667.

27 ibid. f. 131^{v}, 4 June 1667.

28 ibid. f. 136, 17 December 1667. While Ponder had been asked to withdraw the almanack Robert White printed over 6000 copies entitled the Protestant Almanack.

29 Public Record Office SP 29/187/172. Amongst the texts named are The Second, and Third Advice to a Painter (Breda [sic], 1667), Wing M 887A; London's Flames Discovered (1667); and Fiat Lux (1665), Wing C 432.

30 PRO SP 29/187/172, [n.d., c. 1667-8]. Amongst other charges levelled against Royston in the document was that he helped take 'away Darby's Presses for a Quaker's sheet, & Milburn's before that, for ye Catholicks Apology: because they suspect them for Printing ye Company's Coppyes'.

31 Edmund Hickeringhill, A Speech Without Doors (1689), p. 32.

32 The texts make an appearance in the Wardens' Accounts in the following ways:

T P W P, 'Item paid Randolph Malpus alias John Darby for confessing the Printer & disperser of the Poor Whores Peticon & other Pamphletts. 2 00 00' (1667-68);
'Item paid 4 Messengers for Searching for the poor whores Peticon... 02 05 00' (1667-68)

L, '[Oct 6] Item paid him more that hee had Laid out upon the taking downe Mr Redmaines Presse and seizing of the sheetes of the Leviathan. 000 04 06' (1670);
'[March 24] Paid for damasking the Leviathan. 001 13' (1674);
'[Feb 12] Received of Mr John Williams for soe much Expended in the seizure & Damasking part of Hobbs his Leviathan. 002 13 6' (1675)

R T, '[Dec^{b} 2] Item spent on a Search for ye Rehearsall transposed. 001 05' (1672)

T W P A C, '[Feb] 24 Spent in a Search about Toomb's Book & Seizure of 4 Forms of ye Women & Mens Peticons about Coffee. 000 13 5' (1675)

N T, 'Marcij 3 Paid & laid out about another Search for Naked Truth 000 13 10.' (1676);
'[Marcij] 4 Paid Mr Warren for 3 daies attendance searching for Naked Truth 000 09 0.' (1676);
'[Marcij] 22 Paid Mr Garrett for his Bro: Simmons what he laid out for Naked Truths horse hire & other expences. 000 12 6' (1676).

M S o T D M, '[May] 8 Paid & Spent with our Master Mr Norton &^{c} on a Search, & coach hire to Mr Secr^{ty} Coventry &^{c} about Darby' & 'Ponders Pamphlet being part of Mr Smirk. 000 17 0' (1676);

'[May] 9 Paid & laid out in another Search for the residue of Mr Ponders Pamphlett with our Master & others. 000 05 6' (1676).

33 Journals of the House of Commons, vol. viii, 17 October 1666, p. 636.

34 R.C. Latham and W. Matthews, eds, The Diary of Samuel Pepys (11 vols 1970-83), vol. ix, 3 September 1668, p. 298. For an account of the reception of Hobbes see S.I. Mintz, The Hunting of Leviathan (Cambridge, 1962).

35 PRO SP 29/242/79. 30 June 1668.

36 The relationship between the various people who had a vested interest in the publication of the censored book became clear when John Redmayne provided details of the book's printing and seizure to the Secretary of State. See PRO SP 29/279/95^I. 28 September 1670.

37 SCH Court Book D, f. 176. 3 October 1670.

38 For a background to the different editions of the Leviathan see H. Macdonald and M. Hargreaves, Thomas Hobbes: A Bibliography (1952).

39 SCH Box A 3. 'Documents relating to damasking'. This provides the details of the Warden's payment. For Crooke's attempted assignment see Court Book D. f. 244. 22 February 1675

40 For a discussion on shared printing see Prof. D.F. Mckenzie's Sandars Lectures for 1976, privately published as The London Book Trade in the later Seventeenth Century (1976), pp. 20-2; and Peter Blayney's chapter 'Printing-House Methods' in The Texts of King Lear and their Origins (Cambridge, 1982). On the question of Augustan publishing and the meaning of the term 'trade publisher' see Michael Treadwell, 'London Trade Publishers 1675-1750', The Library, 4, 2 (1982) pp. 99-134.

41 SCH Box A. folder A6. Also, Historical Manuscripts Commission, Appendix to Ninth Report, pp. 77-8.

42 SCH Court Book D. f. 174. 5 September 1670.

43 Historical Manuscripts Commission, op. cit. pp. 69-78.

44 SCH Box A. folder A6.

45 See Calendar of State Papers Domestic (1660-1), p. 74, and SCH Court Book D, f. 70^v, 29 March 1662 for Mearne's promotions.

46 SCH Court Book D. f. 139, 14 April 1668.

47 See John Wickham's petition for an account of the search, PRO SP 29/248/88. [October?] 1668. For the grant of the seized press to Mearne see PRO SP 29/239/28. 28 April 1668.

48 SCH Court Book D, f. 139^{v}, 5 May 1668. PRO SP 44/30/32. 8 May 1668.

49 SCH Court Book D. f. 140. 2 June 1668.

50 PRO SP 29/248/88. [October ?] 1668.

51 PRO PC 2/61/106. 13 November 1668.

52 See Historical Manuscripts Commission, op. cit. pp. 77-8. For an account of Randall Taylor as a 'trade publisher' see Michael Treadwell, 'London Trade Publishers 1675-1750', The Library, 4, 2(1982), pp. 99-134.

53 SCH Court Book D, f. 174, 5 September 1670. These original proposals were further refined and modified: ibid. f. 175. 19 September 1670; f. 177^{v}. 17 October 1670; and f. 188-188^{v}. 28 August 1671. On the 'Register' see Court Book D, f. 194^{v}, 27 January 1672, and Court Book E, f. 109, 7 February 1681.

54 See Cyprian Blagden, The Stationers' Company (1960), pp. 193-5 and George Kitchin, Sir Roger L'Estrange (1913), pp. 205-6. See also PRO, SP 29/408/57, 9 December 1678 for a list of publications granted to Seymour in 1669.

55 SCH Box A, folder A6. The document provides a background to the seizure of Rookes's presses and texts.

56 SCH Court Book D, f. 210, 10 January 1673. Although the Company summoned fourteen illegal printers they only listened to the claims of ten; see PRO SP $29/332/96^{I-III}$. 15 January 1673.

57 PRO SP $29/332/96^{I-III}$. 15 January 1673 and Historical Manuscripts Commission, op. cit. p. 77.

58 SCH Court Book D. f. 220. 18 August 1673.

59 Historical Manuscripts Commission, op. cit. p. 77.

60 John Dunton, The Life and Errors (1818), p. 211.

61 PRO SP 29/366/263. 20 December 1676.

62 William Dyer, Christ's Voice to London (1666), Wing D 2942.

63 BL Add MS. Eg, 2231/207.

Robert and Sir Francis Gosling: Eighteenth-Century Bankers and Stationers

Frank Melton

The casual visitor to 19 Fleet Street might neglect to notice a curious piece of fauna, a black spread eagle hovering perilously near three squirrels. The bird sign is familiar as the emblem of Barclays Bank; the animal trio is less well known, being the sign of an old firm - Gosling's Bank - long ago absorbed by Barclays. Gosling's has had a distinguished history, which it claims derives from 1650, when William Pinckney first established its foundation. Within the bank the history of the partnership records various changes until the Gosling family in the eighteenth century began to hold the bank as a family enterprise passing through generations.

The eighteenth-century Goslings were neither goldsmiths nor scriveners, and their banking interests do not derive from either of the two traditions upon which private, deposit banking first emerged during the seventeenth century. The father of the Gosling family, Robert Gosling, was a successful publisher and bookseller, who in another capacity performed certain financial functions which can be called banking. Upon his death his son Sir Francis Gosling gave up the publishing business, took over the lease of the Three Squirrels and became a banker proper. In banking history, Goslings presents a unique example of the first bank in London which arose first from a commercial source. Similarly, in the history of the booktrade Robert and Sir Francis Gosling represent a type of financial activity rare in the annals of publishing.

Robert Gosling was born in 1684 in Whitefriars, Canterbury.[1] His early training as a stationer is unrecorded, but apparently he completed his apprenticeship by 1707, when he published his first book. This initiated a long, successful career, for by the time of his death in 1741, he had published or sold 477 separate titles.[2] These books range the gamut of Augustan taste, even to the curious title by Philander Misaurus, The Honour of the Gout: Or, a Rational Discourse, Demonstrating that the Gout is One of the Greatest Blessings Which Can Befall Mortal Man (1735). The books which Robert Gosling published, sold or printed and distributed can be divided into eleven separate categories:

1)	Religious	76	7)	Historical	50
2)	Classical Subjects and Translations	16	8)	Trade & Commerce	4
3)	Legal - Equity	46	9)	Literary	13
4)	Legal - General	192	10)	Scientific (Geography, Botany and Architecture)	12
5)	Parliamentary Statutes	44	11)	Miscellaneous	18
6)	Parliament	2			

However, if the separate legal and parliamentary categories are reduced from four to one division, they comprise 59% of all the titles Robert Gosling published and sold at his premises near the Old Bailey. These books include Acts of Parliament, both complete as well as for individual sessions, law reports, legal dictionaries and guides to the complexities of diverse branches of law - a variety of titles that found their way to the libraries of the gentry and legal people.

By 1713 the young publisher was acting as a cash keeper for a naval official living abroad, who also remarked upon Gosling's activities in putting his clients' deposits out at interest. It was in this connection as cashier and money broker that his client sought what he termed Gosling's 'multiplicity' of services, and he was not referring to his publishing career.[3] Before 1717 Gosling had a modest record as bookseller and printer, and to some extent he practised banking. But in that year - 1717 - his publishing career took a giant step forward when Elizabeth Nutt sold him half of the patent she and her late husband John Nutt held to publish all statutes and law books. The Nutts' patent had an ancestry from Elizabeth I's grant to Thomas Wright to print for thirty years all law books concerning statute and common law. This privilege descended in a line of patent-holders to Edward Sayer, who then assigned the Nutts as his printers. At John Nutt's death the patent was challenged before Chancery by John Walthoe, bookseller, who had commissioned Nutt to publish Salkeld's Cases. This project was organised as a subscription venture, and at Nutt's death only the first two volumes were in print. When Elizabeth Nutt and Robert Gosling printed volume three of Salkeld's work they did so independent of Walthoe, claiming that by the terms of their patent only they enjoyed the right to its publication.[4]

The Nutts' patent was also challenged by John Baskett, who asked the court whether or not their privilege extended to Rastall and Paulton's abridgements.[5] What the two ambitious publishers Walthoe and Baskett did was to attack the patent in a larger framework than the specific books they mentioned. The original patent extended, so they claimed, to current actions of parliamentary statute and to current decrees in common law. The 'king's printers', from Wright to Sayer, had been authorised to publish the official law of the realm, but this did not extend to the publication of old laws, to law reports or to the many abridgements and commentaries on the law. Works concerning the law, rather than the statement of law itself, did not fall under the patent held by Elizabeth Nutt and Robert Gosling.

From 1717 to 1718 the new co-partners Nutt and Gosling published twenty-three separate titles, which fall into categories suggesting the market they hoped to maintain now that their patent was in jeopardy. During those two years they published five works of Giles Jacob, whose prolific career as a legal writer earned him the description from Alexander Pope as the 'blunderbuss of law'. For the twenty-six separate titles, some in many volumes and several in different editions, Robert Gosling was Jacob's publisher. Jacob published law dictionaries and legal commentaries, but he also published laws arranged under specific topics, and this idea caught their imaginations. Soon they had published volumes of game laws, militia law, laws relating to travelling and poor laws - all designed to attract a public greater than the legal profession.

Nutt and Gosling still upheld their obligations to lawyers and judges. In the two years 1717 to 1718 they published The Law of Evidence, and The Office and Authority of the Justice of the Peace, both by William Nelson of the Middle Temple, as well as a treatise on legal pleas, and both Lutwyche's Cases and Salkeld's. In the years to follow Elizabeth Nutt and Robert Gosling (and he alone after her death) were to publish thirty-four separate law reports, of cases in Chancery, King's Bench and Common Pleas.

Soon Nutt and Gosling adopted another interest to enhance their privilege of printing current parliamentary statutes. This was their interest in publishing all the statues at large, from Anglo-Saxon times to the present, and including ecclesiastical law. In 1720 they printed a digest of the law of England. In Gosling's Bank there is a list of the expenses that Robert Gosling incurred in the publication of these statutes. David Casley was paid for transcribing a copy of Rastall's statutes from Sir Robert Cotton's library, then held at Westminster School.[6] Although the purpose of the transcription was to serve the publication of statutes, it led Gosling to publish as a separate venture Casley's catalogue of the Cottonian library.[7] In another instance Gosling paid Charles Bush £41.4s.0d. for his work in transcribing the Statute Rolls in the Tower of London, specifically the rolls of the reign of Edward I, Edward II and Edward III.[8]

* * *

This output of books followed the growth of the legal profession during the late seventeenth and eighteenth centuries. Not only were there more lawyers under the Georges than there had been under the Stuarts, but also their training was more carefully regulated. Before 1660 many legal actions, especially in the country, were executed by attorneys, the title given to anyone representing the interests of another in court, whether or not he had legal education. Gradually trained lawyers gained control of the attorneys by requiring these men to spend time studying at the Inns of Court. All legal practitioners acquired at least the rudiments of legal practice, while at the same time they were confronted by the bewildering mass of law, particularly as it affected property.[9] Perhaps no person of any legal experience could revive the faith of Oliver Cromwell that the property law of England and Wales could be digested into a pocket book which every man could own.

Lawyers could claim that they knew which conveyances, actions and contracts were likely to be accepted by the courts. Knowing the property law, which was ever in flux, required keeping abreast of the legal decisions of the courts of Chancery and Exchequer. Robert Gosling and the Nutts held a captive audience with the legal profession, but outside the courts and chambers law became a topic of interest, attracting as much apparent fascination as theological dispute provoked during the Reformation. The squires of Walpole's time were likely to purchase law books for use in their everyday affairs, as aids in their duties as J Ps and as reference works to the proceedings in parliament. The vast array of titles in Gosling's shop could satisfy the needs of almost every man of property entering his premises.

Robert Gosling's publishing career must be placed in the context of this change in legal culture. As co-owner of the patent for legal publications Gosling had direct links with the political and legal establishment. In 1738, when the Statutes were finally completed, he delivered copies to the Lord Chancellor, the Master of the Rolls, and the Attorney General as well as twelve separate sets to the Masters in Chancery.[10] One can imagine that the high standards of accuracy which went into the preparation of the legal statutes and other transcriptions and commentaries upon old legal documents inspired confidence in the man who worked so close to the formulation of the printing of the law. He who publishes the law - in Gosling's case statutory as well as equity law - obtains through association a knowledge of the law rivalling that of the best-trained lawyers. What better method to learn the law than to transcribe its original sources, to translate obsolete words into contemporary usage, to set type and correct proofs? From this connection of working closely to the precise meaning of the law Robert Gosling's banking career assumed a closer focus.

Robert Gosling's career in printing legal books and his banking career recall a similar association between the rudiments of law and finance during an earlier stage in English banking history. There are two distinct phases of deposit banking in English history, one medieval, and the other a post-medieval development from which modern banking derives. The first bankers in England followed the Norman kings to their new realm. Then, when the popes were resident at Avignon, during the Babylonian Captivity of the Papacy, the popes relied upon Italian bankers to collect papal taxes. It was during this period that bankers from Lombardy arrived in the City and gave their place of origin to the famous street there, since associated with banking. In the early fourteenth century Edward I expelled his Jewish money lenders and Italian bankers from England and there was a period when there were no deposit banks surviving from one generation to the next.[11] The earliest evidence of a tradition of banking, traceable in an unbroken sequence to the present day, goes back to Shakespeare's time, when a class of petty financiers and conveyancers agreed to accept money on deposit. These were the scriveners, not to be confused with the medieval company of Court Letter Scriveners who were ruined with the invention of the printing press. By 1565 the remnants of the old company were absorbed into the Ironmongers' guild. However, there continued to flourish notaries and other scribes writing petty legal contracts, outside of any guild arrangement, and they called themselves scriveners. Their conveyancing skills brought landowners to these men, who in turn seem to have persuaded their clients to allow them to receive their deposits in London, to be put out on loan. Thus, in this connection legal knowledge carried with it financial acumen, and led scriveners to become loan brokers.[12]

If the scriveners were the first bankers in modern times, their position declined throughout the seventeenth century as the techniques of land transfer became so complex that attorneys and lawyers were able to capture the conveyancing market which the scriveners had once held. With their legal and scribal skills in jeopardy, the scriveners also lost their position as bankers to a branch of the goldsmiths, who, practising as financiers, were known as the goldsmith bankers. One group specialised in loans to the Crown, while at the same time they accepted money on deposit and made loans to and from private clients. The second group of goldsmith bankers were the smaller fry who never acquired the privileges of lending to the Crown. Their days of glory came after Charles II stopped payments from the Exchequer to his bankers in 1672, an act which brought ruin to the cream of the goldsmith bankers. Deposit banking then fell to the lesser goldsmiths, and it is from a handful of these firms that the oldest banks in England today - Hoare's, Coutts's, Martin's and Child's - can trace their origins.

The goldsmith tradition would seem to bear a close affinity to banking, as goldsmiths worked so close to specie. It was no accident that goldsmiths had served as wardens to the royal mint. Even if a goldsmith did not actually make coins, by fashioning gold into precious objects he seemed close enough to coinage to inspire confidence among clients to leave their money on deposit with him. It would seem logical that private banking would proceed from the craft of the goldsmiths, but the actual historical examples are not quite so simple. In fact, only a handful of goldsmith banks managed to survive. At least ninety-three separate goldsmith banks can be accounted for between 1670 and 1700. From 1670 to 1687 at least eleven houses survived, though by 1700 only four of the foundations of 1670 had survived. In the lists of 1677, 1687 and 1700 at least thirty-three new banks appeared. Three of these banks have disputed dates of origin and may have arisen somewhat later in the early eighteenth century. Of the banks remaining, only two foundations lasted beyond 1736. Of the seventeenth century goldsmith banks only five had any permanence - Hoare's, Martin's, Child's, Coutts's and Hankey's.[13]

Private banking before the eighteenth century had shifting foundations. Those few goldsmiths who managed to survive seem to have separated themselves largely from the craft of fashioning specie and specialised in making private loans. Foreign to their training was an expertise in law or writing conveyances. A pamphlet of 1676 said that the goldsmiths had no more knowledge of the law than ordinary citizens.[14] Consequently, the successful goldsmith bankers, trafficking in loans to private individuals, became dependent upon lawyers, and in doing so adopted some of the legal and conveyancing banking traditions the scriveners had prepared some time before. Banking therefore was not a self-contained profession with an expertise peculiar only to itself, such as the church or the army. Bankers relied increasingly upon the conveyancing skills of lawyers, while at the same time lawyers in the country often received deposits and made loans, much like the scriveners of the seventeenth century. When Robert Gosling practised banking alongside his printer's shop he did so in a situation not without parallels in the past, and in a current context where banking had not become firmly established.

The banks' operations are quite different from those banking-like functions which other financiers can perform, such as money lending and discounting notes and bills of exchange. A working definition of banking is a system of money lending beyond an ordinary source of capital. A merchant who lends, say, £100 of his profits is not a banker, since his lending capital - in this case, his profits - is ordinary to his trade as a merchant. Private banking is almost always dependent upon deposits which bankers agree to accept. On the one hand, bankers were cashiers, who kept their clients' accounts and paid some of their clients' debts, in connection with accepting their deposits. On the other hand, bankers also served as loan brokers by finding suitable borrowers for their clients' loans. True bankers, however, are neither simple cashiers nor simple brokers, both of whom merely process money with no other profit to themselves than the fees they charge for their services. In a proper banking situation the banker has the use of his clients' deposits for his own investment. That is, he lends his deposits in his own name between the time that his deposits are received and discharged. Therefore, bankers realised their fortunes, not through the fees they charged for their services as cashiers and loan brokers, but rather through the investment of their clients' deposits in their own names.

As cashiers, bankers receive deposits in return for which they infrequently allow interest. This practice seems to have been uncommon, however, as the bankers Thomas Snow and Thomas Martin related in separate legal depositions in 1722. In lieu of interest, they said, bankers performed a variety of services which went beyond the mere accepting and accounting for the flow of deposits through their hands.[15] They might issue notes, purchase lottery tickets and stock shares, discount bills and notes, accept valuables for safe keeping and act, generally, as London agents for any other affairs their clients might request.

As loan brokers, bankers were brought into the practice of giving credit, one of their distinctive functions. The selling of credit through loans was both simple and complex. Short-term small-scale loans can be secured through surety or, upon certain conditions, through registration. In the early days of banking the conditioned penal bond was used frequently by bankers and ordinary citizens to secure loans. According to this security, if the loan was unpaid at the date set in the contract, the borrower must surrender a draconian fine - often two or three times the amount of the principal - as well as paying the interest. Gradually penal bonds fell into disfavour in Chancery, and upon this turn of events, mortgages began to replace penal bonds in certain lending situations. Mortgages tend to be large-scale loans, and long-term, as long as the rents of the secured property (with other profits) are set to repay the loan. The property is the security for the loan, and at the time of its birth the guarantee of its repayment is set through the rent charges delegated in the mortgage contracts.

Critical in a mortgage negotiation is an accurate assessment of the long-term value of the land secured in the loan. In a penal bond the security is personal, and, as such, is vague since neither the lender nor his banker has any way of determining exactly what a man is worth. However, in a mortgage negotiation credit has a finite value which can be estimated upon an exact system of analysis. There is a two-part inspection of the security. The first stage involves a search through the local land registers and the Chancery rolls to determine that the land is free from liens prior to the mortgage. While his clerks might perform this part of the process of clearing the title, in the second part of the assessment the banker must rely upon either a surveyor or lawyer, or perhaps upon both men.

The survey of the estate was executed at the site. From the manorial rolls the surveyor listed the tenants and the conditions of their leases. At the same time, he noted the legal aspects of the manor, which were the rights and duties of the lords _vis-à-vis_ corresponding dues and privileges maintained by the peasants. The legal franchises of the manor included, for example, fishing rights and the customs relating to hunting. Next, the mensuration of the estate was taken, which included its far-reaching boundaries, as well as the acreage of each tenant. Finally, the tenants themselves were summoned to listen to the surveyor's description of the estate and, if necessary, to challenge his notes. These field notes were then returned to the banker, who determined the value per acre of each holding to be mortgaged.

With the survey and abstract of the title the banker was in a position to make or break a negotiation between his lender and debtor. If he had reason to say that the title was faulty or that the land was worth less than the loan he could wreck the loan but if he could assure his clients that the estate was credit worthy, they were likely to take his advice and the loan would be successfully concluded. Either way, the banker's abilities to determine mortgage credit placed him in a commanding position in the credit process, unlike a passive broker, who acts as no more than a middle-man between the lender and the debtor, who control the process of credit.

The banking part of Robert Gosling's business unfortunately left no accounting ledgers, making it impossible for us to know in quantitative terms how extensive these operations were. Other records survive, however, in the Guildhall Library and at Gosling's Bank, which suggest that Gosling performed the functions of a banker proper, though the question still remains as to how extensive this form of finance was and to what degree it rivalled his bookseller's business. The first suggestion of Gosling's banking operations occurs in a series of letters written to him and a cohort by one of Gosling's kinsmen, Joseph Griffin, who lived abroad where he worked for the Navy. In the letter that he wrote to Gosling on 29 December 1713 he mentioned whether the £160 he had placed on deposit had been put out to loan: '...I can't imagine why you should not promote what you take to be very much your advantage, in placing out your money to a more beneficial account.' Gosling had agreed some time before to manage the operation of a mortgage, to which he and Griffin were both parties. Then, Griffin asked Gosling to redeem another mortgage of houses in the Old Bailey, so that he might pay off his debts in part to Gosling. Gosling then had the lands surveyed and found that the builders were forced to build the houses on a strip of ground so narrow that the tunnels of the chimneys ran into each other, preventing proper ventilation. Also, the houses extended into the jurisdiction of another parish. Gosling issued statements of account only irregularly. After a long silence Griffin wondered whether or not Gosling was really interested in his affairs, for he had heard that Gosling's banking consumed an inordinate amount of his time.[16] Thus, for Joseph Griffin Gosling performed the role of cashier and at the same time he acted as a broker who placed his clients' deposits out at interest.

The next evidence of Gosling's banking is cited in a list compiled by the banker in about 1720, regarding expenses which he incurred while acting on behalf of two parties to a mortgage. Two men were paid £3.15s.0d. to survey the estate. Later, he made a trip north with two other men to inspect and appraise the timber on the property. Gosling was present in Wallop and Romsey when mortgagor and mortgagee agreed to the terms he had arranged.[17] In another example, in 1733, Gosling arranged a mortgage between a Mrs Lawrence and a Mr Russell. He prepared all the preliminaries of credit and arranged all the writings of the conveyances and their registration.[18]

Among the trunks of miscellaneous papers in Gosling's Bank there are papers which contain insufficient notation for the modern researcher to ascribe them either to the business of the Goslings or to the goldsmith bankers who preceded them in the lease of the Three Squirrels. One note lists several orders made for lottery tickets at 5% and interest paid to Lady Day in 1719. On the same document is a copy of a receipt given to John Bennett on 19 August 1719; Bennett is a name unknown in the partnerships of the goldsmith predecessors of the Goslings,[19] though Samuel Bennett was to join Francis Gosling in his banking partnership later. Another document in this assorted collection, however, clearly relates to Robert Gosling's business in discounting bills of exchange: James Mathews wrote to Robert Gosling from Newbury on 27 August 1720 that his brother Thomas 'had waited on you for the money but my not sending you a letter of advice before...was the occasion you did not pay him'.[20] It was the custom for the drawer of a bill to send a letter of advice with the note ordering that the note be paid.

The final evidence relating to Robert Gosling's banking career is reflected in three notes which survive. On 15 November 1735 John Stevens wrote a form which reads: 'Received of Mr. Robert Gosling the sum of £10.10s.0d. for which I promise to be accountable on demand.' That is the form of a simple loan transaction for a small sum which did not require registration. On 4 July 1735 Gosling wrote a promissory note 'to Mr Serjeant Hawkins or Order £24.5s.0d.'. Gosling's name was removed from this simple banker's note when the money was repaid. Another note, for a 'timed' deposit, is dated 22 October 1733 and reads: 'I promise to pay to William Hawkins Serjeant at Law or Order the sum of £93.8s.0d. four months after date for value received.'[21] When the note was paid in, Gosling tore his name from the contract, thus cancelling the obligations he had made in what was clearly a banker's note - one of the distinctiv instruments of banking.

* * *

Robert Gosling died in 1741 and was succeeded in his business for some two or three years by his son Francis, who was to have a different career from his father. Before he ceased his father's publishing operations in 1743 Francis Gosling published nine titles himself. The question arises as to whether or not Francis failed as a publisher, whereupon he then fell back upon, and extended, the banking side of his father's operations. Francis Gosling inherited his father's share in the legal patent, and, until 1743, his name was credited on the title page as being one of the assignees of Edward Sayer. In the same year, however, <u>The Practical Register of the Common Pleas</u> was published for Henry Lintot, who was then designated as the assignee of Edward Sayer, with no similar attribution to Gosling. This suggests that Francis Gosling had either lost or sold his father's share in the patent. Certainly a connection with his publishing background was destroyed on 5 October 1742, when Francis Gosling held an auction sale of his stock. So, after publishing only nine titles, Francis sold off the Gosling's stock - this suggests that Francis did not suffer a decline in the publishing trade but rather took active steps to sell up the printing business for another career.

The publishing catalogue was divided into three parts.[22] Part I consisted of the late Robert Gosling's stock, with ninety-nine separate titles for sale, divided into thirty-four lots, a total of 11,458 separate books. Incidentally, The Honour of the Gout proved not to be a perennial best seller: 670 copies were remaindered in the 1742 sale.

Part II of the auction comprised Robert Gosling's unbound books and the copper plates surviving his death. The plates for both State Trials and Statutes at Large were still around, as befits two such standard references. At the time of his death Robert Gosling had engraved sixty folio plates of Price's Architecture which he never published. In the sale ninety-three books appeared from Francis Gosling's own collection. Titles in the sale catalogue were only briefly described and are difficult to correlate precisely with the formal bibliographical entries accepted today but it appears that Francis Gosling's interest in books extended beyond the stock list his father and himself published.

* * *

The first instance of Francis Gosling's banking makes an abrupt entrance into the partnership of a bank. In the profit and loss accounts, now in Fleet Street, Edward Stanley, on 6 February 1744, was paid fifteen guineas for drawing up a partnership agreement between John Ward, Samuel Bennett and Francis Gosling, and at the Michaelmas reckoning of that year Gosling and Bennett divided profits among themselves of £473.19s.2½d.[23] Francis Gosling had, therefore, bought a share of a bank already in operation. The earliest ledgers were kept by the goldsmiths Abraham Fowler, James Rocke and John Simpson and in these the goldsmiths' work is clearly detailed: fashioning jewellery, making silverware and speculation in bullion are among the features described. At the same time these partners received money from clients who did not call upon their skills as goldsmiths. Their profit and loss accounts do not survive before 1727 but from these records, which are continuous after that time, it is possible to make a comparison with the goldsmith bank of Fowler, Rocke and Simpson and the new partnership which assumed control of the operation in 1744. At that time there is no sharp break in the ledgers; the old customers continued to stay with the new customers. Perhaps more impressive is the size of their clientele. From 1719 to 1722 the bank had 187 clients but from 1751 to 1754 the partnership of Gosling, Bennett and Ward persuaded 480 persons to put their money on deposit with them.[24]

Along with this expansion, the profits of the bank increased dramatically. From 1730 to 1734 the goldsmith bankers Fowler, Rocke and Simpson received into their profit accounts £2164. During a comparable five-year period from 1744 to 1749 the new Gosling partnership more than doubled that amount and £4113 appeared in their accounts as loans and interest repaid, made from their profits as well as from the use of their clients' deposits. The loans books themselves do not survive, and neither do another series of investment ledgers, which were termed the 'stock books'. In the profit and loss accounts, however, there is an incidental reference to the items included in stocks purchased for their customers: the 'Salt Order', lottery tickets and life annuities; but from other references it appears that these bankers, like their successors, were buying shares of Bank of England stock and East India Company stock for their clients, who would have then paid their bankers a commission for this service. From 1730 to 1734 Fowler, Rocke and Simpson recorded that £3516 had been repaid into their stock book from investments made on behalf of their clients. In a comparable five-year period the Gosling partnership increased that record by 3.3 times and £11,739 was repaid into their accounts on behalf of stock purchases made for their clients.

The net profits of the bank are impressive. By 1762 the Gosling partnership had increased the profits, split between the partners, by five times. From 1727 to 1732 Fowler, Rocke and Simpson divided profits which came to a total of £5,211. In the first five years, the Gosling company made a total of £11,552, and this included one bad year - 1747-8 - when they lost £1388. But in a later period, from 1758 to 1762, Gosling recorded £26,795 in profits.[25] The final date is significant in another context, for it is after that time that the numbers of banks practising in London began to increase dramatically. Gosling's bank was well positioned by that time to meet the new competition. Throughout the 1740s and 1750s letters were sent to the bank by clients abroad, even in India. But that story - the growth of the international operations of the bank - has yet to be told.

Notes

1 The few biographical details of Robert and Francis Gosling in print have yet to be organised as a published form, but see *Burke's Landed Gentry*, ed. K.P. Townend (1965), vol. i, p. 325.

2 The analysis of Robert and Francis Gosling's publications was taken from a computer print-out, made in the British Library, of the Eighteenth-Century Short Title list. At this date this project is incomplete, suggesting that the numbers and diversity of titles mentioned in this paper are actually greater than I have indicated.

3 Guildhall Library, MS 8955.

4 Public Record Office C 11/318/28 (Gosling *v.* Walthoe).

5 PRO, C 11/1438/7 (Baskett *v.* Salmon).

6 Goslings Bank, Miscellaneous Papers, 'Moneys disbursed for and upon Account of the Statutes at Large in 6 vols', (26 April 1728 -22 April 1738).

7 David Casley, *A Catalogue of the Manuscripts of the King's Library: An Appendix to the Catalogue of the Cottonian Library... (1734)*.

8 See note 6. *The Statutes at Large, from Magna Charta to the Seventh Year of King George the Second, Inclusive* (6 vols, 1734-5).

9 See R. Robson, *The Attorney in Eighteenth Century England* (Cambridge, 1959); F.M.L. Thompson, 'Land-ownership and economic growth in England in the eighteenth century', *Agrarian Change and Economic Development*, ed. E.J. Jones and S.J. Woolf (1969), p. 54; B.L. Anderson, 'The attorney and the early capital market in Lancashire', *Liverpool and Merseyside Essays in the Economic and Social History of the Port and Its Hinterland*, ed. J.K. Harris (New York, 1969), pp. 50-77

10 See footnote 6.

11 See E.B. Fryde and M.M. Fryde, 'Public credit with special reference to North-Western Europe...', *The Cambridge Economic History of Europe*, (Cambridge, 1963), vol.iii, pp. 430-63.

12 Thomas Wilson, *A Discourse upon Usury...*, ed. R.W. Tawney (1925); A.V. Judges, 'The origins of English banking', *History*, 16 (1931), pp. 138-45; R.D. Richards, *The Early History of Banking in England* (1929); *Records of the Society of Gentlemen Practisers* (1897); F.W. Steer, *A History of the Worshipful Company of Scriveners of London* (London and Chichester, 1973).

13 These figures were compiled from the lists of bankers in F.G. Hilton Price, Handbook of London Bankers (1890-91).

14 The Mystery of the New-Fashioned Goldsmiths (1676), p. 5.

15 PRO, E 133. 145/65 (7710).

16 Guildhall Library, MS 8955.

17 Goslings Bank, Miscellaneous Papers. (List of expenses concerning the sale and mortgage of an estate, c. 1720.)

18 ibid., (William Pocklington's charge for legal services to Robert Gosling.)

19 ibid., 'Several orders in Lottery...Copy of a Receipt given to Jno. Bennett, August 19 1719'.

20 ibid., James Matthews to Robert Gosling, 27 August 1720.

21 ibid. for these three notes.

22 A Catalogue of Books in Quires, and Copies; Being the Stock of Mr. Francis Gosling, Which Will be Sold by Auction to the Booksellers of London and Westminster...on Tuesday, the 5th of October, 1742... (1742).

23 Goslings Bank, Profit and Loss Account No. 664, fol. 58.

24 ibid. These figures are based upon an analysis of the clients' ledgers.

25 ibid. These figures are based upon an analysis of the profit and loss accounts for the relevant periods.

The Personnel of the Stationers' Company, 1800–30: Work in Progress

Michael Turner

It has been my aim for a number of years to collect materials towards the compilation of a biographical dictionary of the London Booktrade between the years 1800 and 1830. This project ambled along in a rather desultory fashion until - on the death of Graham Pollard - I gained easy access to his fine run of the Stationers' Company octavo Livery Lists, which had been owned previously by John Nichols and C.R. Rivington. Looking through these lists I was struck by the size of the Livery in the early years of the nineteenth century, and both by the names that were included and by those that were not. I returned to Cyprian Blagden's account of the Company in order to refresh my memory of its history during this period, for I must admit that I had rather dismissed the Stationers from my thoughts as not having much relevance to the history of the trade by this time. Blagden reminded me that 'The Stationers' Company is one of the very few London Companies which still insists that those buying their freedoms shall be associated with one of its traditional gild trades: bookbinding, bookselling and publishing, printing, paper-merchandising' Also that the Company 'entered the nineteenth century on a wave of prosperity'; that 'the [current] dispute between the masterprinters and their journeymen boosted the intake of apprentices'; that 'even booksellers were taking up their freedoms more frequently'; that 'the Livery, supported in the main by tradesmen other than printers, grew so steadily that it was thought expedient in 1809 to raise the fine to £50'; and that 'in the following year [1810] the number of Livery men reached the record figure of 517 - a size "productive of many inconveniences", the chief of which was that a large number of

Livery men never achieved more than a £40 share in the English Stock'. It was clear that no matter how important or unimportant the Company might have been to the organisation and workings of the trade during the early part of the nineteenth century (1800-30) its archives should provide a rich source of biographical information on a large section of that trade. In 1978, Don McKenzie published the last of his three volumes - Stationers' Company Apprentices - bringing the record in print up to the year 1800.

It became obvious that the 'ambling' should cease and that I should make a systematic attack on the membership of the Stationers' Company for the first thirty years of the nineteenth century. McKenzie's example was before me, and - knowing that he did not intend to go beyond 1800 - it seemed logical that I should begin by carrying on with the apprentices. Although not so distant from the archive as New Zealand, like McKenzie I was only able to visit it infrequently, and, unlike him, I was not particularly helped by the microfilm of the archives made just after the Second World War, because it had clearly been the policy of the makers of that particular set of films to end each sequence of records with the volume that contained the last years of the eighteenth century. Although some of those volumes crept into the nineteenth century, many of them did not creep very far.

So I began with the printed octavo Livery Lists that were available to me in Oxford. Pollard described these lists in his 1955 edition of John Pendred's The London and Country Printers, Booksellers and Stationers Vade Mecum of 1785. The most important run of the octavo series of Livery Lists seems to have been issued around 1 July each year beginning in 1786, the year after Pendred's directory. A broadside series of Livery Lists survives from the year 1721, but I will return to these later. The issues of the octavo series from 1786 to 1797 bear no imprint. From 1798 to 1803 they were printed by March and Teape of Tower Hill; from 1804 to 1862 by Henry Teape at the same address; and after that date by Harrison & Sons of St Martin's Lane. Pollard recorded two sets, the most complete one being at Stationers' Hall which lacks only the issue for 1794. It is a sad fact that neither Robin Myers nor I have ever been able to locate this set. The second set, that is the Nichols/Rivington/Pollard set and the one from which I have worked, starts in 1792, but lacks 1793, 1794, 1799, and 1827 to 1840. For my purpose, therefore, I had a straight run from 1800 to 1826 inclusive. Knowledgeable users of Pendred will know that included in this set were odd issues printed by Harrison & Son published in January - during my period there were examples for 1821 and 1822.

My first illustration shows the title-page of the issue for 1810. The 1 July is the beginning of the Gild Year. The List (second illustration) begins with the names and addresses of the Master, the Wardens, and the Court of Assistants. Note that in the left-hand column every fifth entry is numbered in order of precedence.

The Master and the Upper and Under Wardens would have just been elected by the Court, from the Court, on the Saturday following 29 June (St Peter's Day). The election would normally follow precedence, but an Assistant could avoid holding any further office by paying a fine. The amounts of fines were adjusted from time to time. The Master and Wardens would serve in these offices for the following year; in the case of the death or removal of a Master or either of the Wardens, a special meeting of the Court of Assistants would forthwith elect a replacement. It should be noted that the Assistants who currently hold the office of Alderman take precedence over all other Assistants; a Liveryman, not being an Assistant but becoming an Alderman, is immediately taken into the Court and assumes this level of precedence.

The Assistants are chosen from time to time by the Court from the Liverymen who have either served the office of Renter-Warden, or have paid the required fine in lieu of serving the office. Upon election, an Assistant is required to pay a stipulated fine, those

The title-page of the octavo Livery List of the Stationers' Company issued in 1810.

A

LIST

OF THE

MASTER, WARDENS, ASSISTANTS

AND

LIVERY,

OF

THE WORSHIPFUL COMPANY

OF

STATIONERS.

JUNE 30th, 1810.

LONDON:

Printed by H. Teape, Tower-hill

MASTER.

JOHN CRICKITT, Esq. *Great Knight-rider-street*

WARDENS.

JOSIAH BOYDELL, Esq. *Cheapside*
Mr. THOMAS SMITH, *Bolton-street, Piccadilly.*

ASSISTANTS.

	Sir Matthew	Bloxam, Knt. *Gracechurch-street,* Alderman of London.
5	William	Domville, Esq. *New Ormond-street,* Alderman of London.
	Christopher	Magnay, Esq, *Queen-street, Cheapside.* Alderman of London.
	Mr. Thomas	Hooke, *Thatcham, Berks.*
	Henry	Baldwin, Esq. *Kingston, Surry.*
	Mr. Henry	Clarke, *Gracechurch-street.*
10	Charles	Coles, Esq. *Fleet-street.*
	Thomas	Curtis, Esq. *Camberwell.*
	Mr. William	Stephens, *Throgmorton-street.*
	Mr. Deodatus	Bye, *Peckham.*
	John	Nichols, Esq. F. S. A. *Canonbury.*
15	Mr. Francis	Rivington, *St. Paul's Church-yard.*
	Robert	Raikes, Esq. *Gloucester.*
	Mr. Henry	Isherwood, *Ludgate-hill.*
	Nathaniel	Conant, Esq, *Portland-place.*

called upon election as Aldermen of the City usually paying a greater fee.

The Court is followed by a list of the Stock-keepers: the Master, the Wardens, and six elected members of the Company - two Stock-keepers for the Court of Assistants, two for the Livery, and two for the Yeomanry. These six stock-keepers would have been elected, together with the two other Officers of the English Stock - the Treasurer and the Porter - at a special meeting of the Court of Assistants and the Partners in the English Stock at the beginning of the preceding March. Although elected for the ensuing year the Stock-keepers tended to remain fairly stable from year to year. A member may gradually move upwards from representing the Yeomanry to representing the Court, being replaced by a new member at a lower level.

Next the Clerk and the Treasurer are listed. We have just seen that the Treasurer is elected at the beginning of March along with the Stock-keepers; the Clerk is elected at a Court held at the end of March along with the Beadle and the Renter-Wardens. Like the Treasurer, the Clerk once elected tends to be re-elected year by year until he retires or dies.

We now come to the listing of the Livery at large. The numbering begins again. At the top of the list, of course, will be a number of Liverymen who for one reason or another have never become Assistants. Some will have chosen not to join the Court; others presumably will have failed ever to have been elected. The list proceeds until we reach the Renter-Wardens. A dividing line is usually printed in the lists after the names of the Renter-Wardens and another dividing line occurs after a further group of the Livery. You will remember that the Renter-Wardens are chosen each year at the Court held at the end of March. Usually the Court will summon a number of Liverymen, perhaps eight or nine, from the top

The head of the List in the 1810 issue showing the Master, Wardens and Assistants of the Company.

LIVERY.

Mr. John Martyn, *Maryland, America.*
Mr. Richard Ware, *Richmond-row, East-lane, Walworth.*
Mr. Richard Fuller, *Chertsey, Surry.*
Mr. Henry Fenwick, *Little Moorfields.*
5 Mr. Jacob Wilson, *Little Knight-rider-street.*
Mr. Humphrey Simmons, *George-lane, Pudding-lane.*
Rev. George Strahan, D. D. *Islington.*
Rev. William Tooke, F. R. S. *Great Ormond-street.*
Mr. Jonathan Moore, *Durrington, near Amesbury, Wiltshire.*
10 Mr. Thomas Davidson, *Islington-green.*
Mr. Matthew Brown, *Edward-street, Blackfriers-rd.*
Mr John Bullock, *Hampton, Middlesex.*
Mr. John Miller, *America.*
Mr. Samuel Simmons, *Borough, Southwark.*
15 Mr. William Owen, *Fleet-street.*
Mr. John Frome
Mr. John Wallis, *Warwick-square.*
Rev. John H. Browne, *Eakring, Nottinghamshire.*
Mr. Anthony Collambell, *Goswell-street.*
20 Mr. John Noorthouck, *Peterborough.*
William Timson, Esq. *Moor-park, Surry.*
Mr. John Ramsbottom, *Aldersgate-street.*
Mr. Edwards Lyde, *late of the Strand.*
Richard Ramsbottom, Esq. M. P. *Aldersgate-st.*

of the group listed below the second dividing line just mentioned. Of these, two will be elected to serve as Renter-Wardens for the ensuing year, but most of the others will pay a fine in lieu of serving as Renter-Warden, and some few will choose not to proceed any further in the Livery. In the following year their names will be transferred to the foot of the group listed between the dividing lines, whilst those serving or paying the fine will leapfrog this group and appear at the end of the group preceding the first division. The two Renter-Wardens come last in this section, no matter where their previous precedence would have put them in relation to the leapfrogging group. In the year following their serving as Renter-Wardens, these two will be placed back in their rightful order of precedence among their peers.

If a Liveryman is desirous of making headway in the Company, then he must either serve or else pay the fine for Renter-Warden, for as we have seen already he is not eligible for election to the Court of Assistants, and consequently for higher office, until he has done so. The group between the dividing lines remains in a kind of limbo somewhere in the lower levels of precedence of the Livery, with successively younger and more ambitious or successful Liverymen leapfrogging them every year. I think that I have at least one example of a Liveryman who, having marked time for a year within this group, then made the jump by paying the fine in the succeeding year, but my impression is that once in this 'rump' Liverymen tended to stay there.

The final group of Liverymen, that is those below the second division, will, of course, be headed by those from whom the choice of Renter-Wardens will be made in the following year, and it will end with that group of Liverymen who have been clothed in the previous twelve months. The number of Assistants and the number of Liverymen are then totalled up.

The first page of the List of Liverymen in 1810.

At the end of the list the Beadle is named. Like the Clerk he is elected at the Court at the end of March, and is usually re-elected until such time as he chooses to step down or dies.

The Livery Lists then proceed to list the surviving widows of Liverymen who hold shares in the English Stock. Information concerning the widows of Liverymen in the archives of the Company is proving to be very useful, and I will return to them later on.

Of course, one of the great values of this particular series of Livery Lists is that they record addresses. I have done some work on the London street directories for this period, but as yet I have not analysed them methodically. The Lists, like the directories, must be treated with a certain amount of caution - sometimes the Company clearly looses track of one of its Liverymen, or an address may remain unchanged for the odd year, when other sources indicate that a move has taken place. Furthermore, for the senior members of the Company - and indeed for some others - the addresses given may be residential ones rather than business ones. That in itself is often quite revealing. However, it is very useful to have such an annual recording of addresses - and I believe that especially for those Liverymen who held shares in the English Stock the Company attempted to keep a careful record of their whereabouts, and the whereabouts of their widows.

Before we leave these printed lists I must briefly comment on those issued in January by Harrison & Son, which I mentioned earlier; they are not as useful in that they do not give addresses, nor do they list the widows. However, they do give an additional check on the status of the Livery half-way through the year, and that is very helpful when one is trying to narrow down the date of death of a Liveryman. The same is true of the January broadside lists, which again I mentioned earlier.

With the help of the octavo Livery Lists from 1800 to 1826 and the broadside Lists from 1827 to 1831, I was able to make a full record of all members of the Livery of the Stationers' Company for the first thirty years of the nineteenth century, including all the office holders and members of the Court of Assistants. All told there are just under one thousand individuals involved, or just over a thousand if you include the widows.

In fact, in the course of time, I fed these lists into a computer, which greatly assisted the sorting procedures. For each Liveryman it was possible to print out a profile of his progress through the Livery during this period - and, of course, by extension - if the Lists were available for the necessary years - it would be possible to create such a profile for any Liveryman throughout his career.

These printed Livery Lists are backed up in the archives of the Company by the ledgers known as 'Calls to the Livery': listings here follow the same order of precedence, but the status of the Livery is recorded as of November. Once again we begin with the Master, Wardens, and the Court of Assistants - headed by the serving Aldermen. When we get to the Liverymen themselves there is a very useful addition to the mere listing of the names. The right-hand column gives us the date on which the individual was elected to serve, or was fined for the office of Renter-Warden. This was extremely useful to me in tracking down the history of those members of the Company active before 1800. McKenzie, in an appendix to volume three of his Stationers' Company Apprentices, recorded all the names of the Masters, Wardens and Renter-Wardens up to and including the year 1800; but what I had not known was the years in which others were fined for the office of Renter-Warden. This ledger gives one that information for those who have made the jump of which I have been speaking. For the 'rump', and for those who have not yet been called, the date in the right-hand column is that of clothing (that is the date on which they became members of the Livery). Unfortunately, this volume only goes up to 1814. There is then a gap in the series until 1838 and so it was necessary to resort to other methods of ascertaining the dates on which people were fined for the office of Renter-Warden. It was, of course, possible to work out from the Livery Lists themselves, by looking

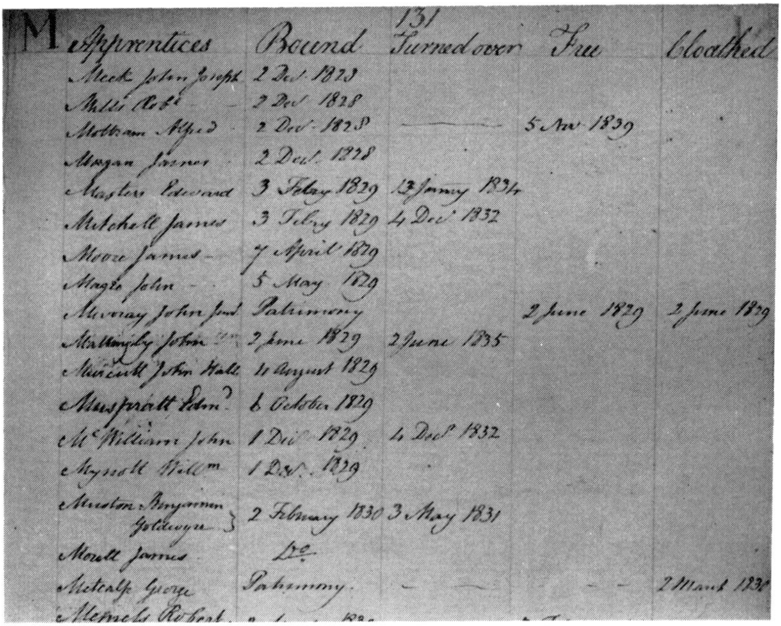

M 131

Apprentices	Bound	Turned over	Free	Cloathed
Meek John Joseph	2 Decr 1828			
Miller Robt	2 Decr 1828			
Mottram Alfred	2 Decr 1828	—	5 Nov 1839	
Morgan James	2 Decr 1828			
Masters Edward	3 Feby 1829	13 Jany 1834		
Mitchell James	3 Feby 1829	4 Decr 1832		
Moore James	7 April 1829			
Magee John	5 May 1829			
Murray John Junr	Patrimony		2 June 1829	2 June 1829
Mattingley John [illegible]	2 June 1829	2 June 1835		
[illegible] John Hall	4 August 1829			
Muspratt Edmd	6 October 1829			
McWilliam John	1 Decr 1829	4 Decr 1832		
Mynott Willm	1 Decr 1829			
Muston Benjamin [illegible]	2 February 1830	3 May 1831		
Morell James	Do			
Metcalf George	Patrimony	—	—	2 March 183[illegible]
Memels Robert	[illegible]			

An extract from *Apprentices Bound, Turned Over, Free and Cloathed 1810–65.*

when they were shown to have 'leapfrogged' up the list; but another was to check the 'Wardens' Accounts' to see who actually paid the fine each year.

As I have indicated, this was work that I could get on with in Oxford, but I did begin to make more frequent visits to Stationers' Hall - a task made much easier by the very good facilities that have now been provided there in the form of the muniment room and the library, and by the presence, at least one day a week, of Robin Myers.

I had to face the task of recording the apprentices. From McKenzie's volumes I knew of the ledgers in the archives called 'Apprentices Bound, Turned Over, Free and Cloathed [sic]'. Two volumes covered my period - the first covering the years 1774-1809, and the second from 1810-65. Here are the entries for the letter 'M' in the second volume. The volumes may be regarded as index ledgers to other parts of the archive. The entries are entered chronologically within alphabetical groups. The surname of the apprentice is followed by his forenames, by the date on which he was bound; by the date (or dates) on which he was turned over (if at all); by the date on which he was made Free of the Company (if he was); and finally, the date he was clothed or became a member of the Livery (if he did). For those entering the Company by Patrimony or Redemption an appropriate entry is recorded. Clearly, this was a very fine place at which to start. If I made an entry for every apprentice bound during my thirty years and linked it into my file for the Livery during the same period, I would have a large proportion of the Members of the Company alive and active during the period I had chosen.

* * *

I began this task in the days before I had access to a computer, but I did plan the work with one in mind. I therefore devised a proforma on which each piece of information was allocated to a single field. The information I decided to attempt to record for each member of the Company was:

Surname
Forenames
Date of First Record - this was usually the date of binding, but could be the date of Freedom for those entering by Patrimony or Redemption
Date of Birth
Date of Death
Father's Forenames with an indication as to whether he was alive or dead at the time of binding
Father's Address
Father's Trade
Master's Surname
Master's Forenames
Master's Address
Master's Trade
Amount (or absence of any mention) of any premium paid
Person paying such a premium
Date of any Turn Over

New Master's Surname &c
(This could be repeated if necessary for subsequent Turn Overs)
A symbol to indicate nature of entry - Servitude, Patrimony, Redemption, Presentation, and I subsequently used this field also to have an identifying symbol for widows
Date of Freedom
Date of Clothing (that is entry into the Livery)

So far - apart from dates of birth and death - this is the information that we are given by McKenzie in his Stationers' Company Apprentices, but I wanted to try to follow each member's progress for the rest of his career, so I added:

Date of serving as (or fining for the office of) Renter-Warden
Date of being called to the Court of Assistants
Date of serving as Under Warden
Date of serving as Upper Warden
Date of serving as Master
Dates of serving as a Stock-keeper
Dates of serving any other office
Apprentices bound
Addresses
References (for example the entry number in McKenzie's third volume for those apprenticed in the eighteenth century).

So with the help of the records already described I created an entry for everyone who was apprenticed between 1800 and 1830, and for everyone who entered the Livery during the same period. The numbers rose rapidly and the file now contains around six and a half thousand entries.

For those whose careers began in the eighteenth century I extracted such information as I could from McKenzie's third volume. Moreover, I read this volume carefully for any indication of other names of members of the Company in the years after 1800, who had escaped my net. Many readers will have realised that there was still an undefined section of the Company that I could not have picked up from the work I have described - that is the Yeomanry alive in 1800 and who never subsequently became Liverymen. To be more explicit - those men who had been apprenticed and freed in the eighteenth century, but who were never to become Liverymen but who were nevertheless alive and active during my period; similarly, those who were apprenticed in the eighteenth century and were made free after the turn of the century, but who likewise were never clothed - though these could be picked up from McKenzie. This remains a problem area - the 'Quarterage Books' of the Company, which recorded the fees paid by the Yeomanry, were lost during the Second World War and there is no easy way of knowing which of them freed in the eighteenth century were still alive in 1800.

Users of the McKenzie volumes will be very familiar with the Company's apprenticeship records, but let us just quickly look at the relevant ledgers in order to see how the material is recorded.

Four 'Memo Books' cover the period: 1794 to 1807; 1807 to 1816; 1816 to 1824; and 1824 to 1835. These are the rough books kept at the Courts when apprentices were bound, turned over and made free; and when Freemen were admitted to the Livery. The illustration shows the entries made on the binding of apprentices, which form the basis of the information provided by McKenzie in his volumes. The name of the apprentice, of his father, his father's trade and address, the master's name, trade and address, length of service and the details of any premium paid are given. On the opposite page are notes of Turn Overs; Freedoms; and Clothings. All of these items of business are the subject of a fee or fine, and at the end of the Court the account is reckoned up. A further entry for the binding of apprentices is made in the Master and Apprentices Calendar. Under each Master is given a list of the apprentices bound to him in chronological order of Court Days. During this period the length of service for an apprentice was invariably seven years; though the sons of some Masters, after being bound to an apprenticeship, were freed by Patrimony before their normal term had run its course. All these proceedings are, of course, minuted in the 'Court Books', and a fair copy of the bindings and turnings over are made in the volume designated 'Apprentices & Turnovers', just as the freedoms are neatly entered into the 'Freeman's Book'. This 'Freeman's Book' runs from August 1796 to December 1830, and was consequently

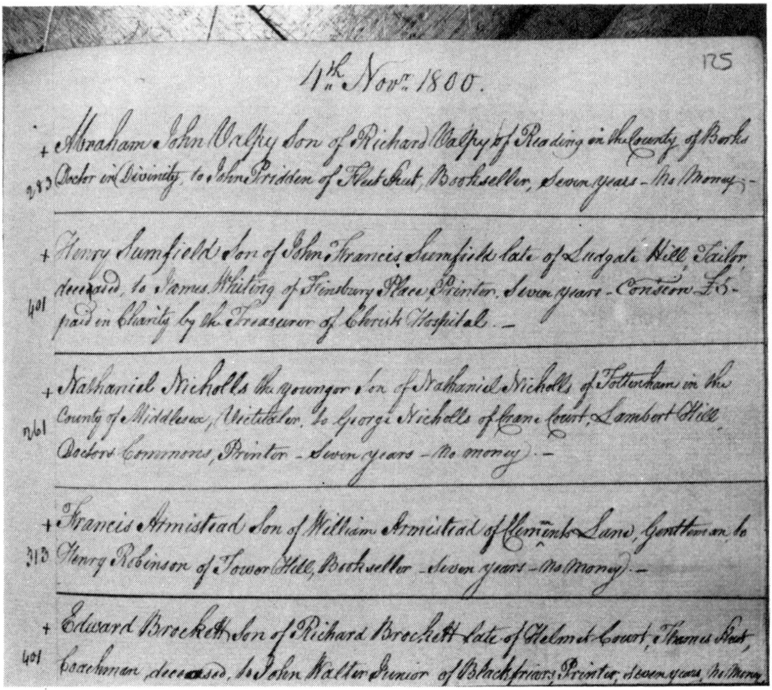
125

4th Novr 1800.

+ Abraham John Valpy Son of Richard Valpy of Reading in the County of Berks
283 Doctor in Divinity, to John Pridden of Fleet Street, Bookseller, Seven years - No Money -

+ Henry Sumfield Son of John Francis Sumfield late of Ludgate Hill, Tailor
401 deceased, to James Whiting of Finsbury Place Printer, Seven years - Consideration £5 -
paid in Charity by the Treasurer of Christ Hospital. -

+ Nathaniel Nicholls the younger Son of Nathaniel Nicholls of Tottenham in the
261 County of Middlesex, Victualler, to George Nicholls of Crane Court, Lambert Hill
Doctors Commons, Printer - Seven years - No money. -

+ Francis Armistead Son of William Armistead of Clements Lane, Gentleman to
313 Henry Robinson of Tower Hill, Bookseller - Seven years - No Money. -

+ Edward Brockett Son of Richard Brockett late of Helmet Court, Thames Street,
401 Coachman deceased, to John Walter Junior of Blackfriars, Printer, Seven years, No Money

An example of the Company's apprenticeship records found in the *Memo Books* showing details of each apprentice.

available to me from the start on the early microfilm. All of these various sources, which may seem quite often to duplicate each other, must be collated in order to be sure that nothing is missed and that inconsistencies are ironed out. I am still working my way through the 'Memo Books' and entering the full details of the apprenticeship bindings, though the freedoms have all been entered.

Once, in the early days, when I was working my way back and forth among these sources - trying to fill in the dates of the various stages of someone's progress through the Company - I remarked to Robin Myers that it seemed to me that there was a missing source. I could not believe that in the day-to-day workings of the Company the officers would not have needed a quick way of checking on a member's overall history. In other words, the file that I was laboriously putting together really should have existed already within the bureaucracy of the Company. 'What', I asked Robin, 'would they do now, down in the Office, if they wanted to find out the date when one of their members was admitted to the Livery?' 'Let's go and ask them', said Robin. 'We would look in the Beadle's Book', said the Clerk, and produced from the office shelf a large ledger that held within its covers not only details of Liverymen as recent as the 1960s but also entries for most of my people at the beginning of the nineteenth century. The Beadle's Book perhaps did not do everything one would have wished, but it proved to be a great find. It appears to have been started in the mid-1830s, a printed title dated 1834 has been provided, but as an entry was then made for all the existing Liverymen it contains information from the late eighteenth century. The illustration shows some of my people under the letter 'B'. Basically, the name is followed by the year in which the person was admitted to the Livery. Often there is an indication of the trade he followed - this is important because it is one of the only places where such a comment occurs, unless he was in the habit of binding apprentices, in which case, his trade would be mentioned in the binding records - remember that men did not always practise the trade to which they themselves had been apprenticed. Then follows an address and a year, which is changed each year until a new address is called for and so on until 1840. After that date years are given only when a change of address takes place. The dates of all offices held are also given, then follows a date on which the person died, and, if he was a shareholder, an indication of the value of the share held; and, if he left a widow, a reference to the entry for the widow appears later in the volume. You see here a couple of sample signatures pasted into the volume, and later in the century the volume does take on something of the nature of a scrap volume, with press cuttings and obituaries pasted in - even the occasional

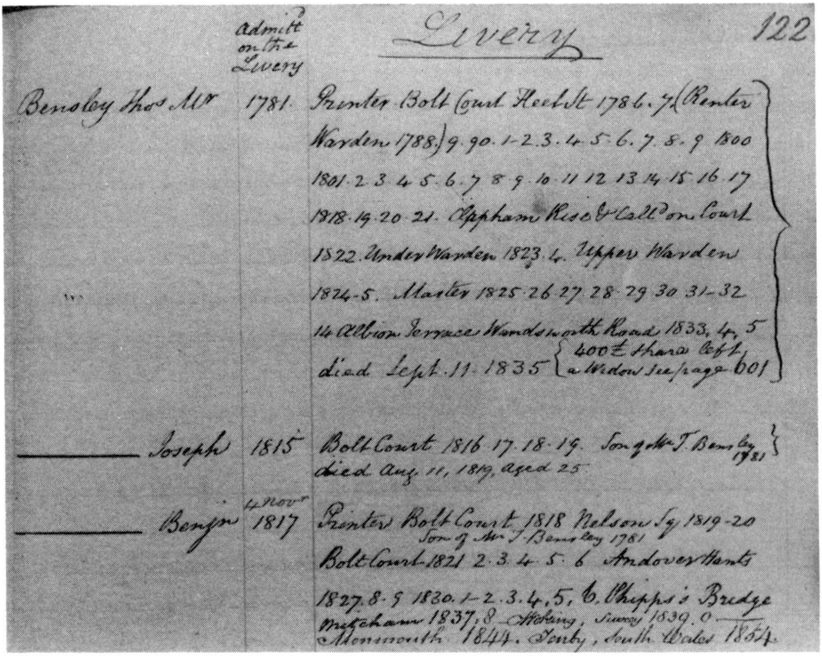

Admitt on the Livery | Livery | 122

Bensley Thos Mr 1781 Printer Bolt Court Fleet St 1786. 7 (Renter Warden 1788) 9. 90. 1-2. 3. 4. 5. 6. 7. 8. 9 1800 1801. 2. 3. 4. 5. 6. 7. 8. 9. 10. 11. 12. 13. 14. 15. 16. 17 1818. 19. 20. 21. Clapham Rise & Call^d on Court 1822. Under Warden 1823. 4. Upper Warden 1824-5. Master 1825. 26. 27. 28. 29. 30. 31-32 14 Albion Terrace Wandsworth Road 1833, 4, 5 died Sept. 11. 1835 {400£ share left a Widow see page 601}

——— Joseph 1815 Bolt Court 1816. 17. 18. 19. Son of Mr T. Bensley 1781 died Aug. 11, 1819, aged 25

——— Benjn 4 Nov 1817 Printer Bolt Court 1818 Nelson Sq 1819-20 Son of Mr T. Bensley 1781 Bolt Court 1821 2. 3. 4. 5. 6 Andover Hants 1827. 8. 9 1830. 1-2. 3. 4, 5, 6. Phipps's Bridge Mitcham 1837, 8 Woking, Surrey 1839. 0 Monmouth 1844. Tenby, South Wales 1854

An extract from the *Beadle's Book*.

letter. Unfortunately, there is not much of that during my period. In the volume for the widows we are given addresses; the name of the husband; more often than not the value of the share held and date of death.

Can I just say how thrilled I always am when I discover a death date? In the past, I have always found it one of the most difficult and frustrating of tasks - to discover when a relatively unimportant person died. Once one can find that out it very often unlocks all sorts of other possibilities for one to continue the search for further information. To be told when a Liveryman died is a great comfort, and to be told the name and address of his widow and her subsequent addresses, down to the date of her death, really does give one a chance. I am constantly amazed, incidentally, by the time-span which my group of people leads me to cover. I have Stationers who were apprenticed in the late seventeen twenties, and I have widows of other Stationers who died in the second decade of the twentieth century.

Whilst on this topic let me say that the Stationers' Company archives turn out to be even more obliging. It was, of course, important to the Company that they should keep a careful record of the shares in the English Stock, and all transfers of shares are carefully recorded. Towards the end of the eighteenth century the Treasurer began to keep notes at the end of one of his ledgers about the wills of partners who had recently died, very often with an indication of what had happened to the share. This obviously proved to be so useful that, just about the beginning of the nineteenth century, he started a new series of notebooks entitled '*Abstracts of Wills*'. The usual form of entry in these notebooks gives one the date of the will (and/or any codicils); some comment on the disposition of the estate, usually confined to the share in the English Stock; the names of the executors; the date of probate and the names of those to whom probate was granted. Clearly, this greatly eases the way forward to a search for the wills themselves, and hopefully to much more information on the relative wealth of these Liverymen, their families and associates. Some of the late-nineteenth-century entries include a note on the value of the estate.

There is quite a lot of miscellaneous information at the beginning of the *Beadle's Book*, and over several pages a number of statistical analyses are attempted. It is all fairly self-explanatory, but I have not as yet checked the figures. Once I have entered all my information into the computer I will be able to accomplish all sorts of sophisticated counts and breakdowns. Two Freedoms by Gift or Presentation were made to two military heroes of the Peninsular Wars - I suspect in connection with their being given the Freedom of the City. The year 1809 seems to be the peak year

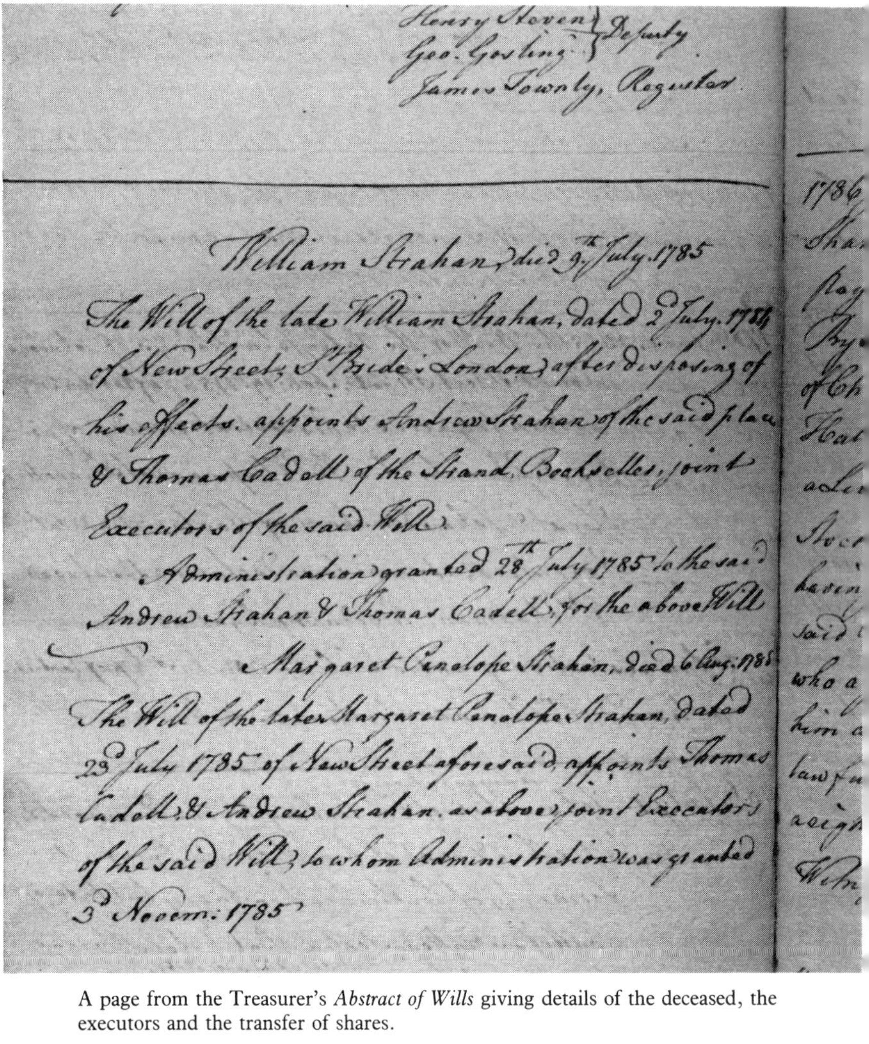
Henry Stevens } Deputy
Geo. Gosling }
James Townly, Register

William Strahan died 9th July 1785

The Will of the late William Strahan, dated 2d July 1784 of New Street, St Bride, London, after disposing of his effects, appoints Andrew Strahan of the said place & Thomas Cadell of the Strand, Bookseller, joint Executors of the said Will.

Administration granted 28th July 1785 to the said Andrew Strahan & Thomas Cadell, for the above Will

Margaret Penelope Strahan, died 6 Aug. 1785

The Will of the late Margaret Penelope Strahan, dated 23d July 1785 of New Street aforesaid, appoints Thomas Cadell & Andrew Strahan, as above joint Executors of the said Will, to whom Administration was granted 3d Novem: 1785

A page from the Treasurer's *Abstract of Wills* giving details of the deceased, the executors and the transfer of shares.

for the Livery - not 1810 as mentioned in the Blagden passage I quoted earlier. There are also other useful listings - for example details of members of the Court of Assistants over the years, and in another section are tabulated the names of the Stock-keepers.

The records discussed up to this point are the ones that I have seriously tackled so far. In order to produce something I have been concentrating on the thousand or so Liverymen and I hope in about a year's time to be able to present a detailed study of the Livery, before I move on and complete the entries for the other members of the Company.

Let us just look at a typical entry for a moment (see Appendixes I and II). I have given each person a unique number under his letter of the alphabet, and his widow has the same number followed by the letter 'W'. This has advantages and saves a lot of time on the computer. For the date of birth, which I know only occasionally, most entries have an approximation. This is usually made from the date of Binding (fourteen years previously), the date of Freedom by Patrimony (twenty-one years previously), and by counting back from an age given at the time of death. The first two of these methods are something of a gamble, but where I have had the chance to check they seem to work fairly well.

When the trade is followed by an asterisk, then that is the trade to which the person was himself apprenticed. If the father was dead at the time of Binding, I say so. The (1) after the date for serving as Renter-Warden indicates that he is listed as the senior of the two, (2) is therefore an alternative here. I have explained the date backwards and forwards at the beginning and end of the _Livery List_ print-out. If the individual became a Liveryman or died within the thirty-year period, then I begin or end the sequence with a line.

The Apprentices are those bound to Bensley. Firstly, there is a reference to any already listed in McKenzie's last volume, followed by those listed in the _Master and Apprentices Calendar_. That volume unfortunately ends in 1807. The rest will have to wait for a computer sorting of the whole file of apprenticeship records. 'Addresses' is supplied for directory or other information that may be found. The _Beadle's Book_ will provide any changes after 1830, and very often the _Abstracts of Wills_ refers to the person as being 'late of...', as under Mary Bensley. If in the course of an entry it is necessary to refer to another person who will himself appear in the file, then the name is printed in bold type.

There are a number of further types of record yet to be dealt with in the archives, and this entry will grow some more before I am finished. Also I expect the number of entries to increase, as I find mention of the Yeomen I mentioned earlier. Having found a new name in this section - then it is back to McKenzie and the eighteenth century.

I am confident that there is going to be a fair amount of information to be gleaned from the records of the English Stock. In the Dividend Ledgers the familiar precedence emerges - this time after the officers, the listing is by the value of the shares held. Such dividends are made twice a year at Midsummer and Christmas - so I will have at least sixty of these lists to deal with. The amounts of dividend drawn by a Stockholder over the years, the transfers of stock, and the reasons for those transfers will all emerge and should help - I trust - to explain some of the attraction of the Company during this period.

I still have a great deal to learn about the workings of the English Stock and I do not want to go too far at this point. In view of the general title of this seminar, I at first suggested that the title of my talk should be: 'Some indicators of personal wealth among the Members of the Stationers' Company in the early Nineteenth Century', but as the time drew nearer I backed off - but this fact will give you some idea of the way that I want to go with my investigations.

If the Dividend Ledgers will tell us something about the wealthier members of the Company - I suspect that the Poor Books or the records of the various Charity payments will tell us something of the less fortunate members of the Company. Perhaps this is where I will find many of the Yeomen.

Finally, there are the Court Books themselves and the Waste Books which lie behind them. Only when I have read these will I really understand the Company during my period, and only then will I be able to flesh out my biographies beyond the bare recital of names and dates. Of course, they will in a large part merely be recording yet again much of the information I have already gleaned from other sources.

I began all this because I really wanted to understand how the Booktrade in London worked during the early part of the nineteenth century. It is, after all, a great period of change - not only were the first major technological changes in the nature of printing since the fifteenth century taking place; but major changes were taking place in the way in which books were being published and sold - the whole structure of the bookselling world was changing from the earlier Conger/Shareholding system into the more familiar world - for us - of separate publishers, and wholesale and retail bookselling. I wanted to know more about the people who brought about these changes, the Fourdriniers, the Walters, the Bensleys and the Hansards, the Longmans, the Murrays, the Simpkins and the Marshalls. Looking at those Nichols/Rivington/Pollard Livery Lists made me wonder why some were in the Company and some were not, what was the attraction of the Company during this period: was it a way into a new social group, or into City politics, or was it still a useful trade connection, with good pickings to be had from the English Stock? I seem at this stage to be somewhat bogged down in the detail - but I hope that in time such a detailed study will produce some worthwhile results.

Appendix I: A typical entry in the work-in-progress analysis based on information in the Beadle's Book.

BENSLEY, Thomas

Born: c.1760 Died: 11 September 1835

Trade: Printer

Son of Thomas, Printer, of the Strand

Stationers' Company Record

Apprenticed on 1 March 1774 to his father Thomas Bensley, Printer, of Strand. No premium mentioned. Freed on 6 March 1781. Clothed on 3 April 1781. Served as Renter Warden 1788 (1). Called to the Cour (Assistant) 1822. Served as Under Warden 1823. Upper Warden 1824. Master 1825. Served as a Stock Keeper 1823/5.

[Livery Lists]
781<<<<<<<<<
800,LIV,133,BENSLEY (Thomas),Bolt Court: Fleet Street
801,LIV,129,BENSLEY (Thomas),Bolt Court: Fleet Street
802,LIV,127,BENSLEY (Thomas),Bolt Court: Fleet Street
803,LIV,118,BENSLEY (Thomas),Bolt Court: Fleet Street
804,LIV,110,BENSLEY (Thomas),Bolt Court: Fleet Street
805,LIV,095,BENSLEY (Thomas),Bolt Court: Fleet Street
806,LIV,093,BENSLEY (Thomas),Bolt Court: Fleet Street
807,LIV,087,BENSLEY (Thomas),Bolt Court: Fleet Street
808,LIV,084,BENSLEY (Thomas),Bolt Court: Fleet Street
809,LIV,078,BENSLEY (Thomas),Bolt Court: Fleet Street
810,LIV,076,BENSLEY (Thomas),Bolt Court: Fleet Street
811,LIV,073,BENSLEY (Thomas),Bolt Court: Fleet Street
812,LIV,066,BENSLEY (Thomas),Bolt Court: Fleet Street
813,LIV,064,BENSLEY (Thomas),Bolt Court: Fleet Street
814,LIV,062,BENSLEY (Thomas),Bolt Court: Fleet Street
815,LIV,060,BENSLEY (Thomas),Bolt Court: Fleet Street
816,LIV,058,BENSLEY (Thomas),Bolt Court: Fleet Street
817,LIV,053,BENSLEY (Thomas),Bolt Court: Fleet Street
818,LIV,037,BENSLEY (Thomas),Bolt Court: Fleet Street
819,LIV,033,BENSLEY (Thomas),Bolt Court: Fleet Street
820,LIV,032,BENSLEY (Thomas),Bolt Court: Fleet Street
821,LIV,026,BENSLEY (Thomas),Bolt Court: Fleet Street
822,ASS,028,BENSLEY (Thomas),Clapham Rise
823,UNW,003,BENSLEY (Thomas),Clapham Rise
824,UPW,002,BENSLEY (Thomas),Clapham Rise
825,MAS,001,BENSLEY (Thomas),Clapham Rise
826,ASS,025,BENSLEY (Thomas),Clapham Rise
828,ASS,020,BENSLEY (Thomas),***
829,ASS,016,BENSLEY (Thomas),***
830,ASS,012,BENSLEY (Thomas),***
831,ASS,011,BENSLEY (Thomas),***
>>>>>>>>>835

By a will dated 15 December 1822, he bequeathed his share [£400] in the English Stock to his wife **Mary**, and appointed her as his sole executrix. Probate was granted to her on 11 March 1836. [Wills B:414]

Apprentices: *McK.3:722 [but cf. father]
4 Aug.1801 Charles Dundas Grant
1 Dec.1801 William Heseltine
2 Nov.1802 Robert Johnson
3 May 1803 Ebenezer Swain
2 Oct.1804 John Goddard
7 May 1804 Robert James Coher
William Cracknell
James Monneypenny
William Munslow
5 Nov.1805 Thomas Bell
5 May 1807 John Barker jr.
4 Aug.1807 James Drummond

Addresses:

References: McK.3:699; Livery Lists; Beadle's Book:122; Wills B:414; Master and Appr.Cal

B044 [W]

BENSLEY, Mary

Born: ? Died: 18 November 1846

Wife and subsequently the widow of **Thomas Bensley**, who died on 11 September 1835.

By her husbands will [prob. 11 March 1836] she had inherited his share in the English Stock [£400]. [Wills B:414] In her own will dated 5 December 1845, she requested her niece Elizabeth Robins to see to the execution of her will. Probate was granted to her on the 5 December 1846. [Wills B:524]

Addresses: 'late of Brighton, Sussex' [Wills]

References: Beadle's Book:601; Wills B:524.

Appendix II: Another typical page of the analysis based on information in the Beadle's Book.

Year	Bindings	Freedom by Patrimony	Redemp.	Gift	Service	Total Freedoms	Clothed	Livery
1800	170	8	4		42	54	25	453
1801	110	9	1		35	45	11	472
1802	108	8	3		43	54	22	468
1803	100	7	5		32	44	12	481
1804	105	5	8		35	48	23	482
1805	208	4	5		28	37	13	488
1806	199	7	3		26	36	10	493
1807	210	10	5		40	55	21	495
1808	170	12	11	2	35	60	26	514
1809	187	8	11		33	52	5	521
1810	186	6	2		38	46	8	517
1811	141	7	4		28	39	11	509
1812	151	5	2		28	35	6	509
1813	155	11	4		47	62	11	500
1814	137	6	2		40	48	7	502
1815	105	12	5		31	48	11	502
1816	127	4	4		38	46	17	501
1817	107	10	1		42	53	13	507
1818	152	8	5		52	65	18	505
1819	162	9	9		52	70	13	498
1820	146	5	2		36	43	9	500
1821	149	6	2		37	45	8	498
1822	171	13	7		39	59	11	492
1823	132	9	5		40	54	18	492
1824	184	28	6		43	77	1	497
1825	234	11	2		46	59	14	500
1826	142	6	0		36	42	14	512
1827	118	11	2		41	54	10	505
1828	129	9	1		45	55	15	502
1829	129	14	3		57	74	11	494
1830	115	5	1		45	51	14	482

The Patent Office as Publisher, 1853–60

John Hewish

In his History of Public Libraries in Great Britain Thomas Kelly - somewhat unexpectedly in such a context - has this to say about Patent Office publications:

> The free distribution of patent specifications and other Patent Office publications, began in 1854, and thanks to the enthusiasm of Bennet Woodcroft, Superintendent of Specifications, was conducted on a generous scale. Most of the recipients at this stage were Mechanics Institutes, learned societies or similar bodies, but the needs of the newly emerging public libraries were not overlooked, and already in 1856 the Commissioners (of patents) were claiming that 'This gift has in most cases laid the foundations of free public libraries where none previously existed'.[1]

The Patent Office was established in 1852, and of course its main function was not to supply free reading matter to public or other libraries but to issue patents and essential patent documentation. In the period to which Kelly is referring the Patent Office went far beyond its brief, undertaking not only one of the most remarkable archival publishing operations of the nineteenth century but also reaching out, as Kelly suggests, to a wider Victorian public. In this it displayed notable originality and considerable extravagance. It was an operation very characteristic of the time, when almost nothing seemed too big to undertake. The Great Exhibition began the decade, and the Great Eastern ended it. On a more mundane level the Office laid the foundations in all essentials of present-day patent documentation. The wider ambition may look somewhat naïve today, but admirable nonetheless. When the Office was set up the main Civil Service reforms had not taken place; it was certainly not typical of government service at the time, and often more resembles a band of irregulars than a part of bureacracy. As so often with irregulars, there were personality clashes and internal stresses.

There were also links with literature: patents, being a kind of royal proclamation, have immemorial links with the Chancery, the royal secretariat. The Patent Office backs onto the Cursitor Street of Bleak House. Dickens and Woodcroft were on the same patent reform committee, and the unreformed pre-1852 system probably contributed something to the Circumlocution Office.

What is an invention patent? It is impossible to improve on the description of one of my predecessors, A.A. Gomme:

> A patent is a grant, on certain conditions, of a limited monopoly to an inventor - it is so called from the form of the grant - the documents received and held by the grantees as their warrants for claiming monopoly rights were called letters patent because they were addressed not to particular individuals but 'to all to whom these presents shall come' and were sealed in such a way that they could be read without breaking the seals - patents of invention form but one series out of a number of such grants of all kinds of privileges by the sovereign - letters patent are today issued for titles of honour and for appointments to certain offices under the Crown...[2]

The present legal basis of invention patents in Britain was hammered out in the courts in the late sixteenth and early seventeenth centuries as a result of popular opposition to abuse of royal privileges. In 1601 Elizabeth proclaimed that subjects wronged by monopolies could go to the common law courts. A year later a man called Darcy sued one Allen for infringeing his monopoly in playing cards. He lost, counsel for Allen declaring:

> Where any man by his own charge and industry, or by his own wit or invention doth bring any new trade into the realm, or any engine tending to the furtherance of trade that never was used before. And that for the good of the realm, that in such cases the King may grant to him a monopoly patent for some reasonable time, until the subjects may learn the same, in consideration of the good that he doth bring by his invention to the Commonwealth; otherwise not...

This definition was written into the law in the Statute of Monopolies of 1624 which permitted:

> any letters patent and grants of privilege - for the term of fourteen years or under, hereafter to be made of the sole working or making of any manner of new manufacture within this realm, to the true and first inventor

provided it was not injurious or inconvenient to the king's subjects in general.

The practice of awarding monopolies for trades or processes was very much older, as the following show:

> 500 BC Sybaris: Monopolies granted to cooks, in order that others might be induced to excel...
>
> 1236 England: Henry III to Bonafusas de Sancta Columba, of Bordeaux, to make cloths of diverse colours, after the manner of the Flemings...
>
> 1449 England: To John of Utynam, for coloured glass, 'No liege of the King learned in such arts shall use them for a term of 20 years, against the will and consent of John...'[3]

The earliest true patent legislation is found in 1474, in Venice, and on very similar principles to our own; over one hundred invention patents were granted in its first seventy-five years. Somewhat earlier, in 1421, Brunelleschi was granted a three-year monopoly for a barge with hoisting gear for blocks of marble so that 'he himself may be urged to further exertion' - surely a superfluity in his case.

In Britain efficient administration of the system lagged far behind its practice. It is paradoxical that the issue of patents, a manifestation of progress, was for centuries the responsibility of one of the oldest and most cumbersome of institutions, the Chancery. Before 1852 a patent for draining mines passed through virtually the same antechambers of state, on its way to the Great Seal, as a patent for appointing an ambassador - though it was easier for the ambassador, as he did not have to hawk it round the Chancery offices, like inventors and minor office holders. H. Harding gives the details in his excellent short history of the Office:

> The unhappy inventor or his agent had to attend at seven different offices, including a Master in Chancery's office, the Home Office (3 times), the Law Officer's chambers, the

> Patent Bill Office, the Signet Office, the Lord Privy Seal's Office, and the Lord Chancellor's Great Seal Patent Office. The application had to pass through ten separate stages, which twice required the personal signature of the Sovereign, and fees had to be paid at each stage, amounting to about £100 for England alone, and over £300 for the three Kingdoms.[4]

At customer level, many of the officials were only deputies, put in by higher officials holding sinecures. Dickens's criticisms of the Prerogative Office, in David Copperfield, apply closely to the Chancery:[5] misuse of fees, inaccessibility, sinecures and so on. This process meant that the documentation of invention patents was dispersed through the public records on the Patent Rolls, or in the form of Privy Seal bills, Signet bills, inventors' petititions, Home Office warrants and the like. The achievement of the nineteenth-century Patent Office can only be understood in the light of the peculiar situation of patent documentation.

Harding includes the Law Officers, the Attorney and Solicitor Genera in his description: they were important in the process, as they were responsible, before the coming of the professional patent agent, for the only examination of patents from a technical and legal aspect. It was work for which they were not very well fitted. As a result the only real test was often in the law courts, in the course of a dispute. The officers did, however, play a part in the emergence of the specification as a separate document in the early eighteenth century. A declaration in more or less - usually less - detail had long been considered part of the bargain between inventor and state as a means whereby the invention could eventually become public property.

Patentees did not like to describe their invention too fully in case someone copied it before the patent was granted, hence the practice grew up of the inventor promising to lodge a separate description (ie. a specification) within a given time. He would 'more particularly explain and describe the nature of the said invention, and the manner in which the same was to be performed in an instrument in writing'. Separate series of specification rolls were established in the records.

* * *

This was the patent system that played its part - a difficult part to assess - in the Industrial Revolution. It is indisputable that it worked after a fashion: the number of patents taken out in 1830 was two-and-a-half times as great as that for 1790. Its abuses led to many complaints. An anonymous eighteenth-century poem, The Patent, gives one popular view:

> Hail to the Patent, which enables man
> To vend a folio, or a warming pan...
> Confers a sanction on the Doctor's pill
> Oft known to cure, but oft'ner known to kill
> What man would scruple to resign his breath
> Provided he could die a patent death.
>
> This too, can make an engine squirt so high
> As to o'erflow the Parlour next the sky.
> That he who sleeps shall wake and start amain
> And think the gen'ral deluge come again;
> Impart a property to all Machines
> To milk of roses and to Magazines;
> To Folly's features give a face of sense
> And raise a trifle into consequence.[6]

That suggestion of the trivial masquerading as the serious anticipates the kind of complaints that were heard when the system was exhaustively investigated during parliamentary enquiries in the nineteenth century. Patents awarded for inventions that did not deserve them were one cause of complaint; another was that it was difficult to get notice of what was being patented in order to oppose an unjustified application. A further major defect was the lack of available information as to what had been patented in the past as a result of the dispersal of inventions in the public records, and in particular in three separate repositories.

One of the architects of patent reform, the lawyer and barrister Thomas Webster gave evidence to the 1851 enquiry that preceded the reforms:

> All specifications enrolled since the 1st of January, 1849, have been enrolled in one office, but the specifications of other existing and expired patents are distributed through three offices. There is not, except at the Great Seal Patent Office, a list or an index...[7]

Another important witness at this enquiry had concerned himself with the Lord Chancellor's office index: he had transcribed it and had processed the entries in three different ways, alphabetically by name, by subject, and in chronological arrangement. He made a great impression when he demonstrated their value to the members of the Commission on Patent Laws. His name was Bennet Woodcroft, and he was the future Superintendent of Specifications, at that time an independent patent consultant and engineer. That commission of enquiry was only the culmination of a long period of agitation for patent reform, by inventors, manufacturers, scientists, lawyers and patent agents. Harding records that by the time of the Great Exhibition there were eleven such committees or associations.[8] One of the most influential was within the Society of Arts. Among its members were Thomas Webster, Bennet Woodcroft, and Charles Dickens. The latter's contribution has been quoted so often that one is hesitant to repeat it - it is spoken in the character of a humble artisan from the provinces:

> Look at the Home Secretary, the Attorney General, the Patent Office, the engrossing clerk, the Lord Chancellor, the Privy Seal, the Clerk of the Patents, the Lord Chancellor's purse-bearer, the Clerk of the Hanaper, the Deputy Sealer and the Deputy Chaff-Wax. No man in England could get a patent for an indiarubber band without feeing all of them. Some of them over and over again. I went through thirty-five stages. I began with the Queen upon the throne. I ended with the Deputy Chaff-Wax.[9]

On the evidence of this sketch, Dickens's plan for issuing patents was, as might be expected, too simple to have worked.

The Patent Law Amendment Act of 1852 was relatively sweeping for its time: it provided for a single Patent Office and for a single United Kingdom patent. It also ordained the publication of provisional and final specifications, the purchase and publication of Bennet Woodcroft's indexes, and the formation of central patent records. All this was to take place under newly created Commissioners, consisting of the Chancellor, the Master of the Rolls, and the two law officers. Unfortunately the Act retained the system of inspection of applications by the latter. The Commissioners were eminent lawyers but they were somewhat remote from the day-to-day work of the office and not well fitted to guide the formation of such a novel undertaking.

Three out of four of them were replaced within a few weeks, when Lord John Russell's administration was succeeded by Aberdeen's.

The new office opened in October 1852, when the Act took effect. At first it was in temporary offices in Quality Court, but at Christmas it moved to the present site, 25 Southampton Buildings, taking over some abandoned offices of the Masters in Chancery.[10] The office was divided into two sections: a Patent Division for taking fees and issuing and sealing the letters patent retained by the inventor, and a Specification Division. There was no proper head of the office and the man who had been the Chancellor's Clerk of the Patents for the previous thirty-two years remained in post to head the patent side. His name was Leonard Edmunds, and he became the focus of the 'Patent Office scandal' of the 1860s. He was also Reading Clerk at the House of Lords.[11]

The first Superintendent of Specifications was Bennet Woodcroft. He is a good example of Victorian upward mobility: his background was not poor - his father was a Manchester textile printer - but he himself had worked at the loom before becoming an independent engineer and patent consultant.[12] He had written a history of steam navigation and edited a de-luxe edition of the Pneumatics of Hero.[13]

Perhaps there was no such thing as a typical civil servant at this period. Woodcroft is reminiscent of some of the new men appointed to reorganise the public records somewhat earlier: well endowed with drive and revelling in his new official powers, yet he was certainly not typical in his impetuosity, tactlessness and capacity for making enemies. He was a remarkable man, but it is sometimes an effort to admit it.

Woodcroft has always been inseparably linked with the Patent Office Library. It opened to readers in 1855, its initial stock being his own collection of books. The first Report of the Commissioners stated: 'The Commissioners have established a public library of research within the Patent Office, to consist of the scientific and mechanical works of all nations.' Woodcroft also brought with him a collection of mechanical models; their story is linked to the origin of the Science Museum. Another foundation collection was lent by a friend of Woodcroft's, the Birmingham engineer Richard Prosser, and was later purchased from his trustees. In 1859 Woodcroft' books were also acquired for the nation for £270 - at least those of them that he did not consider as being only on loan (this situation was the cause of some ill-feeling when he retired in 1876).

That allusion to the 'scientific and mechanical works of all nations' suggests that the new office was a development likely to interest Prince Albert. Within a few months of the library's opening Woodcroft was called to Windsor to be congratulated and to explain his work. Taking the opportunity thus afforded, the engineers of Birmingham and Manchester petitioned Parliament to provide,'in connection with the Patent Office', a library and museum containing scientific and mechanical works of every age and people, for the use of the public.[14] This grand design had to make do with improvised accommodation: the library was at first housed in a ground-floor corridor and was notoriously congested. There were plans, counter-plans and petitions for an adequate building and library for much of the century: it sounds very familiar. (The present building and library were completed in 1901.)[15]

* * *

Under the Act the Patent Office was committed to undertake prompt publication of all patents, and for the first year or so this requirement dominated its publishing activities. Reduced fees and an improved system seem to have encouraged a Victorian patent mania: the number of applications went up from some 600 a year to between two and three thousand. Most inventors now lodged a provisional specification - a short description of the essentials of the invention, on stamped paper like the other documents. Some time later the inventors received their letters patent, and delivered a full specification within the required number of months. Both provisional and full specifications were published. Thus there were two sides to patent documentation, the individual, consisting of the manuscript letters patent with seal attached, and the public, which was published. In its first report, in mid-1854, the Office announced that the specifications were being published within three weeks:

> All the specifications filed in the Office, 3,099 in number, have been printed and published, together with lithographed outline copies of the drawings, and the prints are sold to the public either separately or in the series for the year, at the cost price...the price of a print of the average length of letter press and drawings is eightpence.[16]

The Office chose the familiar imperial octavo 'bluebook' format. The printers were of course the Queen's Printers, Eyre and Spottiswoode, who did all the Office's work, presumably at their East Harding Street works, conveniently close in Holborn. The inventor's text was first copied for the press by stationers' writers, and eventually proof-read by Woodcroft's clerks, working in pairs in the cramped offices. Lithographers from a firm called Malby and Sons transferred the drawings onto the stone, at the Office. Earlier patents not yet printed could be acquired on request, the customer paying for the lithography and the Office for the printing. The Office advertised a coloured version but I have not come across any examples officially produced.[17]

(It is worth mentioning that all inventors' original papers routinely held in the new Patent Office were later destroyed, according to the Destruction Schedules of the Record Office.)

* * *

The Amendment Act had provided for the nation to buy Woodcroft's indexes to the pre-1852 patents. He was paid £1,000 for them, the same sum as his annual salary - the same, incidentally, as Sir Francis Palgrave's salary at the Record Office.[18] The indexes were copied and brought out as soon as possible: the first to appear were a one-volume name index of 647 pages at twenty shillings, and the two-volume chronological index of 1554 pages, at thirty shillings.

The two-volume subject index followed. Another important index for which Woodcroft takes the credit was the Reference Index (1854): it listed patents chronologically from 1617, stating where the records were enrolled, and citing any printed references in journals or Record Office reports. At this time, the inventions dispersed in the public records had not been published. An appendix volume followed this, containing abstracts of inventions for which there were no separate specifications: these were the first substantial abstracts published by the new Office.

Another project officially encouraged was publication of compendiums of patents on subjects of topical concern, such as the following, coinciding with the Crimean War:

> The whole series of specifications of patents for firearms, cannon shot, shells, cartridges, weapons, accoutrements and machinery for their manufacture and the drawings...from the earliest recorded...to the present time...

Other projected series were for reaping machines, sanitary ware, and smoke prevention - also appropriate to the age. The Reaping Machine set has a separate introductory volume by Woodcroft: it was printed by Whittaker at the Chiswick Press, with woodcuts and a dedication to the Prince Consort. It contains the Woodcroft philosophy in its purest form:

> This compilation may, therefore, not only be interesting as a branch of mechanical history, but valuable as giving, as completely as the writer can collect, the accumulated knowledge of mankind in this important department of industry; and by displaying the elementary forms of all known cutters, the combinations of all the parts forming each machine and its mode of action it is to be expected that the machinist will no longer lose his time in reinventing that which is already old...[19]

and concludes with a suggestion to make life easier for the horses. This programme overall was too ambitious: the Firearm set (without an introduction) was certainly completed but the others are not now to be found in the British Library. (Reserve stock of provincial libraries may tell a different story.) Similarly with a projected series of supplements to letters patent, consisting of the reprinting of rare pamphlets - only one volume was published, in 1858, but it is an interesting one.

The Office's only surviving serial publication, other than the patents series themselves, is the Patent Journal or Official Journal, Patents. It was first published in January 1854, in this amazingly prolific early phase, and is still appearing. It contained announcements of new patent applications and items of home or foreign information of interest to inventors. It also published many puffs for the early achievements of the Office.

The series of classified abridgements which became one of the best-known Patent Office publications was also started towards the end of this decade; these were the fore-runners of the ten-year abridgements which are still a standard tool for patent searching. Some of the volumes, such as those for printing or marine engines, had long and didactic prefaces. Outside compilers were usually hired for these volumes and were paid by lump sum.

* * *

The first annual reports for the Office are not easy to interpret, as all the figures for publications, salaries, stationery and copying are for different periods of time. The 1853 report came out in August 1854 and conveniently includes work up to that date which presumably was then included again in the 1854 report. In view of the circumstances and composition of the Office the reports might have been much worse, or not have existed at all. In the first fifteen months, £1288 was spent on stationery and sums of £4962 for printing and £5869 for lithography. Some curious details emerge, such as the £119 for over two thousand tin boxes for holding the seals, and rather more for the wax. (At this time patentees still received the traditional form of grant, a parchment measuring some seventy-five by fifty centimetres, with a lithographed pictorial or decorative border.[20])

One aspect that leaps out of the early figures is the amount paid to the law officers, who received four pounds for each application submitted - £21,000 in the first report. (Well might a footnote add that this sum included compensation for loss of fees to the Attorney-Generals for Ireland and Scotland and would not occur again.) Though the fees were reduced, scandalously large amounts continued to be paid; no less than £142,000 between 1852 and 1867.

* * *

The Office's donations to libraries and other institutions are first mentioned in the 1854 report. In mid-1856 the Patent Journal lists some seventy-three local libraries and nine naval dockyards as receiving the gifts.[21] Woodcroft's terms and conditions are characteristic:

> A Librarian shall be appointed to take charge of the works, who shall be held answerable for their safety and condition. The works to be deposited in a free public library of the town and to be open to inspection by the public at all reasonable hours. No charge to be made or fee of any kind taken, on any pretence whatever...[22]

The Newcastle Literary and Philosophical Society reported that it had modified its rules to meet these conditions. Woodcroft's talents as publicist and self-publicist are evident when he splashed reports of the reception of the gifts in the Patent Journal. There was a well-attended exhibition of printed patents in Manchester Free Library in autumn 1855 and in 1856 the Salford Royal Museum possessed 410 volumes of specifications.[23] There was undoubtedly a genuine professional need for information about patents but I suspect that there was also a Victorian invention fever analogous to the present demand for glossy books on war planes or works such as Jane's Weapon Systems.

Many donations were made to foreign countries. Woodcroft reprinted in the Patent Journal a report in the Washington Daily National Intelligencer 26 April 1856 headed 'A Handsome Present from the British Government':

'On the 20th September ensuing, Professor Woodcroft announced to the Hon. James Buchanan, that the Commissioners of Patents... had decided to present the US Patent Office Library, the works on British Patents now published...' The report included his own letter to the American Patent Office, 'As a servant' (he wrote) 'of the Commissioners...it may appear very presumptuous in me to add any remarks of my own...'. He then adds several remarks on the virtues of publishing specifications and his donations to 'all the libraries in Great Britain'.[24] There is some doubt as to the exact scale of the donations, which may have been smaller than Woodcroft's publicity implies; certainly the industrial towns were sent the specifications but most of them probably received only indexes and abridgements when available. (The policy continues today, as the Patent Information Network.)

The greatest task undertaken by the Office was certainly the retrospective publication of all the patents or, when available, specifications, in a single uniform series from 1617 to 1852, in which year a new annual numbering begins. Woodcroft called it 'the greatest serial scientific work in existence' which may be true in a material, but probably not in a qualitative, sense.[25] The oddity of the starting date has often been remarked upon; it is the date of the first entry in the docket book kept (as mentioned) by the Lord Chancellor's Clerk of the Patents (the predecessor of Edmunds). It shows that Woodcroft's indexes were prepared from this book; the use of dockets or abstracts was essential to cover the ground. 'Mr Woodcroft is no stranger to us' Palgrave wrote to his staff at the start of the work.[26] That Chancery's own abstracts could be used to access the patents shows that there was some method in that administrative labyrinth.

Woodcroft wrote to the Master of the Rolls in early 1853 to complain that the Assistant Keeper at the Rolls Chapel was demanding special authorisation for copying from the rolls in ink, while the Petty Bag and Enrolment offices were not so fussy.[27] This was sorted out but is significant of the new attitude toward the national archives since the beginning of the nineteenth century. It was a time of particular busyness in the reorganisation and centralisation of the records under Sir Francis Palgrave: movement from repositories such as the Tower, the Houses of Parliament and other places was taking place simultaneously with sorting, indexing and publication. The first block of Pennethorne's new building in Chancery Lane was finished in 1856.[28] In 1855 the Office could report: 'The old Specifications number 12,977, and of these 1526 have already been printed, and it is proposed to print at the rate of 2,000 in each succeeding year...'[29]

Invasion by Woodcroft's clerks and lithographers just at this time was clearly not welcomed by the Record Office staff but as both sides were responsible to the Master of the Rolls, they had to be accommodating and seem to have been so without much rancour. The annual reports from the Rolls Chapel for the 1850s often refer to the tribulations of the staff under the impact of Woodcroft's invasion. The long-suffering Assistant Keeper at the Chapel at this time was Henry George Holden, a conscientious and somewhat anxious official. For quantitative purposes he converted the work done for Woodcroft into the terms of ordinary record searches:

> 500 specifications have been copied in ink consisting of 26,800 folios; 1,000 Plans have been copied, and each Plan on the average used five times for distinct purposes, equal to 5,000 inspections.[30]

Holden had to report that what he feared had taken place: several Close and Specification Rolls had been damaged with ink. 'As soon as I had discovered the mischief', he reported, 'I made searching enquiries of all parties how and by whom it had been done, but no one would confess or impeach.'[31] After this, the head of each copying team had to give a list of his men and to take responsibility for what they did. One useful by-product of the mishap is a detailed account in the Record Office's own archives of how the patents were copied on a subject basis. Holden wrote:

> One subject or series is taken up at a time and the Steam Engine or Motive Power is the subject now in hand. Imprimis, Mr Woodcroft's clerks search the calendars from the earliest period to the latest, select references, and give directions for the Specifications to be looked out...[32]

This was, of course, no mere abstracting or calendaring, but transcription verbatim of manuscripts, often running to several skins of parchment each in the scribal forms of the seventeenth- and eighteenth-century Chancery clerks. The drawings, moreover, had to be unstitched for tracing. Holden was particularly worried by the speed at which the work had to be done, and the lack of adequate space. To make things worse, services were still held in the Rolls Chapel during term time. 'This your department only can remedy', Palgrave wrote to the head of the Office of Works, Thornborrow, when asking him to knock a new doorway in the Rolls Chapel wall, so that they could use an adjacent empty office.[33]

Since the records were not arranged by subject, Woodcroft's tackling them on that basis now looks extraordinarily time-wasting and inconvenient; it would surely have been better to have gone through them as enrolled, and done the arrangement later. One sympathises with Holden in his tribulations. For the period before the Specification Rolls existed, the individual invention grants had, of course, to be searched out from the many others.

The cost of the whole operation was very great: for the year 1857 the Patent Office spent £9,000 on stationery and £38,000 on printing and lithography, but these figures cover both retrospective and current publication of patents. Woodcroft's figure of £92,000 for publishing the pre-1852 patents is probably correct.[34] (It was considerably more than the cost of building the first phase of the new Record Office itself.) Nevertheless the Office ended each year comfortably in the black as a result of the fees paid by inventors. Its failure to use the balance in improving facilities for readers was a cause of complaint throughout the nineteenth century.[35] Since the sales of such specialised items as indexes and archival patents were small, the publishing operations in themselves were far from profitable. Earnings from sales of publications remained fairly constant throughout the nineteenth century, at between £1,500 and £2,000 annually.

A culture with a high regard for the diffusion of useful knowledge could not but be enthusiastic about the new Office which began to get a good press, aided by Woodcroft's astute publicity for his donation programme. For a time, patent information was well received as a medium for general and popular instruction. 'The Amendment Act', announced the Morning Post, 'is destined to accomplish results of the highest benefit to the nation':

> It has been instrumental in diffusing an immense amount of useful and interesting knowledge throughout the community at home, in the British colonies, and even in foreign states, by means of the devotion of an accumulation of patent fees to the publication of the specifications of patents...[36]

Dickens, whose satire had appeared in Household Words seven years earlier, now sent his reporter Dodd along to Chancery Lane to see for himself. Under the heading 'A Room Near Chancery Lane' Dodd wrote:

> There is a formidable number of rooms near Chancery Lane, where vexation of spirit attends the steps of those who find themselves involved in proceedings of law and (so called) equity; but one particular room is now in our thoughts - small and neat, indicative of improvement - in one among many things woefully in need of being improved.[37]

He continues with an admirably detailed and understanding account of the Office's activities, spiced with a certain Dickensian scepticism concerning officialdom, for instance on the compendiums of patents:

> The Home Office required the Commissioners to prepare a series of all the hopeless, helpless smoke-consumption patents; and another of all the drainage tile patents whereby we are to become a pure people in the lapse of ages...[38]

* * *

Early in the next decade the press was to take a very different interest in the Office. The Edmunds Scandal or Patent Office Scandal of the 1860s is largely forgotten except by historians of public administration.[39] As it intimately concerned the two senior men in the Office at this time and arose partly because of the pressures of the publishing programme, it is justifiable to mention it. It would be to over-simplify to state that Woodcroft and Edmunds clashed because they represented the new and the old in government service; personality also had a lot to do with it; they were both voluble, self-important and fairly hot-headed. Edmunds was at a disadvantage in that he was a traditional Chancery clerk while Woodcroft's function was new and indispensable. The immediate cause, or one of them, appears to have been - as well it might - the supply of stationery. As the man responsible for this, Edmunds introduced a new system of ordering and the Stationery Office cut off supplies. Woodcroft complained, as always, to the Master of the Rolls about this and other interferences. Edmunds demanded the fullest enquiry into the running of the Office, a step which turned out disastrously for himself. Two Treasury lawyers were appointed to investigate and it was immediately obvious that there was war between Woodcroft and Edmunds, but also that there were irregularities in the Office accounts. Mr Gladstone defined the situation in a later enquiry: 'the Clerk may hold just as much money as he thinks fit, and pay it if he thinks fit, and if he pays nothing at all, there are no means of calling him to account'. Edmunds and his clerk, Roscoe, had been paying the takings from fees and sales into two private bank accounts and transferring them to the Exchequer only when they felt like it. They were also carrying on a practice which they claimed was normal: buying revenue stamps for patent documents at a discount and keeping the difference for themselves. The Report of the Select Committee on the Patent Office Library & Museum, 1864, charged Edmunds with owing the country £17,000.

No short summary can do justice to this affair. Edmunds wanted quietly to resign his two Clerkships, while retaining his pension. At first this was approved by a Lords committee, but the 'scandal of the patent clerk' was now national - even international - news. La Presse, in Paris, commented, 'L'Exchequer de sa Majesté est la chose la plus mysterieuse qui se puisse imaginer'.[40] A full-scale Lords committee under Granville and Derby carried out an exhaustive enquiry. Its report in 1865 confirmed the misdemeanours of Edmunds but was also critical of the original enquiry, the Government and the Treasury. Among the strange material that came to light was the link between Edmunds and Lord Brougham, and his brothers John and William: Edmunds had agreed to commute part of his salary to help pay off a Brougham mortgage.

Edmunds had to resign without a pension, and in the grip of the Treasury. There was a vote of censure on the administration which led to the resignation (due also to other contributory factors) of Lord Derby. Edmunds was imprisoned for debt and spent the rest of his life pamphleteering and appealing in vain for a new enquiry. The affair contributed directly to improved public accounting. Edmonds had some defenders in his lifetime and even now it is difficult to decide the extent of his guilt. He had to handle the finances and present the accounts of Woodcroft's publishing programme, without proper supervision or guidance. At the very time the net was closing in 1864, he was giving evidence at another enquiry into the Library and Patent Museum: it is extraordinary how he and Woodcroft concealed their vehement differences for this purpose, and Edmunds does not appear as the incompetent sinecurist that Woodcroft described. He was, however, a very bad witness, losing his head and provoking his inquisitors. He was also unlucky in having inherited the public morality of the eighteenth century into the Victorian era. He is himself owed a debt in one respect: without the Edmunds Scandal we should know much less about the Patent Office and publications in the mid-nineteenth century.

There have been many changes since this period when the higher staffing and functions of the Patent Office and Library were virtually indistinguishable. In 1878 the first technically qualified staff were appointed (as indexers) and were joined by the first professional examiners in 1884. Under the same Patents Act of 1883 the Commissioners of Patents ceased to exist and the Office came under the Board of Trade with a single Comptroller of Patents, Trade-Marks and Designs. The Patent Office Library -

the senior national science library - became part of the British Museum's Department of Printed Books in 1966 and consequently (as the Science Reference Library) part of the British Library in 1973. The Library's earliest decade - particularly in terms of publishing - forms a unique chapter in its history.

Notes

1 T. Kelly, History of Public Libraries in Great Britain, 1845-1965 (1973), p. 75.

2 A.A. Gomme, Patents of Invention (1946), p. 1, here condensed.

3 Sources illustrating patent evolution, see ibid., pp. 1-15.

4 H. Harding, Patent Office Centenary (1952), p. 5, hereafter cited as Harding.

5 David Copperfield, ch. 33.

6 The Patent, a Poem, by the author of The Graces (1776), pp. 1-3.

7 House of Lords, Select Committee on the Patent Laws (Granville Committee 1852), Report and Minutes, p. 3.

8 Harding, p. 7.

9 Household Words, 2, 30 (1850), pp. 73 ff.

10 Harding, p. 11.

11 Harding, pp. 11-13.

12 For Woodcroft, see Harding, passim; The Engineer (14 February 1879) for his obituary; J. Hewish, The Indefatigable Mr Woodcroft (1980).

13 Sketch of the Origin and Progress of Steam Navigation (1848); The Pneumatics of Hero of Alexandria from the original Greek. Translated by J.G. Greenwood for B. Woodcroft (1851).

14 Harding, p. 12. Copy of draft text in the Science Reference Library.

15 Harding, pp. 12, 13, 33-5.

16 Commissioners of Patents, Annual Reports, 1852/3 (1854), p. 4.

17 ibid. p. 21.

18 ibid. p. 5.

19 B. Woodcroft, Appendix to the specifications of English patents for reaping machines (Patent Office 1853).

20 Commissioners of Patents, Annual Reports, op. cit. pp. 20, 21.

21 Commissioners of Patents Journal, 8 August 1856, pp. 809-12.

22 Commissioners of Patents, Annual Reports op. cit. p. 6.

23 Commissioners of Patents Journal, op. cit. p. 810.

24 Commissioners of Patents Journal, ibid. p. 814.

25 Patent Law Commission, Report 1864 (1865), Appendix 1, pp. 151-2.

26 Public Record Office, PRO 1-19, memorandum, Palgrave to Holden, February 1853.

27 ibid. memorandum, 26 February 1853.

28 See J.D. Cantwell's article, in Society of Archivists Journal, 7 (1984), p. 5; L. Edwards, 'A remarkable family, the Palgraves', in J.M. Shaftesley, ed., Remember the Days (1966).

29 Commissioners of Patents, Annual Reports, 1854 (1855), p. 6.

30 Public Record Office, Reports of the Deputy Keeper (17th: 1856), p. 11.

31 PRO, op. cit., memorandum, Holden to Palgrave, 8 October 1855.

32 ibid.

33 PRO, op. cit., memorandum, Palgrave to Thornborrow, 11 October 1855.

34 Commissioners of Patents, Annual Reports, 1854 to 1858 passim.

35 Parliament Sessional Papers (1863-70); petitions in Science Reference Library, special collections; engineering journals (1863-70); Harding passim.

36 Morning Post, 2 March 1857.

37 Household Words, 15, 21 February 1857, p. 190 seq. (attribution to G. Dodd by Dickens House Museum).

38 Household Words, loc. cit.

39 On Leonard Edmunds: Parliament Sessional Papers, (1863-70); Harding, pp. 16-21; V.G. Alexander, 'A nineteenth-century scandal', Institute of Public Administration Journal, 28 (1950), pp. 298 ff.

40 La Presse, (6 Juin 1865) (from a cutting in Science Reference Library Archives).

Some Bookbinders' Price Lists of the Seventeenth and Eighteenth Centuries

Mirjam Foot

In his List of London Bookbinders 1648-1815, published by the Bibliographical Society in 1950 (pp. xxiv, xxxviii), Ellic Howe mentions the existence of four seventeenth-century bookbinders' price lists. The revised Short-Title Catalogue of Books[1] has brought to light a comparable list (7154.3), and the memorandum book of James Coghlan discovered and discussed by H.M. Nixon in the Journal of the Printing Historical Society (1970) contains three more binders' price lists dating from the eighteenth century.[2] This seems a good opportunity to publish these lists in full, to show how they differ as well as what they have in common, to try to interpret the headings and descriptions - not always perfectly lucid for a twentieth-century reader - and to identify a few of the books listed as examples.

Before embarking on the lists themselves, or on the books and binding styles set out there, I want to point out that these lists cannot be used to establish the original binding price for a specific seventeenth- or eighteenth-century book. They are lists of prices agreed by the bookbinders amongst themselves or, at a later date, between the bookbinders and the booksellers of London and Westminster, in an attempt at establishing a common price for trade bindings. Fine binding is a different subject altogether and the price, dependent on materials used, time taken, and possibly also on the status of the binder, would vary from volume to volume, and might even have been negotiable. There must have been a great many more lists than the seven or eight we know now. But as these lists were ephemeral publications, broadsheets to be discarded as soon as a more up-to-date version had been published, it would not be surprising if the majority had perished. One or two references to other lists exist, and more may well turn up in future.

The prices quoted in the seventeenth-century lists are for books bound in calf, unless otherwise specified. Though Turkey leather had been in use in England since the second half of the sixteenth century, it did not become popular much before the Restoration to the throne of Charles II, and it seems to have been used for bespoke work rather than for trade bindings. Morocco was seldom employed before 1721, and Russia leather, though first mentioned as having been used for binding books c. 1700, was not in common use much before 1730.[3]

The earliest known list, the only surviving copy of which is now in the library of the Society of Antiquaries in London (Lemon 171) is headed 'A generall note of the prises for binding of all sorts of bookes' and is 'Imprinted at London. 1619' (Table 1). It is a broadsheet printed in three columns and, unlike the majority of the lists, the main categories reflect various styles of binding. Within each category the books are priced according to size. The most confusing aspect of this list is the terminology used in the headings. Phrases such as 'Bookes crosse-gilt over', 'All sorts of crosse-bound edges', and 'Bookes crosse-fillets' only become intelligible if one realises that 'crosse' or 'crosse-bound' refers to what we now call dos-à-dos bindings: two small books bound together, back to back, sharing one cover. Usually one finds the New Testament at one end and the Anglican Prayer-book and the Psalms in metre at the other. It will be noted that whenever 'crosse' or 'crosse-bound' occurs in a heading, only books in small format are listed and each time at least two titles are mentioned. If 'crosse' means dos-à-dos, 'one way' must apply to the more usual single-bound books. 'Gilt over' refers to the all-over decoration of the covers in gold, achieved either with small tools or with blocks. In this list no distinction is made between 'gilt over' and 'small tooles', but a design of corner and centre pieces with or without a semis of small tools is quite common at the time. For the smaller formats 'gilt over' may easily refer to decoration in gold with the impression of a single large block, a popular way cheaply to produce expensive-looking trade bindings.[4] 'Gilt, edges and corners' refers to gilding the edges of the leaves and to the use of corner blocks or corner tools on the covers. 'Fillets' are created by running a brass wheel engraved with either one or two lines along the edges of the covers, or slightly further in, to form a panel. Both one-line and two-line fillets are commonly found on trade bindings of the seventeenth century, either used blind or with gold leaf. 'Ovills' are oval centre blocks, also quite common during this period, and 'sheepes leather' speaks for itself. The latter was used only for smaller formats, however, and the Stationers' Company had in fact forbidden the use of sheepskin for large books.[5] 'Bookes in hard bords' is more puzzling than it sounds, unless it means just that: books sewn and laced-in in boards, but not covered. Considering that the term is applied only to Foxe's Book of Martyrs and to bibles, prayer-books and psalters, and considering that this is the golden age of embroidered binding, these may have been provided for the professional embroiderers or for the ladies who occupied their spare time with needlework. Both would require their books in plain boards round which the embroidered covers could be sewn once they were finished.

The majority of the books mentioned on this list are bibles, books of common prayer, and psalm books, in all formats from folio to 32°. Psalm books in 8° and 16° are specified with the word 'Middleborow', perhaps meaning the Middleburg editions of The Psalmes of David in meeter, with the prose (which appears in the margin of the Geneva version), printed by R. Schilders, the 8° edition in 1602 (STC 2507.5) and the 16° in 1599 (STC 2499.9). Nicholas Temperley has argued[6] that the term was used in general for any edition of the English version of the metrical psalms with prose psalms in the margin, based on these Middleburg editions. He also points out that the word 'Psalmes' was commonly used for the metrical version while 'Psalter' was used for the prose version, hence the combination of 'Psalter and Psalmes' in the list. A distinction is also made between a 'Church Bible', the Authorised version printed in Black Letter, and a 'Romane Bible', the Geneva version in Roman letter which was noticeably smaller. Most of the other books on the list can be identified with the help of the Short-Title Catalogue of Books ...1475-1640 (revised edition, vol. 2, 1976, vol. 1 in preparation), A.F. Allison and V.F. Goldschmidt, Titles of English Books, vol. 1: 1475-1640 (1976), R. Watt's Bibliotheca Britannica (1824), and the British Library's Catalogue of Printed Books.[7] It seems pointless to clutter this discussion with long lists of titles - which would become singularly tiresome in the description of some of the later price lists which consist almost entirely of titles, the more so as one cannot be certain that the figure quoted is for the latest available edition of a particular book. I have therefore limited myself to the identification (in footnotes to the individual price lists) of one or two books in each category. These are meant as examples of the kind of book for which a standard price could be established and which in turn could serve as a guideline for other books, not listed. The frequency with which the phrase 'or the like' occurs shows that this was precisely the purpose the bookbinders had in mind.

The next list (Table 2) is of a slightly different character. Unlike the others it is not an 'agreed' list of prices for binding, agreed between the bookbinders and the booksellers, but it is a statement of 'Bookes as they are sold bound' issued by Thomas Downes, the King's Printer for Ireland in or shortly after 1620. It gives the prices for various kinds and sizes of books, bound, decorated ('Bust'), with bosses, with clasps, or with fillets, as charged in London and in Dublin. This is the only list where bosses and clasps are mentioned. The only known copy of this list (STC 7154.3), a half-sheet folio, is held at the Society of Antiquaries and is hidden in a volume of Proclamations concerning Ireland (1572-1670).[8] Unlike the other lists, the prices include the cost of the actual book as well as that of the binding, and those charged '<u>At</u> London' are consistently lower than those charged '<u>At</u> Dublin'.

A copy of the next list, a broadsheet in three columns entitled 'A Generall note of the prises for binding all sortes of bookes', 'Printed at London 1646', is among the Thomason Tracts at the British Library (669.f.10(60)), and has a note in George Thomason's hand indicating that he acquired it on 18 June [1646] (Table 3). Unlike the 1619 list this list is arranged by type of book, an arrangement which remains more or less standard for the rest of the century. The last half column is devoted to 'Sheeps Leather' binding. Under each heading, indicating the kind and size of the book, the various binding styles are listed. Dos-à-dos bindings have gone out of fashion and do not occur on the list, nor do books in boards, though embroidered bindings were still produced.[9] 'Gilt over', 'Corners', 'Edges', 'Fillets', and 'Ovills' we have met before, but a distinction is made here between 'Gilt over' and 'Small tooles ordinary'. As the latter way of decorating is more expensive, it strengthens the interpretation of 'gilt over' as decorated either with a block (for the small formats) or with corner and centre pieces, which are quicker to apply than a number of small hand tools. 'Chequer', slightly more expensive than 'Gilt over' (but cheaper than 'Small tooles'), indicates an all-over pattern made with one or two repeating tools,[10] while 'Rolles' refers to decorating the covers with an engraved brass wheel or roll.

A difference in sewing technique, one more expensive than the other, is indicated by 'double lac'd' and 'single lac'd', referring most probably to sewing on raised bands for which four or five cords were used and sewing on sawn-in or recessed bands for which two thongs or cords were sufficient. On this and more frequently on the later lists sizes are distinguished not only by format but also by paper and type sizes. Here only 'Crown' (15 x 20 in.) and 'pot' ($12\frac{1}{2}$ x $15\frac{1}{2}$ in.) paper are noted and a distinction is also made between 'Bibles in Octavo' and 'Bibles in 8 Minnion'.[11] This seems to be an early use of the term 'minion', a type size between nonpareil and brevier, which is not mentioned in Moxon.[12] The Oxford English Dictionary records as the earliest use of Minion, James Howell's

Vocabulary of 1659 (section L1).

There remains one expression on this list which used to baffle me. Among the prices quoted for 'Sheeps Leather' one of the cheapest is 'All other bookes 8 & 12 guttard'. As the gutter is the inner (spine) margin of the book, the only suggestion I can make is that it refers to 'stabbed' bindings. The practice of stabbing books, a much quicker but also - especially for small formats with a narrow gutter - a much weaker method of holding the sections together than the conventional sewing on thongs or cords on a sewing frame, was restricted by the Stationers' Company to a set maximum number of leaves per format, but it was widely adopted for school books and popular works of limited size.[13]

An indication that these lists were issued more frequently than the small number of surviving copies would lead one to believe, is a reference in Courtbook C of the Stationers' Company:

> At a Court held at Stationers' Hall on the sixth of August 1649...many Bookbinders came and extended a peticion w[i]th a paper of the prizes of binding bookes w[hi]ch they desired might be confirmed by the table. Whereupon the Court declared their willingnesse to helpe them & have desired Mr Robinson and Mr Thrale to yuse the paper and confer with such of them as they shall choose for that and other matters w[hi]ch they desire to make knowne & remedied & then, upon their request the Court will endeavour to give them satisfaction.

The 'table' referred to must have been one of these price lists, almost certainly very similar to the ones we have seen, and indeed on the next list it is spelled out in the title (Table 4):

> A General Note of the Prices of Binding all sorts of Books; Agreed on by the Book-binders, whose Names are under-written. As it was presented to the Master, Wardens, and Assistants of the Worshipful Company of Stationers, August, the 2d, 1669.

This broadsheet is in four columns, and was 'Licensed, September 23. 1669. [by] Roger l'Estrange'. The list, formerly in the library of the Marquess of Bute, acquired by Francis Edwards, Ltd. and presented to the library of Harvard University by Mr Curt H. Reisinger, was edited by W.A. Jackson and a facsimile was presented as a keepsake to members of the Bibliographical Society of America in 1951. The publication of this list enabled the British Library to discover that it possessed a complete copy, but cut up and preserved in two different volumes of the Bagford collection (Harl. 5915 [items 378-83] and Harl. 5960 [item 26], both now in the Department of Printed Books).

Like the 1646 list this list is arranged by type of book, with the prices for binding in sheep together at the end and sub-divided according to size. Under each heading the different binding styles are quoted for and we meet again such specifications as 'Gilt Edges', 'Fillets', 'Ovals', and 'Roll[e]s'. A new distinction is that between 'Edges Extraordinary' and 'Edges Ordinary', made here for the first time and still occurring on the 1695 list. This could refer to gilt edges in both cases, while the covers are left 'ordinary' or plain, or 'extraordinary', ie. decorated with a lot of gold tooling as in the modern 'extra' binding. It could also possibly refer to the decoration of the edges themselves. The practice of painting edges under the gold started circa 1650 and it is possible that 'extraordinary' refers to painted and gilt. As gauffering the edges seems to have gone out of fashion by this date, it is less likely to mean that. However, with painted edges we move somewhat outside the realm of trade bindings, and it is more likely that 'ordinary', if it refers to the edges, means coloured or sprinkled, a quite common way of decorating edges during the seventeenth century, while 'extraordinary' may mean marbled, a novelty at the time.

'Marble Fillets' we find here for the first time. The practice of marbling leather had only recently been introduced in England, and an early marbled calf binding, covering a tract volume bound by Samuel Mearne for Cor. Pigeon in 1655, was illustrated as plate 1 by H.M. Nixon in his <u>English Restoration Bookbindings</u> (1974). On the 1669 list 'marble fillets' on a folio cost 8s. or 10s. It is interesting to see that six years later Samuel Mearne charged £3 per volume for large paper copies of the <u>Book of Common Prayer</u> supplied to the Chapel Royal in 'marble leather'. This is not just another example of Mearne being excessively expensive - though as he much suffered from non-payment of royal bills, his prices may well not have reflected those of the trade. In this case the book itself was included in the price, and as well as with fillets the binding was decorated with the cypher of Charles II at the corners of the panel.

Paper sizes are given again: we find 'Fools-Cap' (13½ x 16¾ in.) as well as 'Crown' and 'Pot', and a distinction is made between 'Bibles in Octavo, Brevere' (brevier, the larger type size) and 'Bibles in Octavo, Nonperil' (nonpareil, the smaller size).

The most notable feature of this 'Note of the Prices' is the list of eighty-two bookbinders 'whose Names are under-written'. Of these eighteen (marked 'a') were booksellers as well as bookbinders; five (marked 'b') were possibly booksellers as well as binders; forty-five (marked 'c') were bookbinders who can be identified from the Stationers' Company's records; and fourteen (marked 'd') are known only from this list.[14] Further information on those men can be found in Ellic Howe's List of London Bookbinders.

The last list of the seventeenth century:

> A General Note of the Prices of Binding All Sorts of Books in Calves-Leather: Agreed on by the Book-Binders, Freemen of the City of London, And by them Presented to the Master, Wardens and Assistants of the Worshipful Company of Stationers, at a Court holden March, 1694/5

exists in two copies (Table 5), both among the Bagford fragments in the British Library. One is a broadsheet in three columns 'London: Printed, and are to be Sold by John Whitlock near Stationers-Hall. 1695', (Harl. 5910 [item 115] kept in the Department of Printed Books), and the other is a not quite accurate and later manuscript copy, (Harl. 5910 [f. 135-7], in the Department of Manuscripts). The Court meeting referred to in the title took place at Stationers' Hall on Monday, 4 March 1694-5 and during this meeting 'A Peticion of severall Bookbinders representing the lowe condition they were brought to by the lownesse of prices and dearness of Lether was exhibited at this Court being their Approbacion to a table of Rates therewith presented'.[15] Like the earlier lists, the books have been arranged by size, but now the secular titles come first, grouped according to size and language, and the last few lines of the list are devoted to 'The antient allow'd Rate of Binding Bibles in Calf'. In this section only the familiar styles 'Gilt Edges', 'Edges Extraordinary', 'Edges Ordinary', 'Fillets', and 'Ovals' are specified and the prices are the same as those for 1669. The main portion of the list gives the titles 'or the like' for which binding prices are quoted, followed by generalisations such as 'All Fools Cap thick', 'All middle siz'd', or even 'All others'. The paper sizes specified here include 'Demy' (17½ x 22 in.) and 'Fools Cap'.

The source for the three eighteenth-century price lists is James Coghlan's memorandum book (Table 6) in which appears a broadsheet in three columns, 'Printed by Edward Bate, in George's Lane near Dame's Street', headed:

> Whereas the BOOKBINDERS of the City of Dublin at a Meeting the 15th Day of September 1743, then held, did Unanimously Agree, that from and after the 29th of the said Month no Books are to be Bound, Paper Gilt or Black'd, for Booksellers, under the following Prices.

This is the earliest surviving evidence of the Dublin bookbinders combining forces to establish a minimum rate of pay for various types of work and when, in the Spring of 1766, a controversy arose between the binders and booksellers of Dublin about a proposed increase in the price of binding amounting to about nine per cent, the 'former Regulations in the year 1743' were recalled. Two years later, on 25 April 1768, a third price increase was published.[16]

This 1743 list resembles the 1619 price list in that it has been arranged according to style or method of binding. Under each heading the prices are quoted for the various sizes, expressed in formats and paper sizes. Very few actual titles are mentioned. The prices 'For the Gilt Work' are on the whole comparable with those for 'Edges Ordinary' on the 1669 and 1695 London price lists[17] and suggest therefore a certain amount, but not a great deal, of gold tooling. 'Gilt Back only', ie. with gold tooling on the spine, is a great deal cheaper, and cheaper still are 'Books Filleted on the Back only with a Tool added thereto', calling to mind the frequently encountered flat spines decorated with double fillets, evenly spaced to suggest bands, with a small tool in each compartment. 'Vellum plain' speaks for itself, and 'Forril', vellum made from unsplit sheepskin, is divided into 'yellow', ie. natural, and 'green'. On p. 43 of his memorandum book James Coghlan tells us how to make 'Green for Velum' by adding 'Viniger' to 'Brass fileings Desolved in Oyl of Viteral' (oil of vitriol: concentrated sulphuric acid), and on p. 63 he gives another 'Aproved Recept' 'To Green Velum, or Foral':

> a Little Vardigrace [verdigris] to half pint of Viniger Best Sort. Take Care Not to put to Much Vardigrace in a Quarter pound is Sufficient to put in a pint & half of Best Viniger. NB: Finding Did not Strike my Velum I put a Little pot ashes [potash: a crude form of potassium carbonate] (viteril [vitriol: a sulphate of iron] answers Better) in it & Used it hot Doing it over Several times it Did.

On the list 'Russia Bands' is placed between 'Books bound in Vellum plain' and 'Forril', and as only large sizes are mentioned it probably does not refer, as I thought at first, to books sewn on cords and bound in Russia leather - an aromatic, diced, usually reddish-brown leather made from calf or cow-hide - but to a form of stationery binding with two or three Russia leather bands sewn across the spine, extending about half way down the sides, as described and illustrated in The Art of Bookbinding.[18] There are separate categories for 'Books bound in Calve's Leather and Letter'd only' [with the title on the spine], for books in 'Plain Sheep' and for 'Books bound in Sheep Banded'. The latter probably refers to sewing on raised cords or bands, a more expensive procedure than either stabbing or sewing on recessed cords.[19]

'Gilt Paper and Black', charged for by the ream, is more likely to refer to gilding or blackening the edges of the paper than to gilding or embossing and colouring black whole sheets. Though funeral services and the like were usually stitched in black paper wrappers, embossed or gilt paper still was not all that common in England at this date. Metallic-varnish paper or embossed paper was made in London from the early 1690s, but it seems improbable to me that it was produced in quantity in Dublin in the 1740s, the more so as most of the embossed paper that was used at the time was imported from Germany.[20] It is just possible that these prices were sales prices for black and (imported) embossed paper. Robert Dossie describes a method 'of gilding proper for the edges of books and paper', suggesting that the edges of whole sheets were gilt.[21] Similarly, in the 1813 London Bookbinders' Price-Book there is a section at the end on 'Gilding and Blacking Paper and Cards', also priced per ream or per pack, and in Parry's Art of Bookbinding of 1818, at the end of the chapter on stationery binding, instructions are given for gilding paper and black-edge paper. The gilding here clearly refers to the edges of the paper, while black-edge paper may be notepaper with a black rim along the edges. John Arnett[22] gives a recipe for blackening the edges of a book with ivory black, lamp black or antimony, mixed with a little paste, and we know that James Coghlan considered '½ lb of Antimoney' among the 'Nessesary Utentials in the Arts of Bookbinding'.[23] Ruling paper for account books or for ledgers was also considered part of a binder's metier and Coghlan, who had acquired a 12-inch ruler and a 'Founting' pen for this task, gives several recipes for red and black ink. Red ink can be made from '3 pints of Stale Bear (rather then viniger) 4 oz of Brazel Dust. Some people puts allom [alum] in it the Butt 1 oz: in this quantety. Simmer these for one Hour together, then Str[ain] it and Bottel it up for Use. Cork it' (p. 32). While the 'Best Recept for Makeing Black Ink for Sail' (p. 33) reads as follows:

> Boyl a pound of Logwood and a quarter of an ounce of allum in five Quarts of water (ale Measure) when the Coulor is is pretty Strong which you may try with a pen, put in half a pound of Galls [gall nuts, containing tannic acid], and let them Simmer allso, trying as Before, then put in 6 ounces of Copras [copperas: ferrous sulphate] & the Same Quantety of Gum Arabeck Let them Steep all Night and then Simmer it ove[r] a Gentle fire. Let it Cool & Strain it off for Use.

In the margin he added 'I should have said Simmer for it Must not Boyl' and again 'NB: it Should Not Boyl at all'.

The remaining two categories, 'Grains' and 'Lacquerd Work' deal with books by the hundred. 'Grains' refers to the grain split or outer split of a sheepskin, the cheapest available leather. 'Testaments Saw'd' (and 'Grammars ditto') indicate an early form of 'perfect binding'. The backs of the sections were sawn in, the cords pressed into the grooves, and the whole was glued up without any previous sewing: a very cheap and very unstable way of holding the book together.[24] 'Lacquerd Work', as we know it from Persian bindings of the seventeenth, eighteenth and nineteenth centuries, seems out of place on a trade list, and it may refer to varnished bindings, though I am not sure whether varnish was used on bindings as early as the first half of the eighteenth century. As described by Arnett (p. 137) varnishing seems quite a complicated operation and would warrant the price of £2.10s. for a hundred prayer-books better than the less labour-intensive habit, fairly common in the seventeenth and eighteenth centuries, of polishing the covers with a polishing iron over one or two coats of glaire. At a guess it may even refer to marbling the leather, several recipes for which are given by Coghlan, such as the one on p. 42: 'Brown for Books Viz What We Call the Prussian Marble on Leather Books Viz Pot ash Steepd or Mixd With Water flung on after the Sperits of Vitriol [a distilled essence of vitriol]'. Another one among his 'Aproved Recepts' reads:

> My Brown for Books is Bound in Calf is Pot Ashes Soked & Weekned with Water thro'd on the Book Standing on its fore Edges Make the Run or Prussion Marble...Oyl of Vitirol is Also Used in My Marblee Weekned with Water a Little Coppris [copperas] in Water is Also What I Marble & Sprinkle with Very Light.

Certainly marbled and sprinkled covers were very popular at the time.

A large variety of paper sizes is mentioned on this list, including for bound books: 'Imperial' (22 x 30 in.), 'Super-Royal' (19¼ x 27½ in.), 'Royal' (19¼ x 24 in.), 'Medium' (18 x 23 in.), 'Demy' (17½ x 22 in.), and 'Propatria' (a watermark most commonly used in eighteenth-century Britain in Foolscap paper: 13½ x 16¾ in.). The paper sizes for writing paper are 'Demy' (15½ x 20 in.), 'Post' (15¼ x 19½ in.), and again 'Propatria' (writing Foolscap: 13½ x 16¾ in.).

One year later, on 14 May 1744, the 'Bookbinders of the Citys of London & Westminster & the libertys thereof' addressed themselves to the booksellers with the statement that 'In Consideration of the exorbitant prices that Leather now Bears...By an Absolute Necessity are Obliged to Come to the following Resolutions in Regard to the Undermentioned prices for the Different sizes of Books.' This price list (Table 7) was copied by James Coghlan on pp. 13-15 of his memorandum book and no printed copy has yet been found. The list starts with prices for binding and lettering books of different sizes indicated by format and paper size. Then follows a section of books bound in calf with or without gilt edges, also priced according to format, paper and type sizes, with a few titles mentioned as examples, followed by 'Sheep Binders prices' per hundred, where mainly individual titles are given. The 'Sowing & Folding Prices' are quoted per 'Alphabett', ie. for the quires A-Z, or per hundred sheets, and a distinction is made between sewing each section separately or all-along ('Sowing only one Sheet at a time'), sewing two-on ('Sowing only two Sheets at a time'), and 'Common Sowing' which may well mean six-on or more. 'Black or Gilt Paper' and 'Ruleing Paper' we have met before. The prices for 'Black or Gilt Paper' given here, however, are noticeably lower than those charged in Dublin the previous year. The paper sizes indicating the sizes of bound books mentioned on this list are 'Royal', 'Demy', 'Crown' (15 x 20 in.), 'Fools Cap', and 'medium'; the sizes for 'Black or Gilt Paper', probably referring to writing paper, are 'post', and 'Fools Cap'; and 'Ruleing Paper' includes 'Pott' (12½ x 15½ in.). The type sizes listed are 'Brevier', 'minion', 'Nonpariel', 'pica', and 'Long primer'.

A copy of the last list to be discussed here (Table 8), addressed 'To the Booksellers of London and Westminster', establishing 'The Prices for Binding agreed on the 2d of June, 1760', was found folded and tipped-in on p. 16 of Coghlan's memorandum book. It is printed in two columns and under each heading indicating the sizes a list of titles is given as examples, followed by the remark 'All Books on the same Paper and Thickness, the like Price'. The paper sizes are familiar. Binding styles are indicated summarily and consist of 'plain Calf', 'Calf', 'Sheep, Rolled', and 'Red Sheep, Rolled'; we encounter 'half bound' here for the first time. Coghlan bought six small calf skins and a pared sheepskin at one shilling each, while red basil, 'sheep skin tanned, used for common bindings', as Arnett puts it (p. 203), cost him ten pence. Bibles and books of common prayer, also arranged by size, are grouped together at the end.

In an attempt to see whether the bookbinders kept to the standard prices quoted in the lists, I looked through a large number of bills for binding work done for Raylton in the 1720s and '30s.[25] I compared these with the London price list for 1744, and notwithstanding the fact that only relatively few titles are mentioned in this list, the comparable entries showed that the prices paid earlier by Raylton were either the same as or slightly lower than those indicated in 1744. I also looked through a quantity of bills of work done for George Hawkins, the bookseller, dating from the 1740s, '50s, and '60s.[26] Not all bills specified in sufficient detail the materials used and the style of binding, and several posts obviously included the price of the books themselves. But a number of bills for binding only (such as those of Wm. Cook, of 1760) quoted the same titles, bound and decorated in the same way as those mentioned in the 1760 list, charging the same price.

In 1787 James Fraser, a master bookbinder, tried to persuade the binders and journeymen to work at piece rates instead of for a settled weekly wage. In an 'Address to the Master and Journeymen Bookbinders of London and Westminster'[27] he breaks down into components the process of binding in calf, lettering (on morocco lettering pieces), and colouring or gilding the edges, of a 12° book of 18 sheets, a crown 8° of 23 sheets, and an 8° of 36 sheets. The cost of the actual work and the materials comes to 'Better than 6d.¾', 'Better than 7d.¾', and 'About 11d.½' for these three sizes respectively. He also lists the overheads (rent, coal, candles, wear and tear, and an errand boy), and gives the fair market price for a 12° in calf, lettered, at 1s., that for a crown 8° at 1s.1d. and that for an 8° at 1s.4d., a rise of about 4d. per volume since 1760 (though the 1760 list does not specify any treatment of the edges). In order to put this in perspective, it may be interesting to note that in 1750 or 1760 a forwarder's wages were 10s.6d. per week. When Jock McKinlay came to London to work as a journeyman, around 1760, he was paid 9s., but he was 'a shocking bad workman'.[28] Finishers were paid more, though according to Laban 'There were very few Finishers then, little or no finishing, except the lettering being required', a statement not borne out by the earlier price lists but pertinent in the light of the 1760 list. In 1786 the rates ranged from 15s. to 18s. per week for a 12½ hour day, a finisher got 21s. and an extremely competent finisher might rise to 24s. This meant that in order to break even and earn his minimum wage, a forwarder in 1760 had to bind at least ten books a week. For a competent craftsman this would not present any difficulties: a state of affairs that prompted R. Pratt, a binder who worked at Buckingham House, to remark that from 1760 to 1780 'Bookbinding was as well paid a Trade as any other'.

A generall note of the prises for binding of all sorts of bookes.

Gilt ouer one way.

Folio.

Bibles folio Roman, or the like —— 11 s.—o d.
Com. and Psalmes: or the like —— 7 s.—o d.

In 4to.

Bibles 4to, or the like —— 5 s.—6 d.
Com, and Psalmes, or the like —— 3 s.—6 d.

In 8o.

Bibles 8o, or th[e lik]e, —— 2 s.—8 d.
Com. Test. & P[sal]mes, or the like, —— 2 s.—6 d.
Com. and Psalmes, or the like, —— 2 s.—o
Psal. 8o Middleborow, or the like, —— 2 s.—o

In 12o.

Bibles in 12o, or the like —— 2 s.—8 d
Com. and Psalmes in 12o, —— 1 s.—8 d.
Practice of [pie]ty, and the like, —— 1 s.—4 d.
Helpe to [illegible] —— 1 s.—2 d

Test. Psalmes 16o. Middleborow, —— 1 s.—2 d.
Psalmes 16o Middleborow, —— 1 s.—o d.
Psalmes 16o common, or the like, —— o—10 d.

In 24to.

Com. Test. Psal. 24o, or of that sort, —— 1 s.—2 d.

In 32o.

Psalmes 32o, Rom. and English, one with another, —— o —— 8 d.

Bookes crosse-gilt ouer.

In 24o.

Com. Test. Psalmes 24o crosse-guilt, —— 1 s.—8 d
Test. Psalmes 16o crosse-guilt, —— 1 s.—8 d.

In 32.

Psalter and Psalmes 32, —— 1 s.—4 d.

Bookes of all sorts gilt, edges and corners.

Church Bible corners in folio, —— 15 s.—o
Bible folio Romane, or the like, —— 8 s.—6 d.
Com. and Psal. folio, or the like, —— 6 s.—o

In 4.

Bible 4. great Rom. —— 4 s.—o
Bible 4, or the like, —— 3 s.—8 d.
Com. and Psalmes 4, or the like, —— 2 s.—6 d.

In 8.

Bible 8, or the like, —— 2 s.—4 d.
Com. Test. Psalmes, or the like, —— 2 s.—4 d.
Psalmes 8. Middleborow, or the like, —— 1 s.—8 d.

In 12.

Bibles in 12, or the like, —— 2 s.—4 d
Test. Psalmes 12, or the like, —— 2 s.—2 d.
Sanctuaries, or the like, —— 1 s.—2 d.

In 16.

Test. Psalmes 16. Middleborow, or the like, —— 1 s.—o

In 24.

Com. Test. & Psalmes, or such other, —— 1 s.—o

In 32.

Psalmes in 32, —— o —— 8 d.

Bookes edges and fillets.

Bibles folio large, —— 10 s.—o
Bibles folio Roman. or the like, —— 6 s.—6 d.
Com. and Psalmes, or the like, —— 4 s.—6 d.

In 4.

Bibles 4 Rom. great letter, —— 3 s.—4 d.
Bibles 4 English, —— 3 s.—o
Com. Psalmes 4, or such like, —— 2 s.—o

In 8.

Bibles 8 or the like, —— 1 s.—10 d.
Com. Test. Psalmes, —— 1 s.—10 d.
Psalmes 8 Middleborow, or the like, —— 1 s.—6 d.

In 12.

Bibles in 12, —— 1 s.—10 d.
Sanctuaries, Dauids Key, and Practice of Piety, and the like, } —— 1 s.—o
Helpe to Deuotion, or the like, —— o—10 d.

In 16.

Test. Psal. 16 Middleborow edges, —— 1 s.—o
Psalmes 16 Middleborow edges, —— o—10 d.
Psalmes 16 com[mon, or t]he like, —— o—8 d

In 24.

Com. Test. Psalmes 24 edges, —— o—11 d
Test. Psalmes 24. or the like, —— o—10 d

In 32.

Psalmes 32, or the like, —— o—7 d.

All sorts of crosse-bound edges.

In 16.

Test. Psal. 16 Middleborow, or the like, —— 1 s.—6 d.

In 24.

Test. Com. and Psalmes 24, or the like, —— 1 s.—6 d.

In 32.

Prayers and Psalmes 32 crosse, —— 1 s.—2 d.

Bookes folio fillets.

Martyrs two volumes, —— 12 s.—o
Church-Bible, —— 6 s.—o
Romane Bible, —— 3 s.—4 d.
Raleighs History, —— 3 s.—6 d.
Perkins, or the like, —— 2 s.—8 d.
All folio's like Babingtons, —— 2 s.—6 d.
All folio's, like Com. & Psalmes, —— 2 s.—4 d.

In 4.

Bibles in 4, large Romane, —— 2 s.—o
Bibles 4. and such like, —— 1 s.—10 d.
Com. & Psalmes, & the like, —— 1 s.—2 d.

In 8.

Bibles 8. or the like, —— 1 s.—2 d.
Com. Test. and Psalmes, & the like, —— 1 s.—2 d.
Test. Psalter, and Psalmes, —— 1 s.—o
All bookes like the Plaine mans path-way, —— 9 d.

In 12.

Bible 12, or the like, —— 1 s.—2 d
Practice of piety, or the like, —— 8 d.

In 16.

Test. Psalmes 16 Middleborow, —— 7 d.
Psalmes 16 Middleborow, —— 6 d.
Psalmes 16 Com. or the like, —— 5 d.

In 24.

Com. Test. and Psalmes, or the like, —— 7 d.

In 32.

Psalmes in 32, or the like, —— 5 d.

Bookes crosse-fillets.

In 16.

Test. Psalmes 16, Middleborow, —— 1 s.—o

In 24.

Com. Test. Psalmes in 24 crosse, —— o—11 d.

In 32.

Psalter and psalmes in 32, —— 9 d.

Bookes in ouills.

Camden with maps, —— 4 s.—6 d.
Church-Bible, —— 5 s —
Raleighs histories, —— 2 s.—6 d.

Plutarch, or the like, —— 2 s.—4 d.
Bible folio Romane, —— 2 s.—2 d.
Perkins, and the like, —— 5 s.—6 d.
Purchas, and the like, —— 1 s.—8 d.
Commines, and the like, —— 1 s.—6 d.

In 4

Bible in 4, and the like, —— 1 s.—2 d.
Smiths sermons, and the like, —— o—10 d.

In 8.

Bibles in 8, and the like, —— o—8 d.
All sorts of Test. psalmes 8 —— o—6 d.
All lattin bookes large, —— o—8 d.
All lattin bookes small, —— o—6 d.

In 12.

Bibles in 12. —— o—8 d.
Test. Psalmes in 12, or the like, —— o—6 d.
All Latin bookes in 16, —— o—5 d.
All Latin bookes in 24, —— o—4 d.

Law-bookes.

Statutes at large, —— 2 s.—6 d.
Rastall Abridgement, folio, —— 1 s.—8 d.
Poultons Abridgement, folio, —— 1 s.—6 d.
Daltons Iustice, folio, —— 1 s.—4 d.
Wests Presidents in 4, —— 1 s.—o
Iustice of peace, in 8, —— o—6 d.

Bookes sheepes leather.

Test. in 8, or the like, —— o—4 d.
Grammers, or the like, —— o—2 d. ob.
Silua, or the like, —— o—4 d.

In 16.

Tullies Orations, or the like, —— o—3 d.
Psalmes in 16 common, —— o—2 d.

In 32.

Psalmes in 32, —— o—2 d.

Bookes in hard bords.

Martyrs, —— 7 s.—o
Bible folio large, —— 4 s.—6 d.
Bible folio small, —— 3 s.—8 d.
Bible medium, —— 2 s.—o

In 4.

Bible in 4, —— 1 s.—2 d.
Test. Com. psalmes in 4, —— 1 s.—o
Com. booke and psalmes in 4, —— o—9 d.

In 8.

Bible 8, —— o—8 d.
Com. Test. psalmes in 8, —— o—7 d.
Psalter, Test. and psalmes, —— o—7 d.
Test psal 8vo —— o—6 d
Com. and psalmes in 16, Com. —— o—4 d.

All sorts of Latin bookes, in folio and quarto.

Bibliotheca patrum, —— 3 s.—6 d.
Tastatus, and the like, —— 3 s.—o
Tremellius bible, —— 2 s.—4 d.
Gorron, or the like, —— 2 s.—o
Stella on Luke, or the like, —— 1 s.—8 d.
Piscator in 4, —— 1 s.—4 d.
Tremellius bible in 4, or the like, —— 1 s.—2 d.
Dictionarium poeticum, —— 1 s.—o
All other small quarto's, —— o—10 d.

FINIS.

Imprinted at LONDON. 1619.

List of binding prices 'Imprinted at LONDON 1619.'

The Price Lists

Table 1

A generall note of the prises for binding of all sorts of bookes.

Gilt over one way.

Folio.

Bibles folio Roman, or the like ——— 11s.— 0d.
Com. and Psalmes: or the like ——— 7s.— 0d.

In 4to.

Bibles 4to, or the like ——— 5s.— 6d.
Com, and Psalmes, or the like ——— 3s.— 6d.

In 8°.

Bibles 8°, or th[e lik]e, ——— 2s.— 8d.
Com. Test. & P[sal]mes, or the like, — 2s.— 6d.
Com. and Psalmes, or the like, ——— 2s.— 0
Psal. 8° Middleborow, or the like, ——— 2s.— 0

In 12°.

Bibles in 12°, or the like ——— 2s.— 8d.
Com. and Psalmes in 12°, ——— 1s.— 8d.
Practice of Piety, and the like, ——— 1s.— 4d.[1]
Helpe to D[evotion,] ——— 1s.— 2d.[2]

[In 1]6°.

Test. Psalmes 16°. Middleborow, ——— 1s.— 2d.
Psalmes 16° Middleborow, ——— 1s.— 0d
Psalmes 16° common, or the like, ——— 0 —10d.

In 24to.

Com. Test. Psal. 24°, or of that sort, — 1s.— 2d.

In 32°.

Psalmes 32°, Rom. and English, one with another, ——— 0 — 8d.

Bookes crosse-gilt over.

In 24°.

Com. Test. Psalmes 24° crosse-guilt, — 1s.— 8d.
Test. Psalmes 16° crosse-guilt, ——— 1s.— 8d.

In 32.

Psalter and Psalmes 32, ——— 1s.— 4d.

Bookes of all sorts gilt, edges and corners.

Church Bible corners in folio, ——— 15s.— 0
Bible folio Romane, or the like, ——— 8s.— 6d.
Com. and Psal. folio, or the like, ——— 6s.— 0

In 4.

Bible 4. great Rom. ——— 4s.— 0
Bible 4, or the like, ——— 3s.— 8d.
Com. and Psalmes 4, or the like, ——— 2s.— 6d.

In 8.

Bible 8, or the like, ——— 2s.— 4d.
Com. Test. Psalmes, or the like, ——— 2s.— 4d.
Psalmes 8. Middleborow, or the like, — 1s.— 8d.

1 Lewis Bayly, The Practise of Pietie, 12°, London, 1619

2 Samuel Hieron, A Helpe unto Devotion, 12°, London, 1618

In 12.
Bibles in 12, or the like, ———— 2s.— 4d.
Test Psalmes 12, or the like, ———— 2s.— 2d.
Sanctuaries, or the like, ———— 1s.— 2d.[3]

In 16.
Test. Psalmes 16. Middleborow, or the like, ———— 1s.— 0

In 24.
Com. Test. & Psalmes, or such other, — 1s.— 0

In 32.
Psalmes in 32, ———— 0 — 8d.

Bookes edges and fillets.
Bibles folio large, ———— 10s.— 0
Bibles folio Roman. or the like, ———— 6s.— 6d.
Com. and Psalmes, or the like, ———— 4s.— 6d.

In 4.
Bibles 4 Rom. great letter, ———— 3s.— 4d.
Bibles 4 English, ———— 3s.— 0
Com. Psalmes 4, or such like, ———— 2s.— 0

In 8.
Bibles 8 or the like, ———— 1s.-10d.
Com. Test. Psalmes, ———— 1s.-10d.
Psalmes 8 Middleborow, or the like, —— 1s.— 6d.

In 12.
Bibles in 12, ———— 1s.-10d.
Sanctuaries, Davids Key,[4] and }
Practice of Piety, and the like, } ———— 1s.— 0
Helpe to Devotion, or the like, ———— 0 — 10d.

In 16.
Test. Psal. 16 Middleborow edges, ———— 1s.— 0
Psalmes 16. Middleborow edges, ———— 0 — 10d.
Psalmes 16 Com. or the like, ———— 0 — 8d.

In 24.
Com. Test. Psalmes 24 edges, ———— 0 — 11d.
Test. Psalmes 24. or the like, ———— 0 — 10d.

In 32.
Psalmes 32, or the like, ———— 0 — 7d.

All sorts of crosse-bound edges.
In 16.
Test. Psal. 16 Middleborow, or the like, 1s.— 6d.

In 24.
Test. Com. and Psalmes, 24, or the like, 1s.— 6d.

In 32.
Prayers and Psalmes 32 crosse, ———— 1s.— 2d.

Bookes folio fillets.
Martyrs two volumes, ———— 12s.— 0
Church-Bible, ———— 6s.— 0
Romane Bible, ———— 3s.— 4d.

3 either: John Hitchcock, A Sanctuary for Honest Men, 12°, London, 1617
or: Sir John Hayward, The Sanctuarie of a Troubled Soule, 12°, London, 1618

4 Richard Middleton, The Key of David, 12°, London, 1619

Raleighs History, —— 3s.— 6d.[5]
Perkins, or the like, —— 2s.— 8d.
All folio's like Babingtons, —— 2s.— 6d.[6]
All folio's, like Com. & Psalmes, —— 2s.— 4d.

In 4.
Bibles in 4, large Romane, —— 2s.— 0
Bibles 4. and such like, —— 1s.-10d.
Com. & Psalmes, & the like, —— 1s.— 2d.

In 8.
Bibles 8. or the like, —— 1s.— 2d.
Com. Test. and Psalmes, & the like, —— 1s.— 2d.
Test. Psalter, and Psalmes, —— 1s.— 0
All bookes like the Plaine mans path-way, —— 9d.[7]

In 12.
Bible 12, or the like, —— 1s.— 2d.
Practice of piety, or the like, —— 8d.

In 16.
Test. Psalmes 16 Middleborow, —— 7d.
Psalmes 16 Middleborow, —— 6d.
Psalmes 16 Com. or the like, —— 5d.

In 24.
Com. Test and Psalmes, or the like, —— 7d.

In 32.
Psalmes in 32, or the like, —— 5d.

<u>Bookes crosse-fillets.</u>
In 16.
Test. Psalmes 16, Middleborow, —— 1s.— 0

In 24.
Com. Test. Psalmes in 24 crosse, —— 0 — 11d.

In 32.
Psalter and Psalmes in 32, —— 9d.

<u>Bookes in ovills.</u>
Camden with maps, —— 4s.— 6d.
Church-Bible, [in ms reads —— 5s]
Raleighs histories, —— 2s.— 6d.
Plutarch, or the like, —— 2s.— 4d.
Bible folio Romane, —— 2s.— 2d.
Perkins, and the like, —— 5s.— 6d.[8]
Purchas, and the like, —— 1s.— 8d.[9]
Commines, and the like, —— 1s.— 6d.

In 4.
Bible in 4, and the like, —— 1s.— 2d.
Smiths sermons, and the like, —— 0 — 10d.

In 8.
Bibles in 8, and the like, —— 0 — 8d.
[altered in ms to read —— 9d.]
All sorts of Test. psalmes [8]
[4 deleted, 8 in ms] —— 0 — 6d.

5 Sir Walter Raleigh, <u>The History of the World</u>, fol. London, 1617

6 Gervase Babington, <u>Workes</u> (4 parts), fol. London, 1615

7 Arthur Dent, <u>The Plaine Mans Path-way to Heaven</u>, 8°, London, 1619

8 William Perkins, <u>Works</u> (3 vols), fol. London-Cambridge, 1616-1618

9 Samuel Purchas, <u>Purchas his Pilgrimage</u>, fol. London, 1617

All lattin bookes large, —— 0 — 8d.
All lattin bookes small, —— 0 — 6d.

In 12.
Bibles in 12. —— 0 — 8d.
Test. Psalmes in 12, or the like, —— 0 — 6d.
All Latin bookes in 16, —— 0 — 5d.
All Latin bookes in 24, —— 0 — 4d.

Law-bookes.
Statutes at large, —— 2s.— 6d.
Rastall Abridgement, folio, —— 1s.— 8d.
Poultons Abridgement, folio, —— 1s.— 6d.[10]
Daltons Iustice, folio, —— 1s.— 4d.[11]
Wests Presidents in 4, —— 1s.— 0
Iustice of peace, in 8, —— 0 — 6d.

Bookes sheepes leather.
Test. in 8, or the like, —— 0 — 4d.
Grammers, or the like, —— 0 — 2d.ob. [obolus = half penny]
Silva, or the like, —— 0 — 4d.[12]

In 16.
Tullies Orations, or the like, —— 0 — 3d.
Psalmes in 16 common, —— 0 — 2d.

In 32.
Psalmes in 32, —— 0 — 2d.

Bookes in hard bords.
Martyrs, —— 7s.— 0[13]
Bible folio large, —— 4s.— 6d.
Bible folio small, —— 3s.— 8d.
Bible medium, —— 2s.— 0

In 4.
Bible in 4, —— 1s.— 2d.
Test. Com. psalmes in 4, —— 1s.— 0
Com. booke and psalmes in 4, —— 0 — 9d.

In 8.
Bible 8, —— 0 — 8d.
Com. Tes. psalmes in 8, —— 0 — 7d.
Psalter, Test. and psalmes, —— 0 — 7d.
[In 16 deleted; whole entry in ms:-
Test. psal. 8to —— 0 — 6d.]
Com. and psalmes in 16, Com. —— 0 — 4d.

All sorts of Latin bookes, in folio and quarto.
Bibliotheca patrum, —— 3s.— 6d.
Tastatus, and the like, —— 3s.— 0
Tremellius bible, —— 2s.— 4d.

10 Michael Dalton, The Countrey Justice, fol. London, 1619

11 William West, Simboleography...with divers presidents, 4to, London, 1615, 1618

12 Simon Pelegromius, Synonymorum Sylva, 8o, London, 1619

13 John Foxe, Book of Martyrs (2 vols), fol. London, 1610

Gorron, or the like,	[2]s.	0	Tremellius bible in 4, or the like,	1s.	2d.
[1 altered in ms to read 2]			Dictionarium poeticum,	1s.	0
Stella on Luke, or the like,[14]	1s.	8d.	All other small quarto's,	0	10d.
Piscator in 4,	1s.	4d.			

FINIS

Imprinted at LONDON. 1619.

14 Didacus Stella, In...Evangelium secundum Lucam enarrationum tomus primus/secundus (2 vols), fol. Antwerp, 1608

Table 2

Bookes as they are sold bound,	At London. li.	sh.	d.	At Dublin. li.	sh.	d.
Church Bible in folio Bost, Bust, and Claspt	1	12	00	2	00	00
Communion and Psalmes folio bound	0	07	00	0	09	00
Bible in 12° with Psalmes & Geneal. in fill.	0	06	06	0	08	00
Bible in fol. Roman old with notes fill.	1	00	00	1	04	00
Bible in folio median with Psalmes and Genealog. fill.	1	00	00	1	04	00
Bible in quarto great Rom. new, with Psal. & Geneal. fill.	0	14	06	0	18	00
Bible in quarto small Rom. with fillets	0	11	06	0	13	04
Bible in quarto new Engl. with Psal. & Geneal. fill.	0	11	06	0	13	04
Bible in octavo Psal. & Geneal. fillets with Service	0	07	00	0	08	06
Testament and Psalmes in quarto fill.	0	05	06	0	06	08
Testament and Psal. in octavo boords clasp.	0	02	06	0	03	00
Communion Booke and Psalmes quarto fill.	0	04	00	0	05	00
Communion Booke and Psalmes oct. clasp.	0	02	08	0	03	04
Communion Booke and Psalmes 16° claspt	0	01	10	0	02	04

Ciceronis Officia octavo sheepes leather,	0	01	00	0	01	04
Ciceronis Sententiæ in duodecimo bound	0	01	00	0	01	04
Ovidij Metamorphosis oct. bound	0	01	00	0	01	04
Ovidij Epistolæ octavo bound	0	01	00	0	01	04
Pallingenius in octavo bound[1]	0	01	02	0	01	06
Setoni Dialectica in octavo bound[2]	0	01	00	0	01	06
Aphthonius in octavo	0	01	00	0	01	04
Salustij Historia in octavo bound	0	01	00	0	01	04
Æsopi Fabulæ in oct. bound	0	00	07	0	00	10
Mantuanus in octavo bound	0	00	07	0	00	10
Castaleonis Dialogi oct. bound	0	00	10	0	01	02
Terentius octo bound	0	00	09	0	01	[0] 0
Primmers plaine	0	00	04	0	00	04
Other small Schoole-bookes.						
Corderius in octavo	0	00	04	0	00	04
Isocratis ad Demonicum in oct.[3]	0	00	04	0	00	06
Nowelli Catechismus medius.	0	00	04	0	00	06
Ovidius de Tristibus	0	00	04	0	00	06
Sturmij Epistolæ octavo	0	00	04	0	00	04
Vivis Exercitationes Ling. Lat.[4]	0	00	04	0	00	06
Catones in octavo	0	00	03	0	00	04
Epitome Colloquiorum Erasmi[5]	0	00	03	0	00	04

With all other Priviledged Bookes according to these differences in their prizes.

1 Marcellus Palingenius, Zodiacus Vitae...opus, 8°, London, 1616

2 Joannes Setonus, Dialectica, 8°, London, 1617

3 Isocrates, Oratio ad Demonicum, 8°, Louvain, 1551 (?)

4 Joannes Ludovicus Vives, Linguæ Latinæ exercitatio, 8°, London [? 1612] or Edinburgh, 1620

5 Desiderius Erasmus, Epitome Colloquiorum, 8°, London, 1608

A Generall note of the priſes for binding all ſortes of bookes

Bibles in follio *London* or the like.

	li	s	d
Gilt over, or double lac'd	0	11	0
Corners, or ſingle lac'd	0	8	0
Edges and Fillets	0	6	6
Fillets	0	3	6
Ovills	0	2	6

Bibles in quarto great Roman or the like

Small tooles ordinary	0	8	0
Gilt over, or double lac'd	0	5	6
Chequer	0	5	10
Corners, or ſingle lac'd	0	3	8
Gilt edges	0	3	0
Fillets	0	2	0
Ovills	0	1	4

Bibles in quarto ſmale or the like

Smale tooles ordin.	0	8	0
Gilt over, or double lac'd	0	5	4
Corners or ſingle lac'd	0	3	6
Gilt edges	0	2	10
Fillets	0	1	10
Ovills	0	1	2

Bibles in 8 Minnion or the like.

Smale tooles ordin.	0	5	0
Gilt over, or double lac'd	0	3	0
Corners or ſingle lac'd	0	2	6
Chequer	0	3	2
Gilt edges	0	2	0
Fillets	0	1	3
Ovills	0	0	10

Bibles in Octavo or the like

Smale tooles ordinary	0	4	6
Chequer	0	2	10
Gilt over or double lac'd	0	2	8
Corners or ſingle lac'd	0	2	4
Edges gilt	0	1	10
Fillets	0	1	2
Ovills	0	0	9

Bibles in 12 or all other ſmale Bibles.

Smale tooles ordinary	0	4	0
Chequer	0	2	8
Gilt over or double lac'd	0	2	6
Corners or ſingle lac'd	0	2	0
Gilt edges	0	1	8
Fillets	0	1	0
Ovills	0	0	8

Teſtament and Pſalmes in 24 or the like

Gilt over	0	1	0
Gilt Edges	0	0	9
Fillets	0	0	6

Pſalmes in 8 Middleborough or the like.

Gilt over, or lac'd	0	2	4
Gilt Edges	0	1	6
Fillets	0	0	10
Ovills	0	0	8

Pſalmes in 24 or the like

Gilt over, or lac'd	0	0	9
Gilt Edges	0	0	7
Fillets	0	0	5

Pſalmes in 32 or the like

Gilt over	0	0	9
Gilt Edges	0	0	7
Fillets	0	0	5

Bookes in Folio lattine.

Atlas major 3 voll. or the like fillets		1	10	0
Lyra 6 voll large, Ariſt. Opera 2 voll, Plutarchi Opera 2 voll. or the like.	Fillets a voll.	0	5	6
	Rolls	0	4	0
Hutteri heb. Biblia, Buxtorph. heb. Biblia, Buxtorph. Concord. or the like.	Rolles a voll.	0	3	6
Montanus Biblia Ent., Eraſmi Epit. 1 vol., Mendz. in Reg. 1 vol., Grotius in ver. Teſt. or the like.	Fillets	0	4	4
	Rolles	0	3	0
Gerrard. Harm. Mathew Paris. Scapula Lex. Eſtius in Epiſt. or the like.		0	2	6
Gerrardi Loci Com. 4 vol. Grot. in ver Teſt. 3 vol. Sibelii Opera 5 vol. or the like.	Rolles	0	2	0

Bookes in quarto Lattine.

Sculteri Medulla. Mellificium Hiſtoricum. Voſſii Gram. Hiſpan: Biblia. or the like.	Rolles	0	1	4
All Latine bookes 4 if large paper		0	1	0
If thick at		0	1	2
All latine bookes 4 pot paper rolles		0	0	10
If thick at		0	1	0

Bookes in 8 12 & 24.

Buxtorphi Lexicon, Paſſoris Lexigon, Lumbard in Senten. or the like.	Rolles	0	0	8
All thinne latine bookes 8 rolles		0	0	7
All latine bookes 12 & 16 rolles		0	0	5
All bookes 24 & 32 Fillets		0	0	5

Bookes in follio Engliſh

Atlas 2 voll. or the like in Fillets		1	0	0
Haackſons Chron. or the like. Rolles		0	3	0
Gerrards Herball, Parkinſons Herball and the like.	Fillets	0	4	4
	Rolles	0	3	0
Booke of Martyrs or the like, fil.		0	12	0
Rolles.		0	8	0
Newmans Con. Turkiſh Hiſt. Rawleighs Hiſtory Andrews Sermons, or the like.	Rolles	0	2	6
Annotations. Survey of London. Joſephus Hiſt: Perkins Workes 3 vol. or the like.	Rolles	0	2	0
Sands Ovid. Bakers Chron: or the like.	Rolles	0	1	10
Hackwells Apol: Cotgraves Dictionary. Hierons Works Boyſes Workes, or the like.	Rol.	0	1	8
Canterburies Doome. Hookers Policie. Pembles Workes. Feild of the Church, or the like.	Rolles	0	1	6
Daltons Juſtice Henry the 7. Holy State. Holy War or the like.	Rolles	0	1	4

Bookes in 4 Engliſh

Riders Dictionary Piſcator in N: Teſt. or the like.	Rolles	0	1	4
Weſts Preſidents Thomas Dict. Diodates Notes or the like.	Rolles	0	1	2
Goodwins W: Caryls Workes. or the like.	Rolles	0	1	2
Weymes workes 4 vol. Wills and Teſtam. Crittica Sacra. or the like.	Rolles	0	1	0
All ſmale 4 pot paper, Rolles		0	0	10

Bookes in Octavo Engliſh

Souls Conflict. Records Arethmat: or the like.	Rolles	0	0	7

Bookes in 12 Engliſh.

Scudders daily Walke Mirour of Martyrs Practice of Piety or the like.	Rolles	0	0	5

Sheeps Leather

All ſmale Follio pot paper	0	0	10
All thinne Crown, in quarto at	0	0	7
All thick pot paper in quarto at	0	0	6
All thinne pot paper in quarto at	0	0	5
Hunts Arethmaticke 8, Records Arethmaticke 8, Smetius 8, Large Teſtaments 8 and the like.	0	0	4
All thinne Crown, one with another	0	0	3 ob
Teſtaments in 8 and 12, Virgill. 8, Quarles Poems 8 and the like.	0	0	3 ob
All other bookes 8 & 12 guttard	0	0	3
All ſortes of ſmale bookes, as Gramers Pſalters & the like	0	0	2 ob
Pſalter Teſtament pſalmes in 8	0	0	7
Teſtament Pſalmes 8	0	0	6
Teſtament Pſalmes 12	0	0	5
All ſortes of thinne bookes, ſheeps Leather fillets, as Grammers, Pſalters, ſmale 12, 24 and 32.	0	0	4
Primers gilt the Groſſe	1	0	0
Primers plaine the Groſſe	0	10	0

Printed at London 1646.

FINIS

List of binding prices 'Printed at London 1646.'

Table 3

A Generall note of the prises for binding all sortes of bookes

Bibles in follio London or the like.

	li	s	d
Gilt over, or double lac'd	0	11	0
Corners, or single lac'd	0	8	0
Edges and Fillets	0	6	6
Fillets	0	3	6
Ovills	0	2	6

Bibles in quarto great Roman or the like

Small tooles ordinary	0	8	0
Gilt over, or double lac'd	0	5	6
Chequer	0	5	10
Corners, or single lac'd	0	3	8
Gilt edges	0	3	0
Fillets	0	2	0
Ovills	0	1	4

Bibles in quarto smale or the like

Smale tooles ordin.	0	8	0
Gilt over, or double lac'd	0	5	4
Corners or single lac'd	0	3	6
Gilt edges	0	2	10
Fillets	0	1	10
Ovills	0	1	2

Bibles in 8 Minnion or the like.

Smale tooles ordina.	0	5	0
Gilt over, or double lac'd	0	3	0
Corners or single lac'd	0	2	6
Chequer	0	3	2
Gilt edges	0	2	0
Fillets	0	1	3
Ovills	0	0	10

Bibles in Octavo or the like

Smale tooles ordinary	0	4	6
Chequer	0	2	10
Gilt over or double lac'd	0	2	8
Corners or single lac'd	0	2	4
Edges gilt	0	1	10
Fillets	0	1	2
Ovills	0	0	9

Bibles in 12 or all other smale Bibles.

Smale tooles ordinary	0	4	0
Chequer	0	2	8
Gilt over or double lac'd	0	2	6
Corners or single lac'd	0	2	0
Gilt edges	0	1	8
Fillets	0	1	0
Ovills	0	0	8

Testament and Psalmes in 24 or the like

Gilt over	0	1	0
Gilt Edges	0	0	9
Fillets	0	0	6

Psalmes in 8 Middleborough or the like.

Gilt over, or lac'd	0	2	4
Gilt Edges	0	1	6
Fillets	0	0	10
Ovills	0	0	8

Psalmes in 24 or the like

Gilt over, ot [sic] lac'd	0	0	9
Gilt Edges	0	0	7
Fillets	0	0	5

Psalmes in 32 or the like

Gilt over	0	0	9
Gilt Edges	0	0	7
Fillets	0	0	5

Bookes in Folio lattine.

Atlas major 3 voll. or the like	fillets	1	10	0
Lyra 6 voll large Arist. Opera 2 voll Plutarchi Opera 2 voll. or the like.	Fillets a voll.	0	5	6
	Rolls	0	4	0
Hutteri heb. Biblia Buxtorph. heb. Biblia Buxtorph. Concord. or the like.	Rolles a voll.	0	3	6

Montanus Biblia Ent. Erasmi Epit. 1 vol. Mendz. in Reg. 1 vol. Grotius in vet. Test. or the like.	Fillets	0	4	4
	Rolles	0	3	0
Gerrard. Harm. Mathew Paris. Scapula Lex.[1] Estius in Epist. or the like.		0	2	6
Gerrardi Loci Com. 4 vol. Grot. in vet Test. 3 vol. Sibelii Opera 5 vol. or the like.	Rolles	0	2	0

Bookes in quarto Lattine.

Sculteti Medulla.[2] Mellificium Histor- icum. Vossii Gram. Hispan: Biblia. or the like.	Rolles	0	1	4
All Latine bookes 4 if large paper		0	1	0
If thick at		0	1	2
All latine bookes 4 pot paper rolles		0	0	10
If thick at		0	1	0

Bookes in 8 12 & 24

Buxtorphi Lexicon[3] Passoris Lexicon Lumbard in Senten. or the like.	Rolles	0	0	8

1 Johannes Scapula, Lexicon Graeco-Latinum, fol. London, 1637

2 Abraham Scultetus, Medulla Theologiæ Patrum Syntagma, 4°, Francfurt, 1634

3 Johannes Buxtorfius, the elder, Lexicon Hebraicum et Chaldaicum, 8°, London, 1646

All thinne latine bookes 8	rolles	0	0	7
All latine bookes 12 & 16	rolles	0	0	5
All bookes 24 & 32	Fillets	0	0	5
Bookes in follio English				
Atlas 2 voll. or the like	in Fillets	1	0	0
Isaacksons Chron.[4] or the like.	Rolles	0	3	0
Gerrards Herball	Fillets	0	4	4
Parkinsons Herball and the like.	Rolles	0	3	0
Booke of Martyrs or the like, fil.		0	12	0
Rolles.		0	8	0
Newmans Con. Turkish His. Rawleighs History Andrews Sermons,[5] or the like.	Rolles	0	2	6
Annotations. Survey of London. Josephus Hist: Perkins Workes 3 vol. or the like.	Rolles	0	2	0
Sands Ovid. Bakers Chron:[6] or the like.	Rolles	0	1	10
Hackwells Apol: Cotgraves Dictionary. Hierons Works Boyses Workes. or the like.	Rol.	0	1	8
Canterburies Doom.[7] Hookers Policie. Pembles Workes. Feild of the Church. or the like.	Rolles	0	1	6
Daltons Justice Henry the 7. Holy State.[8] Holy War. or the like.	Rolles	0	1	4
Bookes in 4 English				
Riders Dictionary[9] Piscator in N: Test. or the like.	Rolles	0	1	4
Wests Presidents Thomas Dict. Diodates Notes[10] or the like.	Rolles	0	1	2

4 Henry Isaacson, Saturni Ephemerides, sive Tabula Historico-chronologica, fol. London, 1633

5 Lancelot Andrewes, XCVI Sermons, fol. London, 1641

6 Sir Richard Baker, A Chronicle of the Kings of England, fol. London, 1643

7 William Prynne, Canterburies Doome, fol. London, 1646

8 Thomas Fuller, The Holy State, fol. Cambridge, 1642

9 John Rider, Rider's Dictionarie, 4°, London, 1640

10 Giovanni Diodati, Pious Annotations, upon the Holy Bible, 4°, London, 1643

Goodwins W: Caryls Workes, or the like. Rolles	0	1	2
Weymes workes 4 vol. Wills and Testam. Crittica Sacra. or the like. Rolles	0	1	0
All smale 4 pot paper, Rolles	0	0	10
Bookes in Octavo English Souls Conflict.[11] Records Arethmat: or the like Rolles	0	0	7
Bookes in 12 English. Scudders daily Walke[12] Mirour of Martyrs Practice of Piety or the like. Rolles	0	0	5
Sheeps Leather			
All smale Follio pot paper	0	0	10
All thinne Crown, in quarto at	0	0	7
All thick pot paper in quarto at	0	0	6

All thinne pot paper in quarto at	0	0	5
Hunts Arethmaticke 8 Records Arethmaticke 8[13] Smetius 8 Large Testaments 8 and the like.	0	0	4
All thinne Crown, one with another	0	0	3ob
Testaments in 8 and 12 Virgill. 8 Quarles Poems 8[14] and the like.	0	0	3ob
All other bookes 8 & 12 guttard	0	0	3
All sortes of smale bookes, as Gramers Psalters & the like	0	0	2ob
Psalter Testament psalmes in 8	0	0	7
Testament Psalmes 8	0	0	6
Testament Psalmes 12	0	0	5
All sortes of thinne bookes sheeps Leather fillets. as Grammers, Psalters, smale 12. 24 and 32.	0	0	4
Primers gilt the Grosse	1	0	0
Primers plaine the Grosse	0	10	0

Printed at London 1646.

FINIS

11 Richard Sibbes, The Soules Conflict with it selfe, 8°, London, 1636

12 Henry Scudder, The Christians Daily Walke, 12°, London, 1642

13 Robert Record, The Ground of Arts. Teaching...Arithmeticke, 8°, London [1646]

14 Francis Quarles, Divine Poems, 8°, London, 1642

Table 4

A General Note of the Prices of Binding all sorts of Books;

Agreed on by the Book-binders, whose Names are under-written.
As it was presented to the Master, Wardens, and Assistants
of the Worshipful Company of Stationers,
August, the 2d, 1669.

Ogilby's Bibles in Folio, or the like.	l.	s.	d.
Gilt Edges in one Volumn	01	00	00
Fillets only	00	12	00
Plain Ovals	00	08	00

Bibles in small Folio, London, or the like.			
Edges and Fillets	00	06	06
Fillets	00	03	06
Ovals	00	02	06

Bibles in Quarto, Cambridg, or the like.			
Edges Extraordinary	00	05	00
Edges Ordinary	00	03	06
Fillets	00	02	06
Ovals	00	01	06

Bibles in Octavo, Brevere, or the like.			
Edges Extraordinary	00	03	06
Edges Ordinary	00	02	04
Fillets	00	01	06
Ovals	00	01	00

Bibles in Octavo, Nonperil, or the like.			
Edges Extraordinary	00	02	10
Edges Ordinary	00	01	10
Fillets	00	01	02
Ovals	00	00	10

Bibles in 12.			
Edges Extraordinary	00	02	06
Edges Ordinary	00	01	06
Fillets	00	01	00
Ovals	00	00	08

Bibles in 24.			
Edges Extraordinary	00	02	06
Edges Ordinary	00	01	06
Fillets	00	01	00
Ovals.	00	00	08

Service-Book, Testament, and Psalms, Brevere, Octavo.			
Edges Extraordinary	00	02	10
Edges Ordinary	00	01	10
Fillets	00	01	02
Ovals	00	00	10

Service Brevere in 12.	
& Psalms, or otherwise.	
Edges Extraordinary	00 01 08
Edges Ordinary	00 01 02
Fillets	00 00 09
Ovals	00 00 06
Service in 24. With Psalms, &c.	
Edges Extraordinary	00 01 02
Edges Ordinary	00 00 10
Fillets	00 00 08
Plain	00 00 06
Books in Folio, Latin.	l. s. d.
Atlas Major, 3 Vol. or the like, Rolls	1 10 00
Aristot. 2 Vol. Rolls	0 11 00
Lexicon Poliglott, or the like, 2 Vol.	0 12 00
Item, in one Vol. Rolles	0 08 00
Plutarchi Opera, 2 Vol. or the like, Rolls	0 08 00
Lipsius in Senecam Lipsius in Jacitum [sic] Buxtorph. Heb. Bib. } or the like	0 03 06
Corpus Juris Civ. one Vol.	0 04 00
In 2 Vol. or the like	0 06 00
Critici Sacri, 9 Vol.[1] or the like, Rolles	1 10 00
Scapulae Lexicon, Grotius in Vet. Test. or the like	0 03 00

Ravanella. S. 3 Vol.	0 09 00
Estius in Epist. or the like, one Vol.	0 02 06
Brennius in Bib. Gerardi Loci Com. 4 Vol. or the like	0 08 00
Books in Quarto, Latin.	
Sculteti Medulla Mellificium Hist. Vosii Gram.[2] or the like } Rolls	0 01 04
All Latin Books in Quarto, Large & thick	0 01 02
If not thick	0 01 00
All Latin Books, Pot-paper, Rolls, Thick,	0 01 00
If not thick	0 00 10
Books in 8. 12. and 24.	
Screvelius's Lexicon,[3] Octo. large	0 00 10
Virgil, Horatius vel Paterculius, and the like } Rolls	0 00 10
All thick Octo. Latin, Rolls	0 00 08
All thin Octo.	0 00 07
All Twelves and Sixteens	0 00 06
All Twenty fours	0 00 05
Books in Folio, English.	
Ogilby's China, Virgil, all his other Books, or the like in single Vol. Marble Fillets }	0 08 00

1 John Pearson, Critici Sacri, 9 vols, fol. London, 1660

2 Gerardus Vossius, De arte grammatica libri, 4°, Amsterdam, 1662

3 Cornelius Schrevelius, Lexicon Manuale Graeco-Latinum, 8°, London, 1663

	l. s. d.
Æsop compleat in one, Iliads and Odysses[4] in one, or the like, Marble Fillets	0 10 00
The same Books plain	0 07 00
The same Books single	0 05 00
Kings Works, or the like	0 03 06
Hammond on N. Testament Poultons Stat. or the like, Rolls	0 03 00
Davila's Hist.[5] Rawleighs Hist. or the like	0 03 00
Plutarchs Lives Heylins Cosmog. or the like	0 02 06
Cotgraves Dict. Bakers Chronicle, Taylors Cases of Conscience, Rolls	0 02 00
Life of Christ, Rolls	0 01 10
Hammond on Psalmes Spotswood Hist, or the like	0 01 08
Cassandra, or the like	0 01 06

Small Folio.

Fullers Holy War[6] Hubbards Reports Baccalin, and the like All Pot Folio's small	0 01 04

Books in Quarto, English.

Goldman, or the like, Rolls	0 01 06
Hughs Grand Abridgment, being 3 Vol. Rolls	0 04 00
Wests Presidents. Thomas Dict. or the like	0 01 02
Carills twelfth part, or the like	0 01 00
Baxters Saints Rest[7]	0 01 02
Baxters Reasons, Rolls. And all such English Quarto's thick	0 01 00
All small Pot-paper Quarto's Rolls	0 00 10

Books in Octavo, English

All large Octo. Decay of Piety, or the like	0 00 09
Taylors Living and Dying,[8] or the like-	0 00 08
All thin Crown Octavo's	0 00 07
All Pot Octavo's, Quarles Poems, &c	0 00 06

4 Homer, Iliad, fol. London, 1669; Homer, Odyssey, fol. London, 1665: price quoted for in one, ie. bound together, and for single

5 Enrico Caterino Davila, The Historie of the Civill Warres of France, fol. London, 1647, 1648

6 Thomas Fuller, The Historie of the Holy Warre, fol. [Cambridge] 1651

7 Richard Baxter, The Saints Everlasting Rest, 4°, London, 1669

8 Jeremy Taylor, The Rule and Exercises of Holy Living, 8°, London, 1663; Idem, The Rule and Exercises of Holy Dying, 8°, London, 1655

Books in 12. and 24.	
All large Twelves	0 00 06
All small Twelves and Twenty-four's	0 00 05
Sheeps Leather, Folio's	
Ottaman Empire, or the like, Rolls	0 01 02
Noyes Reports,[9] or the like, Rolls	0 01 00
All thick Pot Follio's	0 01 00
All thin Pot	0 00 10
Large Quarto, Sheep.	s. s. d. [sic]
Placita Redivia, or the like, Rolls	0 00 10
All thin Crown Rolls	0 00 09
All Fools-cap, or the like, Rolls	0 00 08
Quarto's Pot-paper, Sheep.	
Stillingfleets Origines Sacra,[10] or the like, rolls	0 00 08
All thick Pot	0 00 06
All thin Pot	0 00 05

Octavo's Large.	
Decay of Piety, or the like	0 00 05
Gent. Callings,[11] or the like	0 00 04
Records Arithm. Erasmus Colloq. Testaments Octo. Rom. or the like	0 00 04
All thin Crown, and all Fools-Cap	0 00 03½
Octavo Pot.	
Test. Octo. Com. Quarles Poems. Randolphs Poems. Hools Corderius,[12] or the like	0 00 03
All thin Pot	0 00 02½
Large Twelves.	
Present State of Eng. Pr. of Piety, or the like	0 00 03
Meads almost a Christ.[13] Ac. of Com. the like	0 00 02½
Redemption of Time, or the like	0 00 02
Pot Twelves.	
Baxters Call.[14] Doct. Bible, or the like	0 00 02½

9 Sir William Noye, Reports and Cases, fol. London, 1669

10 Edward Stillingfleet, Origines sacrae, 4°, London 1666

11 [? Richard Allestree], The Gentleman's Calling, 8°, London, 1668

12 Charles Hoole, [ed], Maturinus Corderius's School Colloquies, 8°, London, 1657

13 Matthew Mead, The Almost Christian Discovered, 12°, London, 1664

14 Richard Baxter, A Call to the Unconverted, 12°, London, 1663

Twenty-four's.	
Practice of Piety, or the like	0 00 03
Gerrards Meditat, Crums of Comf.[15] the like	0 00 02½
All thin Twenty-four's	0 00 02

All sorts of Thin Books, Sheeps-Leather Fillets, As Grammars, Psalters Small 12s, 24s, and 32s.	0 00 04
Primmers Gilt, the Gross	1 00 00
Primmers Plain, the Gross	1 10 00

15 Michael Sparke, The Crums of Comfort, 24°, London [? 1650], and part: London, 1652

Thomas Hunt.[c]
Samuel Mearn.[a]
Thomas Raw.[a]
George Eversden.[a]
George Calvert.[a]
William Richardson.[c]
Edward Powel.[a]
Robert Cutler.[a]
Hilliam Harris.[c]
William Rands.[a]
Humphry Toy.[c]
William Branch.[c]
Edward Gough.[b]
Francis Hyarne.[c]
Henry Evans.[c]
Joseph Moore.[a]
John Downs.[d]
William Sherington.[c]
Robert Deevs.[c]
Thomas Hodyson.[b]

Thomas Cooper.[d]
William Terry.[c]
Joseph Cater.[c]
John Homersham.[d]
Nathan Brookes.[c]
Edward Eccleston.[b]
Christopher Lingerd.[c]
Stephen Cope.[c]
Richard Oliffe.[d]
Thomas Allsop.[a]
William Potter.[d]
Thomas Lammas.[c]
William Redmayne.[c]
Peter Scarlet.[d]
Robert Smith.[c]
John Fletcher.[c]
Thomas Kequick.[c]
Richard Dew.[c]
John Bishop.[c]
Walter Dunn.[c]

William Mason.[c]
John Mendey.[c]
William Stephens.[c]
William Willis.[c]
Walter Davis.[a]
Martin Barnham.[d]
Langlie Curtis.[a]
Robert Cox.[c]
Jonathan Adams.[d]
Richard Littleton.[d]
John Hewet.[c]
John Shepherd.[c]
Richard Barnes.[c]
William Baker.[c]
Thomas Hartley.[b]
Samuel Freeman.[c]
William Curtis.[c]
William Veery.[d]
Samuel Cook.[c]
Joshua Mitchel.[a]

Joshua Conuiers.[a]	George Bale.[c]	Robert Finnis.[d]
Samuel Sprint.[a]	William Bishop.[c]	John Major.[c]
John Grover.[c]	Adam Winch.[c]	Nathaniel Oldfield.[c]
William Charles.[c]	Thomas Brown.[a]	Daniel Barber.[c]
Richard Sympson.[a]	James Parkhurst.[c]	James Hatton.[d]
William Hilliard.[d]	John Shrimton.[c]	William Goff.[d]
Richard Janua.[a]	John Spicer.[a]	
Gregory Pool.[c]	Richard Hewes.[b]	

Licensed, September 23. 1669. ROGER L'ESTRANGE.

a Bookseller and bookbinder.

b Possibly bookseller; certainly bookbinder.

c Bookbinder found elsewhere in Stationers' Company records.

d Bookbinder known only from this list.

A General Note of the Prices of Binding

All Sorts of

BOOKS in CALVES-LEATHER:

Agreed on by the

BOOK-BINDERS,

Freemen of the City of *London*,

And by them Presented to the Master, Wardens and Assistants of the Worshipful Company of *Stationers*, at a Court holden *March*, 169$\frac{4}{5}$.

Books in Folio, Latin.

	l.	s.	d.
Lexicon Polyglotton *in Two Vol. or the like*	00	15	00
Grotii Opera, *in 4 Vol. or the like*	00	14	00
Eusebius, *&c. in 3 Vol.*	00	12	00
Euripides	00	02	09
M. T. Ciceronis Opera *in 2 Vol.*	00	06	06
Limborch Theolog.	00	02	06

Quarto, Latin.

	l.	s.	d.
Cambridge Dictionary, *or the like*	00	02	00
All thin Quarto Demy	00	01	06
All Fools Cap thick	00	01	06
All Fools Cap thin	00	01	04

Octavo, Latin.

	l.	s.	d.
All Variorum's *thick*	00	01	02
All thin	00	01	00
Coles Dictionary	00	01	00
All middle siz'd	00	00	09
All Fools Cap	00	00	08
Cambridge Phrases	00	01	02

Twelves, Latin.

	l.	s.	d.
Gradus ad Parnassum	00	00	08
Ovidii Metamorphosis	00	00	08
All thin Twelves *Large*	00	00	07
All Small	00	00	06
Comp. Prayer *Latin*	00	00	08

Twenty Fours, Latin.

	l.	s.	d.
Ovidii Opera, *or the like*	00	00	07
All others	00	00	06

Folio, English.

	l.	s.	d.
Camden's Britannia *large*	00	12	00
Camden *small*	00	06	00
Clark on the Bible	00	04	00
Josephus	00	03	06
Hammond's Works 4 *Vol.*	00	14	00
Geograph. Dictionary	00	04	06
Manton's Works 4 *Vol.*	00	15	00
Bp. Reynold's Works	00	04	00
Bp. Taylor's Life of Christ	00	03	00
Duty of Man's Works	00	03	00
Baker's Chronicle	00	02	09
Dryden's Juvenal	00	02	04

Folio, Fools Cap.

	l.	s.	d.
Burnet's Theory *complete*	00	02	04
Oxford Com. Prayer	00	02	06
Laud's Life *Fol.*	00	02	04
Watson's Body of Divinity	00	02	00
L'Estrange's Esop	00	02	00
Burnet's History of the Reformation, *in 2 Vol. with Cuts*	00	05	06
Prince Arthur	00	02	00
Pearson on the Creed	00	02	00
Brown's Works	00	02	00
Acts for One Session of Parl. *large*	00	02	06
The same *Small*	00	02	00

Quarto, English.

	l.	s.	d.
Complete Clerk	00	01	06
Baxter's Saints Rest	00	01	06
Dr. Sherlock of the Trinity	00	01	02
Bp. Patrick on Genesis	00	01	04

Octavo *Large*, English.

	l.	s.	d.
Burnet's Abridgment	00	00	10
Gibson's Anatomy	00	01	02
Duty of Man	00	00	10
Plutarch's Morals 5 *Vol.*	00	04	02
Plutarch's Lives 5 *Vol.*	00	05	00
Dr. Sherlock of Death	00	00	09
Lock of Education	00	00	08
Terence *in English*	00	00	10
Jure Maritimo	00	01	00
Salmon's Dispensatory	00	01	00
Peche's Storehouse	00	01	00
Parson's Counsellor	00	00	10
Wingate's Abridgment	00	00	10
Hales's Contemplations	00	00	10
Dr. Scott's Christian Life 3 *Vol.*	00	02	06

All Fools Cap Octavo's.

	l.	s.	d.
Allen's Persuasive, *&c. in 4 Vol.*	00	03	04
Peche's Herbal	00	00	08
Pia Desideria	00	00	08
Chamberlain's State of *England*	00	00	08

All Large Twelves.

	l.	s.	d.
New State of *England*	00	00	08
Duty of Man	00	00	08
Devout Christian	00	00	08
Busbequius Epist. English	00	00	08

All thin Twelves.

	l.	s.	d.
Lake of the Sacrament	00	00	07
Devout Communicant	00	00	07
All small Twelves *and* Twenty Fours	00	00	06

The antient allow'd Rate of Binding *Bibles* in *Calf*.

Ogilby's Bibles Folio, or the like.

Gilt Edges	01	00	00
Fillets only	00	12	00
Plain	00	08	00

Bibles Quarto, *Cambridge* or the like.

Edges Extraordinary	00	05	00
Edges Ordinary	00	03	06
Fillets	00	02	06

Bibles Octavo, Brevere.

Edges Extraordinary	00	03	06
Edges Ordinary	00	02	04
Fillets	00	01	06

Bibles Octavo, Nonpareil.

Edges Extraordinary	00	02	10
Edges Ordinary	00	01	10
Fillets	00	01	02

Bibles Twelves and Twenty Fours.

Edges Extraordinary	00	02	06
Edges Ordinary	00	01	06
Fillets	00	01	00
Ovals	00	00	08

LONDON: Printed, and are to be Sold by *John Whitlock* near *Stationers-Hall*. 1695.

List of binding prices 'LONDON: Printed, and are to be Sold by *John Whitlock* near *Stationers-Hall*. 1695.'

Table 5

A General Note of the Prices of Binding All Sorts of Books in Calves-Leather:

Agreed on by the BOOK-BINDERS, Freemen of the City of London,
And by them Presented to the Master, Wardens and Assistants
of the Worshipful Company of Stationers,
at a Court holden March, 1694/5.

	l. s. d.
Books in Folio, Latin.	
Lexicon Polyglotton in Two Vol. or the like	00 15 00
Grotii Opera, in 4 Vol. or the like	00 14 00
Eusebius, &c. in 3 Vol.	00 12 00
Euripides	00 02 09
M.T. Ciceronis Opera in 2 Vol.	00 06 06
Limborch Theolog.[1]	00 02 06
Quarto, Latin.	
Cambridge Dictionary, or the like	00 02 00
All thin Quarto Demy	00 01 06
All Fools Cap thick	00 01 06
All Fools Cap thin	00 01 04
Octavo, Latin.	
All Variorum's thick	00 01 02
All thin	00 01 00
Coles Dictionary[2]	00 01 00
All middle siz'd	00 00 09
All Fools Cap	00 00 08
Cambridge Phrases	00 01 02
Twelves, Latin.	
Gradus ad Parnassum[3]	00 00 08
Ovidii Metamorphosis	00 00 08
All thin Twelves Large	00 00 07
All small	00 00 06
Comp. Prayer Latin	00 00 08
Twenty Fours, Latin.	
Ovidii Opera[4], or the like	00 00 07
All others	00 00 06

1 Philippus a Limborch, Theologia Christiana, fol. Amsterdam, 1695

2 Elisha Coles, A Dictionary English-Latin, 8°, London, 1692

3 Gradus ad Parnassum, 12°, London, 1691

4 Publius Ovidius Naso, Opera, 24°, Amsterdam [1674]

Folio, English.	l. s. d.
Camden's Britannia large	00 12 00
Camden small	00 06 00
Clark on the Bible	00 04 00
Josephus	00 03 06
Hammond's Works 4 Vol.[5]	00 14 00
Geograph. Dictionary	00 04 06
Manton's Works 4 Vol.	00 15 00
Bp. Reynold's Works	00 04 00
Bp. Taylor's Life of Christ[6]	00 03 00
Duty of Man's Works	00 03 00
Baker's Chronicle	00 02 09
Dryden's Juvenal	00 02 04

Folio, Fools Cap.	
Burnet's Theory complete[7]	00 02 04
Oxford Com. Prayer	00 02 06
Laud's Life Fol.	00 02 04
Watson's Body of Divinity	00 02 00
L'Estrange's Esop	00 02 00
Burnet's History of the Reformation, in 2 Vol. with Cuts[8]	00 05 06

Prince Arthur	00 02 00
Pearson on the Creed	00 02 00
Brown's Works	00 02 00
Acts for One Session of Parl. large	00 02 06
The same Small	00 02 00

Quarto, English.	
Complete Clerk	00 01 06
Baxter's Saints Rest	00 01 06
Dr. Sherlock of the Trinity[9]	00 01 02
Bp. Patrick on Genesis	00 01 04

Octavo Large, English.	l. s. d.
Burnet's Abridgment[10]	00 00 10
Gibson's Anatomy	00 01 02
Duty of Man	00 00 10
Plutarch's Morals 5 Vol.	00 04 02
Plutarch's Lives 5 Vol.	00 05 00
Dr. Sherlock of Death	00 00 09
Lock of Education	00 00 08
Terence in English	00 00 10

5 Henry Hammond, Works (4 vols), fol. London, 1684

6 Jeremy Taylor, Antiquitates Christianæ; or the History of the Life...of...Jesus, fol. London, 1684

7 Thomas Burnet, The Theory of the Earth, fol. London, 1690

8 Gilbert Burnet, The History of the Reformation of the Church of England (2 vols with plates), fol. London, 1681, 1683

9 William Sherlock, A Vindincation of the Doctrine of the Holy...Trinity, 4°, London, 1694

10 Gilbert Burnet, The Abridgment of the History of the Reformation of the Church of England, 8°, London, 1683

Jure Maritimo	00 01 00
Salmon's Dispensatory	00 01 00
Peche's Storehouse	00 01 00
Parson's Counsellor	00 00 10
Wingate's Abridgment	00 00 10
Hales's Contemplations[11]	00 00 10
Dr. Scott's Christian Life 3 Vol.	00 02 06
All Fools Cap Octavo's.	
Allen's Persuasive, &c. in 4 Vol.	00 03 04
Peche's Herbal[12]	00 00 08
Pia Desideria	00 00 08
Chamberlain's State of England	00 00 08
All Large Twelves.	
New State of England	00 00 08
Duty of Man[13]	00 00 08
Devout Christian	00 00 08
Busbequius Epist. English	00 00 08
All thin Twelves.	
Lake of the Sacrament[14]	00 00 07
Devout Communicant	00 00 07
All small Twelves and Twenty Fours	00 00 06

11 Sir Matthew Hale, Contemplations Moral and Divine, 8°, London, 1695

12 John Pechey, The Compleat Herbal, 8°, London, 1694

13 [Richard Allestree], The Whole Duty of Man, 12°, London, 1695

14 Edward Lake, Officium Eucharisticum, 12°, London 1690

The antient allow'd Rate of Binding Bibles in Calf.

Ogilby's Bibles Folio, or the like.

Gilt Edges	01 00 00
Fillets only	00 12 00
Plain	00 08 00

Bibles Quarto, Cambridge or the like.

Edges Extraordinary	00 05 00
Edges Ordinary	00 03 06
Fillets	00 02 06

Bibles Octavo, Brevere.

Edges Extraordinary	00 03 06
Edges Ordinary	00 02 04
Fillets	00 01 06

Bibles Octavo, Nonpareil.

Edges Extraordinary	00 02 10
Edges Ordinary	00 01 10
Fillets	00 01 02

Bibles Twelves and Twenty Fours.

Edges Extraordinary	00 02 06
Edges Ordinary	00 01 06
Fillets	00 01 00
Ovals	00 00 08

LONDON: Printed, and are to be Sold by John Whitlock near
Stationers-Hall. 1695.

Table 6

Whereas the BOOKBINDERS of the City of Dublin at a Meeting the 15th Day of September 1743, then held, did Unanimously Agree, that from and after the 29th of the said Month no Books are to be Bound, Paper Gilt or Black'd, for Booksellers, under the following Prices.

N.B. By unanimous Consent, it was the Day aforesaid further Resolved, That all Octavos shall be charg'd Ten Pence, Twelves Eight Pence (at least) and so in Proportion for Books of Larger Size, as rated underneath, to all Gentlemen, Authors or others.

For the GILT WORK.

	l.	s.	d.
Imperial Folio Bible	1	2	9
Super-Royal	0	18	0
Royal Folio ditto	0	16	3
Medium	0	14	0
Demy Folio ditto	0	10	0
Propatria, or Paper of that Size	0	8	0
Bibles, Quarto, with Cuts	0	6	6
Ditto without	0	5	0
Bibles, large Octavo	0	2	6
Ditto large Twelves	0	1	6
Ditto smaller Twelves	0	1	4
Ditto Eighteens	0	1	2
Royal Folio Common-Prayers	0	10	0
Medium ditto	0	6	6
Common-Prayers Quarto	0	3	6
Ditto Octavo	0	1	10
Ditto large Twelves	0	1	4
Ditto the next Size Twelves	0	1	2
Ditto the long Lines Twelves	0	1	0
Ditto the short Lines Fine Paper	0	0	10
Ditto the common Sort	0	0	9
Ditto Twenty-fours	0	0	10

Books bound in VELLUM plain.

FOLIOS.

Imperial	0	6	6
Super-Royal	0	5	6
Royal	0	4	6
Medium	0	3	6
Demy	0	2	6
Propatria	0	2	0
Pocket Books Demy	0	0	9
Ditto Propatria	0	0	7

RUSSIA BANDS.

Imperial	0	16	0

	l.	s.	d.
Super-Royal	0	14	0
Royal	0	12	0
Medium	0	10	0
Demy	0	8	0

FORRIL.

	s.	d.		s.	d.
Medium Fol. yellow	1	9	green	2	0
Demy Fol. ditto	1	4	ditto	1	6
Propatria Fol. ditto	0	10	ditto	0	11

Pocket Books common Size	0	0	3

Quartos, long or broad, the one half Price of Folio's, in either Vellum or Forril.

Books GILT BACK only.

	l.	s.	d.
Imperial Folio	0	2	0
Super-Royal ditto	0	2	0
Royal ditto	0	2	0
Quartos of the above Sizes each	0	1	0
Medium Folios, and under that Size	0	1	6
Quartos Medium and under that Size	0	0	10
Royal Octavo	0	0	7
Medium Ditto	0	0	5
Twelves of all Sizes	0	0	4

GILT Paper and BLACK.

Demy in Quarto the Rheam	0	9	0
Thick Post ditto the Rheam	0	7	0
Thin Post ditto the Rheam	0	4	6
Propatria Folio the Rheam	0	5	0
Ditto Quarto the Rheam	0	5	0
Post Paper Octavo the Rheam	0	6	0

Books bound in Calve's Leather and Letter'd only.

FOLIOS.

Imperial	0	8	0
Super-Royal	0	6	6
Royal	0	5	0
Medium	0	3	6
Demy	0	2	10
Propatria	0	2	4

QUARTOS.

Imperial	0	4	0
Super-Royal	0	3	3
Ditto Musick twelve Sheets	0	2	0
Royal	0	2	6
Medium	0	1	9
Demy	0	1	5
Propatria	0	1	2

OCTAVOS.

Royal	0	1	2
Medium	0	0	9

TWELVES.

Without Distinction	0	0	7

N.B. All Dictionaries, such as Coles, Boyer, Bailey, Dyche, Schrevelius's Lexicon, and all Octavo Bibles, bound plain are to be Ten-pence, and no Quarter Book of any Sort whatsoever to be allowed.

GRAINS.

	l.	s.	d.
Testaments Saw'd per 100	0	12	6
Grammars ditto per 100	0	10	5
Burton's Books and Psalters per 100	0	8	4
Countess of Morton,[1] and others per 100	0	8	4

LACQUERD WORK.

	l.	s.	d.
Common-Prayers and Manuals per Hundred, whereof one Quarter to be Shagreen	2	10	0

In a single Quarter six to be Shagreen.

Books FILLETED on the Back only with a Tool added thereto.

	l.	s.	d.
Imperial Folio, Super-Royal ditto, Royal ditto, each Book	0	0	6
Medium ditto	0	0	4
Demy ditto	0	0	3
Propatria ditto	0	0	3
Quartos of all Sizes	0	0	2
Octavos Royal, and all under	0	0	1
Twelves of all Sorts each	0	0	1
For lettering the Volume in Black on the second Pannel of Folios and Quartos, each Book	0	0	2
For all Octavos and Twelves ditto	0	0	1
For Filleting and Rolling all Octavos and Twelves each	0	0	3

Books bound in SHEEP Banded.

FOLIOS

	l.	s.	d.
Coasting Pilot	0	3	0
Royal	0	2	9
Medium	0	2	6
Demy	0	2	0
Propatria	0	1	8

QUARTOS.

	l.	s.	d.
Royal	0	1	4
Medium	0	1	3
Demy	0	1	0
Propatria	0	0	9
Octavo, if Letter'd	0	0	7
Twelves	0	0	4
Testaments of each Sort	0	0	4

Plain SHEEP.

	l.	s.	d.
Testaments single 2½d. each, per 100	1	0	10
Grammars ditto 2¼d. each, per 100	0	18	9
Burton's Books and Psalters 2d. each, per 100	0	16	8
Countess of Morton's,[1] and others of or near that Size, 1½d. each	0	12	6

1 Anne Douglas, Countess of Morton, The Countess of Morton's Daily Exercise, 12°, London, 1689

RUL'D PAPER.

All Ruling, except the common Pounds Shillings and Pence on Six penny and Propatria Paper, to be one Penny per Hundred.

Printed by EDWARD BATE, in George's Lane near Dame's Street.

Table 7

may 14th 1744.

To the Booksellers of London & Westminster. &c:

Gentlemen, At a Considerable meeting of the Bookbinders of the Citys of London & Westminster & the libertys thereof In Consideration of the exorbitant prices that Leather now Bears by the Scarceness of that Commodity. By an Absolute Necessity [we] are Obliged to Come to the following Resolutions in Regard to the Undermentioned prices for the Different sizes of Books. These Gentlemen, we hope may appear Reasonable to you, haveing Lost by all the work lately Undertaken, &c.

The Prices are as follows:- Viz:

	s.	d.		s.	d.
Royal folio Letterd	7 :	0:	Roy 4to Lett^{d}	3 :	0.
Demy D^{o}	4 :	0:	Demy D^{o}	2 :	0.
Crown D^{o}	3 :	0.	Crown D^{o}	1 :	9.
FoolsCap D^{o}	2 :	9.	Fools Cap letterd 4to	1 :	6
Chambers's Dict: per Vol & Books of that size Letterd)	4 :	6.	Roy: 8vo plain	1 :	2
			Demy D^{o}	0 :	10

12^{ismo} D^{o} —— 0 : 7

All (Dictionarys or Lexicons 4to —— 2 : 0
(8vo Ditto —— 1 : 0
(Magazines & Books of y^{t} Size —— 1 : 0
(8vo Sheep rould —— 0 : 7
(12^{ismo} D^{o} —— 0 : 5.

<u>NB: that Books of all Sizes with Cutts are to be considered.</u>

The Edges Binders Prices in Calves Leather

	l	s	d
Bible Royal Edges ——	0	14	0
D^{o} plain Royal ——	0	7	0
Ditto Small fol^{o}: ——	0	3	6
Ditto Edges ——	0	7	0
Large 4to plain ——	0	2	3
D^{o} in Edges ——	0	4	6.
Small 4to plain ——	0	1	9
D^{o} Edges ——	0	3	6
Octavo Brevier plain ——	0	1	2
D^{o} Edges ——	0	2	0.
minion plain ——	0	0	9.
D^{o} Edges ——	0	1	2.
Nonpariel plain ——	0	0	7.
D^{o} Edges ——	0	0	11.

	s	d.
Common prayer Royal plain ——	5	6.
folio medium plain ——	3	0.
folio Demy plain ——	2	6.
Ditto Edges ——	5	0-
4to Royal plain ——	2	6-
Small 4to plain ——	1	3-
Ditto Edges ——	2	6-
8vo Large Letter Edges ——	1	6-
8vo pica Edges ——	1	1-
D^{o} with Testament ——	1	6-
8vo Ditto plain ——	0	9.
Brevier Edges ——	0	7½
D^{o} with Testament Edges ——		10-
Small 12^{ismo} ——	0	6-
24°. Edges ——	0	5-
D^{o} with Testament ——	0	7½
Bible Nonpariel fine paper Cambridge Edges) ——	1	0-
D^{o} plain ——	0	8-
Com[m]on prayer Cambridge Brevier ——	0	9-

All Common prayer with Cutts 2 pence More
All Sacrament Books Black Calf Under the
Size of the new Week's preparation[1] —— 0 : 6.
Size of the New —— 0 : 7.
All Common prayers in Sheep a halfpenny Less

Sheep Binders prices p[er] C neat

	l	s	d
Oxford Testament ——	0	18	0.
Long primer Testament ——	1	6	0-
Psalters ——	0	15	0.

1 <u>The New Week's Preparation for a Worthy Receiving of the Lord's Supper</u>, 12°, London [1744]

Lillys Grammers with the Construction	0	16	0.
Ward's Ditto	0	18	0-
Dyches Spelling Book[2] and all such	0	16	0-
Chapman's Book & Accedents	0	14	0.
All printed Down of 12: Sheets each and Under	0	16	0.
All above 12 Sheets	0	18	0.
New Week's preparation	0	17	0.
Hoppus Meshuring[3]	0	18	0.
London Spelling, Weald Ditto. Watts Songs London New Meathod &c:	0	13	0.
New Year's Gift. Mortons Devotion Devout Companion		13	0
Common prayer 24°, Old psalms Almo [?] Beza's Testament &c:		16	0

Sowing & Folding Prices

Folio's 1 farthing an Alphabett F[olding?] S[ewing?]

4^{tos} & 8^{vos}: 1 halfpenny a hundred Sheets. folding & 12^s: 1 penny folding 18^s 1 penny halfpenny a hundred folding - 4^{tos} 8^{vos} 12^s 18^s Common Sowing 1 penny p[er] C Sheets: for Sowing only two Sheets at a time three half pence. & for Sowing only one Sheet at a time 2 pence for Every hundred Sheets the Sowing -

NB: that the Above is the very full price. Some women will work Cheeper. -

Black or Gilt Paper

	s	d
Thick post 4to	1	6-
La Thin D^o:	1	3-
Fools Cap D^o	1	3-
Small thin 4to P[er] Ream	1	0-
Thick Post 8vo	1	0-
Thin 8vo	0	10-

Ruleing Paper

	s	d
Folio Pott or Fools Cap p[er] Rm	1	0-
4to D^o p[er] Rm	2	0-
fo^o. For foulding & Sowing p[er] D^o	0	6
4to p[er] Ditto	0	10-

NB: that 3 hund & 84 Lines is one q^r. we Charge or by the thousand — 6-

2 Thomas Dyche, A Guide to the English Tongue, 12°, London, 1713 (possibly a later edition)

3 Edward Hoppus, Practical Measuring Made Easy, 8°, London, 1738

Table 8

TO THE BOOKSELLERS OF LONDON AND WESTMINSTER.
GENTLEMEN,
In Consideration of the great Advance on both Sorts of Leather, the Bookbinders of London and Westminster, by a general Agreement, have fixed the following Prices for Binding; which the Support of Ourselves and Families will oblige us strictly to observe.

The PRICES for BINDING agreed on the 2d of June, 1760.

	l.	s.	d.
FOLIO'S, Imperial Paper.			
ALBINUS's Tables, Calf, lettered[1]	1	2	0
Ditto, half bound, lettered	0	11	0
Catesby's Carolina, per Vol. lettered	0	16	0
Atlas Maritimus, lettered	0	16	0
Palmyra, or Balbec, lettered[2]	0	10	0
Heads and Lives of illustrious Persons, gilt and lettered	0	14	0
All Books on the same Paper and Thickness, the like Price.			
FOLIO'S, Royal Paper.			
Campbell's Vitruvius, per Vol. lettered[3]	0	8	0
Religious Ceremonies, per Vol. lettered	0	8	0
Gibbs's Architecture, lettered	0	7	6
Clarendon, lettered	0	7	0
Norden's Travels, per Vol.	0	8	0
All Books on the same Paper, &c. the like Price.			
FOLIO'S, Demy.			
Harrison's Voyages, per Vol. lettered	0	6	3
System of Geography, ditto, lettered	0	6	3
Stow's Survey, per Vol. lettered	0	6	9
Ware's Architecture, lettered	0	6	9
Maitland, per Vol. lettered	0	6	9

1 Bernardus Siegfried Albinus, Tables of the Skeleton and Muscles of the Human Body, fol. London, 1749

2 Robert Wood, The Ruins of Palmyra, fol. London 1753; Idem, The Ruins of Balbec, fol. London, 1757

3 Colin Campbell, Vitruvius Britannicus, 3 vols fol. London, 1717-1725

Rapin with Heads, &c. lettered	0	5	3
Statutes at Large, lettered	0	5	3
Universal Traveller, lettered	0	5	9
Bailey's Dictionary, lettered	0	5	9
Chamber's Dictionary, per Vol. lettered	0	5	3
James's Dictionary, per Vol. lettered	0	5	9
Burkitt with Cuts, lettered	0	5	3
without Cuts, lettered	0	4	3
Stackhouse's Bible, per Vol.[4]	0	5	3
Sloan's Jamaica, per Vol.[5]	0	8	6
Illustration of the Bible	0	6	9

All Books on the same Paper, &c. the like Price.

FOLIO'S, Crown.

Stackhouse's Body of Divinity, lettered[6]	0	3	9
Taylor's Life of Christ with Cuts	0	4	0
Jacob's Law Dictionary, lettered	0	3	6
Wood's Conveyancer, lettered	0	3	6
Tillotson's Sermons, per Vol. lettered	0	3	6
Bion's Instruments	0	3	6

All Books on the same Paper, &c. the like Price.

FOLIO'S, Fool's-Cap.

Peere Williams's Reports	0	3	3
Viner's Abridgment[7]	0	3	3
Ludlow's Memoirs	0	3	3

All Books on the same Paper, &c. the like Price.

QUARTO'S, Royal Paper.

Smollett's Don Quixote, lettered[8]	0	3	3
Jarvise's Don Quixote, lettered	0	3	6
Pope's Works, lettered	0	3	0
Bolingbroke	0	3	0

All Books on the same Paper, &c. the like Price.

QUARTO'S, Demy.

Ainsworth's Dictionary, lettered[9]	0	2	9
Boyer's Dictionary, lettered	0	2	6
Cruden's Concordance, lettered	0	2	6
Heister's Surgery, lettered	0	2	6
Addison's Works, per Vol. lettered	0	2	3
Hook's Roman History, per Vol. with Cuts, lettered	0	2	6

4 Thomas Stackhouse, A New History of the Holy Bible, 2 vols fol. London, 1752

5 Sir Hans Sloane, A Voyage to the Islands...and Jamaica, 2 vols fol. London, 1707-1725

6 Thomas Stackhouse, A Complete Body of Divinity, fol. London, 1734

7 Charles Viner, A General Abridgment of Law and Equity, 24 vols fol. Aldershot, 1747-1758

8 Miguel de Cervantes Saavedra, The History and Adventures of the Renowned Don Quixote. Translated ...by T. Smollet, 4°, London, 1755

9 Robert Ainsworth, A Compendious Dictionary of the Latin Tongue, 4°, London, 1751

Gravesand's Philosophy, per Vol. lettered	0	2	6
Taylor on the Romans, lettered	0	2	3
Philosophical Transactions, lettered	0	2	3
Emerson's Mechanics, lettered[10]	0	2	3
All Books on the same Paper, &c. the like Price.			

OCTAVO'S, Royal Paper, in plain Calf.

Clarendon's History, Calf[11]	0	1	3
Molloy's De Jure Maritimo	0	1	3
Owen's Dictionary,			
—— in 4 Vols. plain, per Vol.	0	1	9
—— in 8 Vols. plain, per Vol.	0	1	6
Ainsworth's Dictionary,			
—— plain, in 1 Vol.	0	2	0
—— Ditto, in 2 Vols. per Vol.	0	1	6
Robertson's Navigation,			
—— per Vol. plain	0	1	3
—— in 1 Vol. plain	0	1	6
Shervin's Tables	0	1	3
All Books on the same Paper, &c. the like Price.			

OCTAVO'S, Demy, Calf.

Boyer's Dictionary	0	1	2
Bailey's Dictionary	0	1	2
Schrevelius's Lexicon	0	1	2
Magazines	0	1	2

Crouch's and Saxby's Rates	0	1	1
Burn's Justice, per Vol.[12]	0	1	0
Complete Housewife	0	1	0
Smollett's History of England,			
11 Vols. plain, per Vol.	0	1	2
Ditto, 7 Vols. with Cuts, per Vol.	0	1	2
New Duty of Man	0	1	1
Peerage of England, per Vol.	0	1	1
Virgil, Delph.	0	1	1
Martin's Philosophy, per Vol.	0	1	1
—— Grammar	0	1	1
Prussian Infantry and Cavalry	0	1	1
Bland's Discipline	0	1	0
Gordon's Grammar	0	1	0
Duty of Man	0	1	0
Salmon's Grammar	0	1	1
And all Octavo's, such as Sherlock's Sermons, &c.	0	0	11
Tillotson's Sermons, per Vol.	0	1	0
All Books on the same Paper, &c. the like Price.			

Crown OCTAVO'S, Calf.

Hervey	0	0	9
Pope's Works, per Vol.	0	0	9
New Duty of Man	0	0	9
Bartlet's Farriery[13]	0	0	9
All Books on the same Paper, &c. the like Price.			

10 William Emerson, The Principles of Mechanicks, 4°, London, 1758

11 Edward Hyde, 1st Earl of Clarendon, The History of the Rebellion, 3 vols 8°, Oxford, 1720-1721

12 Richard Burn, The Justice of the Peace, 3 vols 8°, London, 1758

13 John Bartlet, The Gentleman's Farriery, 8°, Eton, 1754

Demy TWELVES, Calf.

Nature display'd	0	0	10
Dryden's Virgil[14]	0	0	10
Martin's and Salmon's Gazetters	0	0	10
New Manual	0	0	9
Milton's Paradise Lost and Regain'd	0	0	9
Theobald's Shakespear, per Vol.	0	0	9
Spectators, Tatlers, and Guardian, &c.	0	0	8

All Books on the same Paper, &c. the like Price.

Small TWELVES, Calf.

Rasselas, Shandy, and Pope's Works[15]	0	0	7
Gay's Fables with Cuts	0	0	9

All Books on the same Paper, &c. the like Price.

OCTAVO'S, Sheep, Rolled.

Drelincourt on Death[16]	0	0	8
Wingate's Arithmetic	0	0	8
Wild's Surveying	0	0	8

All Books on the same Paper, &c. the like Price.

Large TWELVES and Crown OCTAVO'S, Sheep, Rolled.

Salmon's and Martin's Gazetters	0	0	8
New Duty of Man	0	0	7
New Manual	0	0	7
Marshal on Sanctification, &c[17]	0	0	7
Bartlett's Farriery	0	0	7

All Books on the same Paper, &c. the like Price.

Demy TWELVES, Sheep, Rolled,

Hawney's Measurer	0	0	6
Croxall's Æsop	0	0	6
Beveridge's Thoughts[18]	0	0	6
Harrison's Cookery, &c.	0	0	6

Red Sheep, Rolled.

Letter Writer	0	0	6
Rider and List	0	0	5
Dodsley's Gent. and Baldwin's Journal, &c.	0	0	6
——— Lady's	0	0	4½

All Books on the same Paper, &c. the like Price.

14 Publius Virgilius Maro, The Works of Virgil...Translated by Mr Dryden, 12°, London, 1730

15 Alexander Pope, Works, 12°, London, 1757

16 Charles Drelincourt, The Christian's Defence against the Fears of Death, 8°, London, 1751

17 Walter Marshall, The Gospel-Mystery of Sanctification, 8°, Edinburgh, 1733 (or possibly a later edition)

18 William Beveridge, Private Thoughts upon Religion, 2 parts 12°, London, 1752

Small TWELVES, Sheep, Rolled.

Miss's Magazine	0	0	5
Young Lady's Magazine, per Vol.	0	0	5
Howe's Meditations[19]	0	0	5
All Books on the same Paper, &c. the like Price			

BIBLES.

Royal Bible	0	9	0
Medium Bible	0	6	6
Small Folio Bible	0	4	3
Large Quarto Bible	0	2	6
Small Quarto Bible	0	2	0
Octavo Bible	0	1	4
Minion Bible	0	0	11
Nonpariel Bible	0	0	9
Twenty-fours Bible	0	0	8

COMMON-PRAYERS.

Royal Prayer	0	5	0
Folio Prayer Medium	0	4	0
——— Demy	0	3	6
Quarto Prayer	0	1	9
Octavo Prayer	0	1	0
Brevier Twelves Prayer	0	0	8
Small Twelves Prayer	0	0	7
Twenty-fours Prayer	0	0	6

19 Charles Howe, _Meditations_, 12°, Dublin, 1754

Notes

1 A.W. Pollard & G.R. Redgrave, A Short-Title Catalogue of Books... 1475-1640 (1926), (revised edn. of vol. ii, 1976).

2 At the end of this fascinating article in which Coghlan's binding equipment and stationery stock are described, H.M. Nixon announced a second article intended to deal with the binders' price lists and some of the recipes. He then kindly and generously handed this material over to me, and, though it is a disappointment not to have his comments on these lists, it may be useful to put them into perspective by publishing all known lists at the same time. I am also grateful to the editor of the Journal of the Printing Historical Society for relinquishing his claim.

The present article was first published in G. Colin, ed., De libris compactis miscellanea (Brussels, 1984). A few additions and amendments have been made since.

3 For this and much of the information used throughout this article I am indebted to G. Pollard, 'Changes in the style of bookbinding, 1550-1830', The Library, Ser. 5, 11 (1956), pp. 71-94, and to Bernard Middleton, A History of English Craft Bookbinding Technique 2nd edn. (1978), passim. See also Bernard Middleton, 'The Bookbinders case unfolded', The Library, Ser. 5, 17 (1962), pp. 66-76, and H.M. Nixon, Five Centuries of English Bookbinding (1978), p. 48.

4 See H.M. Nixon, Broxbourne Library: Styles and Designs of Bookbinding (1956), pp. 126-7, 118-20.

5 E. Arber, A Transcript of the Registers of the Company of Stationers, 1554-1640 (5 vols, 1875), vol. i, p. 100. W.A. Jackson, Records of the Court of the Stationers' Company 1602-1640 (1957), p. 176.

6 N. Temperley, 'Middleburg Psalms', Studies in Bibliography (1977), 30, pp. 162-70.

7 I am grateful to the President and Council of the Bibliographical Society for making the typescript and proofs of vol. i available for research. For the post-1641 lists, D. Wing, Short-Title Catalogue of Books...1641-1700 (New York, 1945-51, revised edns of vols i and ii, New York, 1972, 1982) and A.F. Allison and V.F. Goldschmidt, op. cit., vol. 2: 1641-1700 (1977) have been used, as well as Watt and the British Library Catalogue.

8 I am very grateful to Mr John Hopkins, Librarian of the Society of Antiquaries, for his help in finding this list.

9 eg. H.M. Nixon, op. cit., p. 132, pp. 143-4.

10 eg. G.D. Hobson, English Bindings 1490-1940 in the Library of J.R. Abbey (1940), pl. 28.

11 The sizes in inches given here and below are the approximate sizes per sheet, and are taken from E.J. Labarre, Dictionary and Encyclopaedia of Paper and Paper-Making (Amsterdam, 1952); P. Gaskell, 'Notes on Eighteenth-Century British Paper', The Library, Ser. 5, 12 (1957), pp. 34-42, and An Alphabetical List of the Names of the Several Species of Writing Papers, Printing Papers...with their Size and Value per Ream (1781) (broadsheet, BL 510.i.6[7]).

12 J. Moxon, Mechanick Exercises (1683-4). See also W. Savage, A Dictionary of the Art of Printing (1841), pp. 802-3.

13 D. Foxon, 'Stitched books', The Book Collector, vol. 24 (1975), pp. 111-24.

14 H.R. Plomer, A Dictionary of the Booksellers and Printers who were at Work in England...1641-1667 (1907); idem, A Dictionary of the Printers and Booksellers...1668-1725 (1922). D.F. McKenzie, Stationers' Company Apprentices 1605-1640 (Charlottesville, Va., 1961); idem, Stationers' Company Apprentices 1641-1700 (Oxford, 1974).

15 Stationers' Company Court Book F. f. 218[b].

16 J.W. Phillips, 'The Origin of the publisher's binding in Dublin', Transactions of the Cambridge Bibliographical Society, 2 (1954), pp. 92-4.

17 The price for a Bible, 'Quarto, without Cuts' is 5s., the same as that for 'Edges Extraordinary' for the same size Bible in 1669 and 1695.

18 H. Parry, The Art of Bookbinding (1818), pp. 44-6, frontispiece.

19 See A.N.L. Munby, 'Chirms banded bindings', Transactions of the Cambridge Bibliographical Society, 1 (1950), pp. 181-6.

20 R. Dossie, The Handmaid to the Arts (1758), vol. i, pp. 392-4 contains a section on how to make embossed and metallic-varnish paper, but the author also complains that 'The manufactures of the gilt and marbled papers have not been so much cultivated in our own country, as it were to be wished, since very great sums have been always annually paid, both to Germany and Genoa, on this account.'

21 ibid. p. 397.

22 J. Arnett, Bibliopegia (1835), p. 53.

23 H.M. Nixon, 'The memorandum book of James Coghlan', Journal of the Printing Historical Society, 6 (1970), pp. 39-41. This and quotations concerning Coghlan's binding equipment below are taken from the 'Catalogue' printed in this article. The price lists and the recipes are quoted from the manuscript.

24 I am grateful to Dr Nicholas Pickwoad and to Mr David Foxon for information on these points.

25 I am grateful to Mr Michael Harris for providing me with xerox copies from originals in the Public Record Office C 114/182 PT II.

26 These bills are at the Stationers' Company. I am grateful to Miss Robin Myers for drawing them to my attention.

27 Published in full in E. Howe, The London Bookbinders 1780-1806 (1950), appendix iii.

28 ibid. p. 9 for this and the information and quotations below; and J. Jaffray, A Collection of Manuscripts Relating to the Art and Trade of Bookbinding, 4 (1864), (not published). A typescript of this is in the British Library 667.r.19, pp. 190-1, 216-7, 224-5.

Moses Pitt and Insolvency in the London Booktrade in the Late-Seventeenth Century

Michael Harris

The framework of this paper will be provided by the career of Moses Pitt, a London bookseller of considerable interest and surprising obscurity. The materials for an analysis of his shifting financial position are quite rich. Not only was he involved in a series of historically fruitful law suits but payments for his correspondence and other manuscript items concerned with his business survive from as early as the mid-1660s. In conjunction with the comments on his personal circumstances published by Pitt towards the end of his life, notably in his striking publication The Cry of the Oppressed (1691), a quite detailed picture emerges - despite the many intolerable loose ends and ambiguous chronologies.

Pitt was not a typical bookseller as his financial interests took him further outside the trade than most. However this in a way gives his career a special interest as it links the business of bookselling with some of the other areas of commercial activity which make up the mosaic of economic life in London. At the same time during his lifetime Pitt passed from comfortable affluence to total ruin and in examining how and why this came about it is possible to give some focus to a consideration of the issue of insolvency in the booktrade as both a threat and a reality.

To provide a reasonable context for a gloomier side of Pitt's career it may be useful to say a few words about his background and the period of upswing in his commercial life. Success and failure in trade cannot easily be separated arising as they do out of the same motives and actions mediated by a range of often unknowable variables including individual character, personal circumstances or blind chance. Pitt was born about 1639 and brought up in Cornwall.[1] In 1654 he was apprenticed to Robert Littlebury, bookseller and member of the Haberdashers Company, an organisation of which Pitt became free in November 1661. Unlike many of his contemporaries Pitt declined to exchange to the Stationers and although he experienced some minor difficulties over the binding and freeing of apprentices, as well as through legal action by the City in the mid-1680s, the impact on his business activities was limited.

By the mid-1660s he was established at the sign of the White Hart in Little Britain where he combined the interests of bookseller and publisher. His location may have contributed to his early success as he seems to have been largely unaffected by the Great Fire which wiped out some members of the trade and gave a considerable impetus to the demand for books. The Fire also brought into his neighbourhood some of the major City booksellers including Richard Royston and Pitt's long-term associate Richard Chiswell, and this in itself may have provided an opportunity for extending contacts in the trade.[2] Part of Pitt's rise to prosperity was based on his broad range of personal associations. One of his earliest imprints links his name with a series of leading booksellers on a law patent item.[3] Even more valuable in terms of publishing were his contacts with the prolific members of the cultural élite focused in the Royal Society. Pitt's earliest correspondence, dating from February 1666, shows that he was already working closely with Dr John Pell, insolvent mathematician and founder member of the Royal Society, organising the printing and the casting of figures for a work on algebra.[4] Such connections continued to provide a base for Pitt's publishing enterprises. A large proportion of his output was made up of books in Latin concerned with science and mathematics which he published in association with the Society.[5] It seems likely that from the first he combined this side of the business with the importation of continental Latin books which, during the 1670s, became one of the staples of his trade and led to trips abroad to accumulate stock.[6]

A symptom of Pitt's commercial success appeared in his decision to move his business into the City, still very much in the throes of rebuilding, although he seems to have kept some warehouse accommodation in the neighbourhood of his original premises in St Bartholomews' Close. The first entry in the Term Catalogues to give his address as 'the Angel in St Paul's Churchyard' occurs in 1673 and is characteristically for a collection of Robert Boyle's essays.[7] Whether his continued use of the address indicates a settled location is not clear. However by the mid-1670s he was established in premises standing next to a paved area at the corner of Pater-Noster-Row and Paul's Alley, a byway leading down to St Paul's Cathedral.[8] A shop in this location was hard to come by and was of considerable value in developing and maintaining an effective turnover. The lease passed from the owner, Sir Thomas Davies, to a series of booksellers: in 1669 to Richard Royston, in 1673 to Richard Chiswell and subsequently - for 'a great sum of money' - to Moses Pitt.[9] According to his own account Pitt spent an even greater, but still unspecified, sum on wainscotting, shelving and general fittings before moving in his 'great stock of books and other things to the value of Six or Seven Thousand pounds'. At this address the two components of Pitt's business continued to flourish. On the publishing side his circle of contacts, established largely through his associates in the Royal Society, steadily widened. Robert Boyle, for example, introduced him to Glibert Burnet[10] who was apparently among the first of a sequence of dignitaries in the Church of England to have some business connection with Pitt. His output in this area clearly chimed with the highly developed sense of orthodox religions which appeared in all his personal writings.

During the mid-1670s therefore Moses Pitt was in good commercial and financial shape. With a wide range of contacts, a growing stock and a well-placed retail outlet, business was flourishing. Wing lists eighteen items from 1676 with his name on the imprint, a high point in terms of the quantity of books published.[11] However

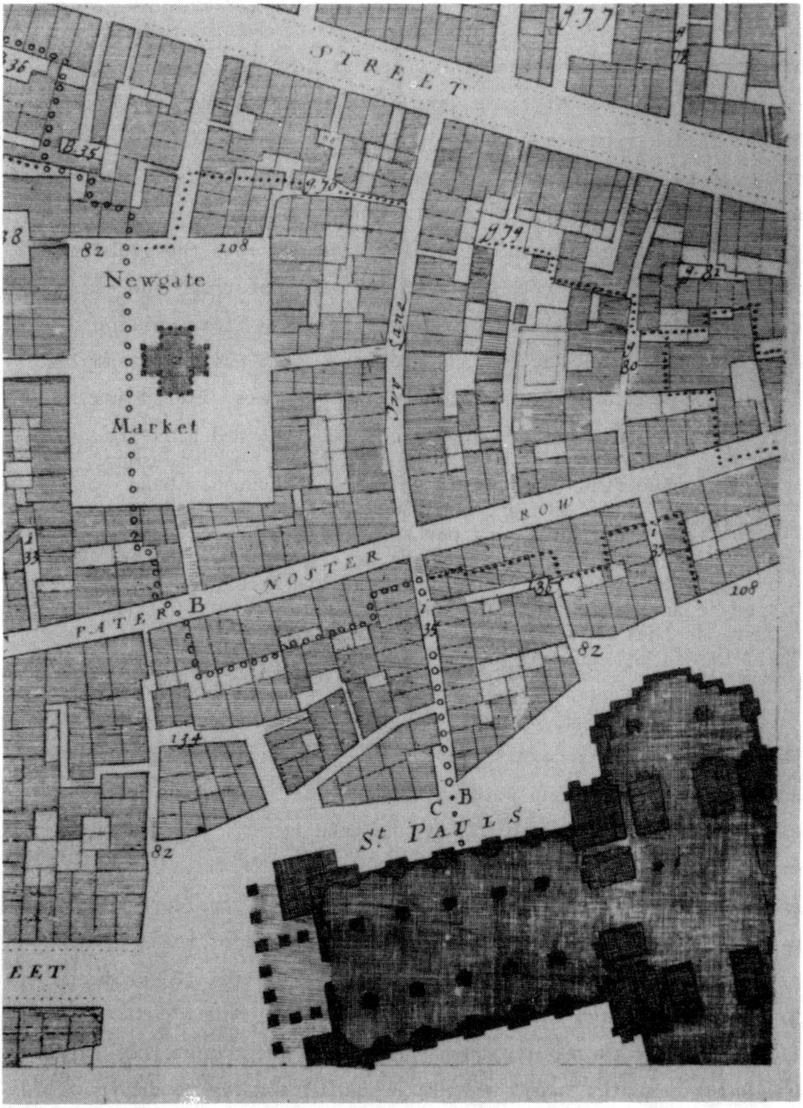

Detail from John Ogilby and William Morgan: 'A New and Accurate Map of the City of London', 1676, showing the location of Pitt's shop at the junction of Pater-Noster-Row and Pauls Alley (i 35).

it was this very level of success that was pushing Pitt towards dangerous waters. One of the paradoxes of commercial success was that it invariably contained the seeds of disaster. The ever-present insecurities of trade were clear enough to Daniel Defoe who had fallen from a considerable financial height in 1692 and continued to stagger from crisis to crisis throughout his variegated career.[12] In his excellent treatise the Compleat English Tradesman, first published in 1725 and gradually expanded into the 1730s, Defoe devoted a chapter to the need for the honest and successful tradesman to guard against over-commitment.[13] After dwelling on the vulnerability of success and providing some pregnant examples of sudden collapse he went on to urge the successful tradesman:

> to be cautious still of not launching out beyond himself: Nothing of its kind is more common than for the Tradesman, when he once finds himself grown rich, to have his Head full of great Designs and new Undertakings. He finds his Cash flow in upon him, and perhaps he is fuller of Money than his Trade calls for; and as he scarce knows how to employ more Stock in it than he does, his Ears are the sooner open to any Project or Proposal that offers itself; and I must add that this is the most critical Time with him in all his Life; if ever he is in danger of Ruin, 'tis just then.[14]

Defoe was, as might be expected, highly sympathetic to those that gave way: 'tis next to impossible', he wrote, 'for such a Man to sit still, and do nothing, to see the World flow up to his very Teeth, and not open his Mouth to take it in, 'tis against the very Current of his Blood; he cannot do it'.[15] These remarks, like many of his others, could be said to apply with considerable force to Moses Pitt who found himself in 1678 at the crossroads of his career and suddenly drawn into a series of interrelated projects which carried a high level of commercial risk.

The first of these, which gradually came to dominate his entire publishing capacity, was the notable and ultimately notorious English Atlas.[16] In some ways picking up this grand project was a logical extension of Pitt's established interests. The plates of the Jansson world Atlas became available to him through his Dutch booktrade contacts and support for the scheme was provided on a semi-official basis by a committee of the Royal Society. The dangers should perhaps have been even more evident. Map production was notoriously expensive. The high cost of materials and specialist workmanship was bound to involve a large capital investment and during the eighteenth century a number of quite notable map specialists broke themselves on relatively modest projects.[17] In Pitt's case, as someone who had neither the experience nor the premises on which to carry out the work, the scheme can only be called Utopian. It is tempting to draw a parallel with the bookseller-publishers who became involved in massive university projects, Robert Scott at Oxford and John Owen at Cambridge, which proved well beyond their capacity and led to extreme financial difficulty.[18] In the early stages the eleven large folio volumes of the *Atlas* were intended to contain 900 leaves of text with 600 printed plates. Payment was to be by subscription at forty shillings per volume, Pitt himself depositing money with the secretary of the Royal Society to guarantee publication. The work was to be completed in three years and Pitt seems to have launched himself into it with his usual energy. In his early *Proposals*, for example, he claimed that he had 'sent a Man beyond the Seas, to the Paper-Mills to take care about making the Paper, and providing him with other things that may be necessary for carrying on this work'.[19] This probably included finding skilled labour.

However his main effort, and the principal side effect of the *Atlas* project, was Pitt's move to take over the printing office in the Sheldonian Theatre at Oxford. Pitt was able to get a sub-lease on the premises, partly at least through his agreement to purchase John Fell's unsold books, rejected by the Stationers' Company, at the asking price of £3,800.[20] Pitt's main, if not his sole, interest was in publication of the *Atlas* and it made commercial sense to spread the costs. Consequently Pitt brought in, under terms of partnership, three other London booksellers, first William Leake, and shortly after, Thomas Guy and Peter Parker. In September 1678 the four signed a three-year lease on the Theatre at £200 per annum.[21]

The agreement between the partners themselves was complex. The stock of books was divided, half to Pitt, perhaps in association with Leake, and half to Parker and Guy.[22] Although the printing office contained some of the necessary materials, the booksellers had to provide others. Each supplied a different font of type - Pitt, for example, 'Primer and English Roman' - while Leake was also to provide two printing presses and Guy all the cases and chases. According to Pitt, Parker and Guy were given full control of the general printing office and made all the decisions about the books produced, Pitt paying his contribution to the expenses and receiving a fourth share of the books and profits. A separate area at the Theatre may have been set aside for production of the Atlas and Pitt certainly undertook some other publishing ventures on his own account.[23] The intricacies of such an agreement were pregnant with difficulties.

While Pitt was struggling to meet his commitments over the Atlas - volume one with the Oxford imprint limped into existence in May 1680 - and attempting to auction off his share in the moiety of Fell's books, he was also moving into a new area of financial speculation.[24] In 1678 his relative Richard Mill died childless, having appointed Pitt as sole executor to his estate, of which a prime slice of Westminster property was the principal asset.[25] In this rather haphazard way Pitt was drawn into the active but financially dubious area of property speculation. At all commercial levels attempts to boost profits and to secure against financial disaster led to some diversification of interest. Among booksellers this could involve the provision of a variety of financial and other services or more simply the sale of alternative commodities, such as patent medicines, alongside books. However within the middling and upper levels of the trade, diversification was centred on those areas of investment which attracted successful businessmen generally. The details of individual and group investment are extremely difficult to pin down but in broad terms the choice for the deployment of surplus capital outside trade lay between land and government securities. The merchant community in general seems to have moved away from land and it has been suggested that merchants rarely held a large percentage of their non-trade assets in freehold or leasehold urban property.[26] The established difficulties of investment in houses and land - the need for a high level of supervision, risk of fire, the generally low capital value and the perennial difficulty of uncovering concealed or delayed incumbrances - diverted the flow of money into other channels. Where the evidence is available, property does not seem to figure very largely in the assets of individual booksellers. Thomas Bennet, for example, when he died in 1706, was said to be worth £10,000 - of which £9,000 was in cash and the remainder in a freehold in Fleet Street, the leases of three houses in the Old Bailey and a coffee house in Birchin Lane.[27] Corporate ownership of property could be extensive and the Stationers' Company held blocks of property adjacent to the Hall, although this can hardly be said to have played a large part in the Company's investments. On the other hand among the most financially successful members of the booktrade were those, like Thomas Guy, whose fortunes were based on speculation in securities - in his case in seamen's pay tickets and subsequently in South Sea stock. Success was far from certain in either area but property, perhaps surprisingly, seems to have carried the greater risks.

Pitt's excursion into property was therefore not in itself particularly unusual although the scale of his subsequent involvement certainly was. Richard Mill's estate, known as the Blue Boars Head estate, stood in the block between King Street and Duke Street and was held by Mill from the Dean and Chapter of Westminster under a forty-year lease, at an annual rent of twenty shillings.[28] It consisted of a number of houses in a rather dilapidated condition and some open plots, but the possibilities were clear enough. Pitt seems almost immediately to have begun to extend his interest in this area - acquiring, in particular, a stake in the property around Antelope Alley and on the St James's Park side of Duke Street. During the 1680s, although the Westminster estate provided the

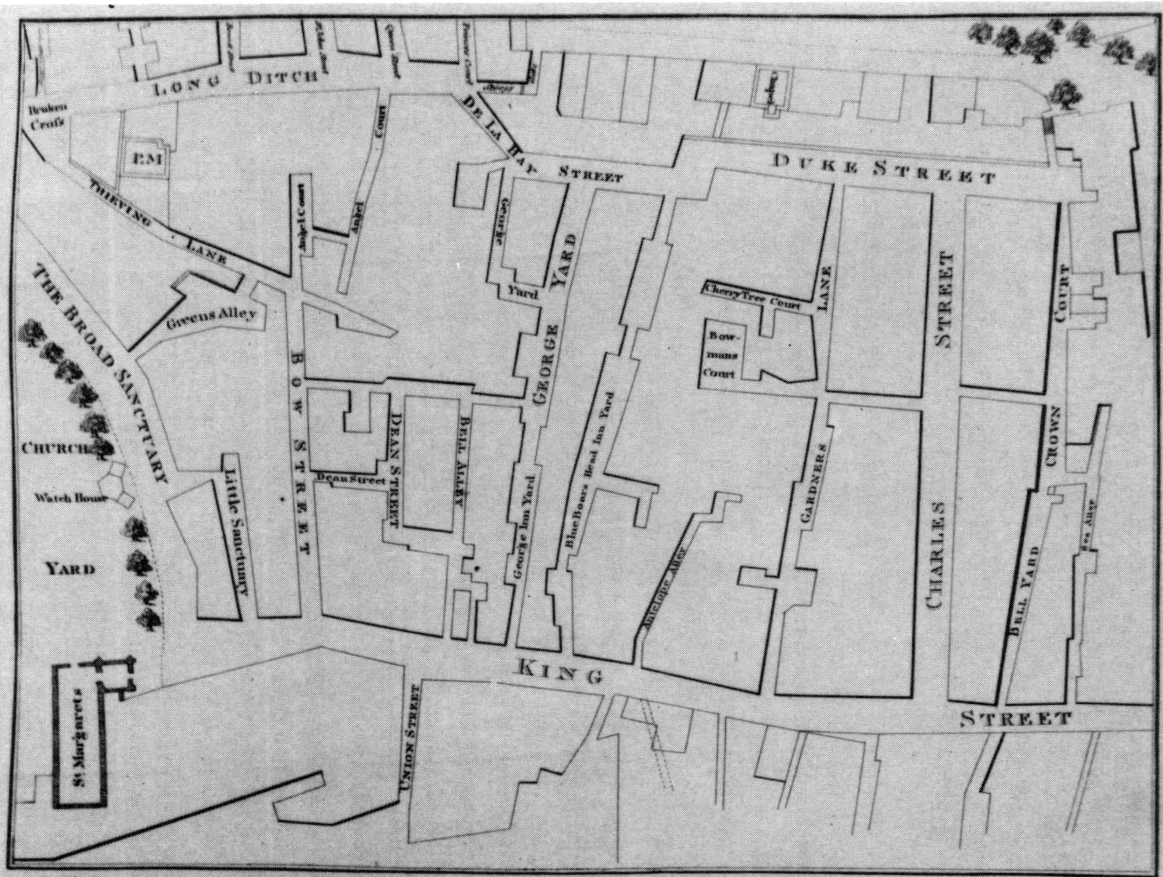
LONG DITCH
Broken Cross
DE LA HAY STREET
DUKE STREET
THIEVING LANE
Angel Court
Angel Court
George Yard
GEORGE YARD
Greens Alley
THE BROAD SANCTUARY
BOW STREET
Cherry Tree Court
LANE
Bowmans Court
STREET
COURT
CHURCH
Watch House
Little Sanctuary
Dean Street
DEAN STREET
BELL ALLEY
George Inn Yard
Blue Boars Head Inn Yard
GARDNERS
CHARLES
CROWN
YARD
Antelope Alley
BELL YARD
KING
St. Margarets
UNION STREET
STREET

focus for his development plans, he also acquired an interest in several detached and 'straggling' properties in various parts of London and in the provinces.[29]

By the end of the 1670s Pitt was therefore becoming deeply committed in a variety of projects any one of which could have made his fortune. The remainder of this paper will attempt to trace the process by which the opposite took place and led with almost Grecian inevitability towards the debtors' prison.

The first fissure in the grand structure which Pitt had been so busily putting together had no direct bearing on any of his main projects but concerned the tenure of his shop. It seems that as Pitt's commercial commitments built up so he became increasingly accident-prone and even if, as on this occasion, the elements of cause and effect are not at all clear, the circumstances must have contributed to a sense of general uneasiness.[30] Pitt's London shop remained the focus of his working life and by 1680 he claimed that it held 'a stock of bookes of papers manuscripts & Copyes to the value of near Tenn thousand poundes'. The problem arose from the fact that although he had taken on the premises as a corner shop, the paved area at the junction of Paul's Alley and Pater-Noster-Row was not the property of his landlord. This stark truth emerged some time in the late 1670s when Pitt suddenly found building under way on the area he had used for the display and sale of books. Not only was a substantial length of shop window subsequently blocked off but his rooms at the back of his house were 'quite darkened & stopped up & made like a Dungeon'. Worse than this Pitt's landlord in rebuilding after a fire had pushed the East wall of the house into the adjacent plot. Consequently Pitt's new and very active neighbour began to dismantle the entire wall 'to the ruine and utter demolishing of the said house and the utter spoyling and destruction of y^{r}. Orators goods'. Pitt claimed that the removal of parts of the wall had exposed his books 'to the damage of raine and snow' and that he had suffered £500 worth of damage through the attendant stopping-up of a water course. Worst of all he had been forced at great expense and with great difficulty to find alternative accommodation in the area and was 'much dampnified...by the breaking spoyling & disordering of his goods & books & by being forced for some time to discontinue his trade whilst his present house & shop were fitting up' at the cost, he claimed, of £150. His new premises were apparently closer to the cathedral.[31] From all this it can be suggested that Pitt began the 1680s in a state of some personal confusion.

In fact all Pitt's major commitments were beginning to cause trouble. The Atlas was increasingly bogged down under its own enormous costs, later calculated by Pitt at £1,000 for each part.[32] At the same time disagreements with the Royal Society sponsors, particularly Robert Hooke, non-payment by subscribers and the problems of long-distance oversight were all taking their toll.[33] Volume 2, when it appeared at the end of 1681, was riddled with faults and it may have been Pitt's inability to meet the terms of a financial agreement with his Dutch colleagues that led to the removal of their names from the plates of volume 3. The Oxford arrangements themselves were another source of pressure. Pitt seems to have dropped out of the partnership in 1683 when he took a protracted and unexplained trip to Ireland. On his return he was faced with a series of financial demands from his former associates which led to the seizure of his Oxford warehouse and his own arrest.[34] In a series of counter-charges Pitt accused Parker and Guy of falsifying the accounts and of cheating him over the division of Fell's books. Instead, he claimed, of taking 'Bibles & such other Bookes as were proper for their way of trade...[they]...did pick & choose out of the said Bookes for themselves the most choice & valuable', leaving Pitt about £500 down on the transaction.[35]

The complications of Pitt's business life, which included a series of law suits over encumbrances on the Westminster estate,[36] were set against an increasingly uneasy political background. In the mid-1680s the upheavals surrounding the accession of James II, the sharpening up of the Catholic issue and the 'Revolution' which brought in William and Mary were accompanied by a series of shock waves which reached far down into the business life of the nation. This was particularly damaging in a community which relied heavily on an elaborate system of credit. The low quality and limited amount of coin and the absence of formal financial institutions meant that almost everyone was involved in an unending sequence of credit transactions. Defoe enquired 'how many thousand of families wear our their cloathes before they pay for them, and eat their dinner upon tick with the butcher?'.[37] This system of credit had considerable dangers for members of the trading community, not only in the accumulation of personal debts but through direct involvement in those of others. As Defoe pointed out it was hardly possible for tradesmen 'to go through the World in their Business without being bound for one another',[38] and he particularly identified the practice of standing surety for someone else's debts as potentially fatal. John Dunton, who 'was over persuaded, upon some extremities, to become surety for a Brother and Sister-in-law, at several times for about 1200 l.', experienced some of the worst effects of such arrangements.[39]

In the booktrade credit was as prevalent as in many other areas of commercial life. While booksellers, including Pitt, often relied on barter with their colleagues to acquire new stock, in the intricate structure of relations between complementary areas of the trade, as well as between the tradesmen and their customers, credit was an inevitable component.[40] Dunton claimed that during his prosperous period as a bookseller he settled his accounts regularly at six-monthly intervals and that this was the usual period of credit allowed in the trade.[41] In practice, however, most individuals seem to have suffered and inflicted vast delays in payment which often extended over years. For such arrangements to work, a stable economic environment was essential and it seems clear that the booktrade as a whole was going through a bad time in the mid-1680s as political tension increased. Dunton refers to the 'universal damp upon Trade' which accompanied Monmouth's rebellion in 1685 and credits the event with his speculative trip to America.[42] Many individual instances of financial ruin date from this period and Plomer, in his Dictionary, lists at least twenty cases between 1682 and 1687 in which prosecutions for debt involving booksellers were heard in the Court of Common Pleas.[43] Many were between London and provincial booksellers and clearly the need for the settlement of outstanding accounts was felt to have become a matter of some urgency. An aside on the edginess of the mid-1680s appears in the careers of a few minor booksellers such as Samuel Palmer, Dunton's ex-apprentice, who 'preferred shooting to bookselling', joined the army in about 1686 and was drowned; or Benjamin Alsop who, 'being a wild sort of a Spark', left his shop to get a commission in Monmouth's army'.[44] From the end of the decade the effects of involvement in a protracted Continental war were cumulative and damaging. Many members of this merchant community, including Defoe, succumbed to the related difficulties and the Stationers' Company records reflect a build-up of bankruptcies in the 1690s which touched even the most substantial booksellers.

These circumstances must have impinged on Pitt's commercial life and may have played a part in his decision in the mid-1680s to carry out a general restructuring of his business. In doing so he came increasingly to rely on the support of Adiel Mill, an ominous figure in Pitt's career whose name became inextricably linked with his in the mythology of the late seventeenth-century booktrade. Mill was presumably a relation of the late Richard Mill and was certainly a first cousin of Pitt himself, a further reminder that family relationships often lay at the heart of the financial disasters of this period.[45] Although he emerges from Pitt's writing in a highly unfavourable light and was certainly the instrument of his final ruin, Mill seems to have had a higher status in the booktrade than Pitt suggests. Having transferred from the Haberdashers to the Stationers' Company he took an active part in company affairs during the 1670s, becoming one of the principal tenants of the property near the Hall, and taking on a sequence of booktrade apprentices including the son of Robert Littlebury, Pitt's former master.[46] In 1685 he was elected to the livery, though his name had been struck off the list by 1689, and this timing, taken together with his position as executor of Henry Hills Senr, may indicate some Catholic sympathies.[47] (An Irish background is indicated and his catch phrase, identified by Pitt as 'I hate a trick' has a slight Celtic ring to it.) Mill dealt mainly in paper from his premises at the sign of the Peacock, Amen Corner, supplying Pitt among others, but he was also involved in a variety of miscellaneous activities which may have included some rather obscure publishing. The 'A.M.' imprints in Wing reach a peak in 1685, and Mill's name was spelt out at length in at least two works issued in 1689.[48] He was also active in a range of other commercial areas, including an unspecified trade to Jamaica and was described by one of his associates in the late 1680s as 'the best Projector in England'.[49] It was to Mill that Pitt increasingly trusted his business affairs. By the mid-1680s he was acting as his agent or 'cashier', a role distinct from that played by Sir Richard Hawkins, a member of the Grocers' Company, who provided Pitt with a variety of banking services and figured prominently in his accounts.[50]

The most important decision taken by Pitt in the restructuring process was to play down or even abandon his involvement in bookselling in order to concentrate on the development of the Westminster estate. He consequently embarked on a programme of stock clearance. In 1685 he held two auctions in the City. The first in November, run by Edward Millington, was described in a fifty-two-page catalogue.[51] Among the mixed collection of books was a considerable variety of bibles, prayer books and related items from the Oxford days and it was claimed that this was the first time such works had been offered at auction. The charitable possibilities of this were highlighted in the catalogue. The second sale the following month was devoted entirely to religious material printed at Oxford, some of which had evidently suffered from lying around in some of Pitt's warehouses as several sheets were said to have been run off to replace those in the 12mo bibles which 'were mildew'd and rotton'.[52] At the same time Pitt decided to move to Westminster and about 1686 let his 'House in St. Pauls Church-Yard, to Mr Joseph Watts, and Sold him a Considerable Quantity of Books and Household-Stuff', accepting bonds in payment.[53] The move not only enabled him to dispose of a further quantity of stock but also to escape pressure from the City where the Court of Aldermen had moved against him for practising as a 'Stationer' while outside the Company.[54] The removal to Duke Street also provided Pitt with direct oversight of his building programme: his switch from one area of commercial activity to another was far from complete. He intended to continue his involvement with the Atlas. Indeed he could hardly do otherwise given the scale of his investment, although the project had remained dormant since the publication of volume 4 in 1682. He also continued to dabble in other areas of publishing, particularly in works on travel, but his output from 1685 was very slight. He may also have kept a quantity of stock at the 'Great Warehouse in St Batholomews Close', though the evidence for this is rather sketchy. A manuscript volume in the British Library labelled 'Catalogue of M. Pitt's Library' contains a list, on 167 folios, of books in Latin and other continental languages and some large multiples of a few works in English.[55] The item is not clearly dated. Most of the books were published before 1684 including, for example, a sequence of the 'Mercure Hollandais' running erratically from 1672 to that date. However a small number of others are from the later 1680s and one of the last leaves is headed 2 January 1691.[56]

The inextricable confusion that developed between the property of Pitt and Mill, who had his own line of booktrade interest, cannot be sorted out, but it seems possible to suggest that these books, or some part of them, were left over when Pitt disposed of his stock in 1685. The level of Pitt's continued investment in the booktrade was clarified in his statement at the end of the decade when he described his property as held a few years previously.[57] This included

> divers Stocks Impressions parcells and quantityes of bookes bound and in quires and of several parcells and quantityes

> of paper for the Printing of the bookes called or intitled the Atlas and of other bookes and Copyes of bookes and Copper plates and of divers presses letters utensills and other materialls for printing to the value of fourteen thousand pounds.

Referring specifically to his stock as held in 1688 later in the same document, Pitt estimated the total value at £20,000. These figures may be highly speculative, and they are not repeated in the Cry but they do at least suggest that his break with the trade was far from clear cut. Pitt's movement away from bookselling seems to have left the way clear for the build-up of Samuel Smith's commercial activity in exactly the same area. Smith had been Pitt's servant and apprentice in the 1670s, although freed by a member of the Stationers' Company in 1682.[58] His business centred around Continental imports and scientific publications and he must have picked up many of his contacts by way of Pitt. It was to Smith that Pitt's former associates in Holland applied at the end of the 1680s to find out what was happening to the Atlas project and to ask him to intervene on their behalf.[59] Ironically, and perhaps typically, Smith seems to have taken a hand in Pitt's downfall in spite of what must have been considerable personal obligations.

Selling up his books and calling in his debts, estimated by Pitt at about £5,000, was part of his attempt to get to grips with the development of the Westminster estate. However, neither the money raised, much of it probably already owed by Pitt, nor the rising income from rents that accompanied the improvements were enough to support Pitt's schemes. His costs, which included the expensive renewal of the lease and an apparently never-ending series of law suits, as well as the building itself, required access to large sums of ready money. Consequently he began to raise loans against the property from all quarters, utilising his personal contacts and becoming enmeshed in a highly elaborate web of financial obligations.[60] Amongst many such transactions, he raised £3,800 on a general mortgage of the whole estate from Lady Elizabeth Jones, £1,000 from Edward Stillingfleet, when Dean of St Pauls, and a further £1,000 from John Tillotson, Dean of Canterbury. In 1686 he even borrowed £2,000 from his former partner and legal adversary in the booktrade, Thomas Guy. Clergy of the Church of England and booksellers seem to have been Pitt's main sources of finance. Although his contacts in the trade remained sound, however, he was probably not able to tap the resources of the Stationers' Company which engaged in a certain amount of institutional money-lending. The Company provided a modest service for members of the trade, issuing bonds of up to £100 against heavy security for a fixed term.[61] Through its officers it seems also to have been involved in a variety of much less formal engagements as the case of Adiel Mill, graphically described in the Cry, indicates. Mill, as a member of the Livery and friend of the Treasurer John Leigh, was clearly in a special position. Nonetheless the transaction suggests how casually sums of money could be acquired from such a major institution. Leigh's wife claimed that Mill often borrowed money through her husband:

> and that a Week before he Died, he being so well as to be up and down in his House, and she herself not being well, was in her Bed, her Husband coming in to their Bed-Chamber, opens the Chest where the Money lay, and taking out [a] One Hundred Pound Bag, she Ask'd him, What Husband, are you going to pay away Moneys? He Answer'd, No, but Mr Mill wanted 100 l. and he was carrying it down to lend him.[62]

The drift of the story was that Mill never paid it back.

The loans raised by Pitt were translated into bricks and mortar during the late 1680s, and in the Cry he claimed to have 'Laid out about Twelve Thousand Pounds in Buildings, whereby I have made Westminster as Healthy a place, as any other parts about London, and as Commodious for Gentry to Live in, which has brought a Considerable Trade to that part of the Town'.[63] It should perhaps be added that a good deal of Pitt's building consisted of stabling. Speculation on this scale was a dangerous affair and the difficulties which were inherent in the credit system applied with proportionally greater force as the range of borrowing was extended. Legal action was a far from effective way of obtaining money from a debtor as the process itself was likely to mop up any money available for payment.[64] Nonetheless the law was an ever-present threat and the far-reaching apparatus of the courts, continually crowded with individuals under process, often for very small sums, heightened the sense of hazard. The debtor remained entirely at the mercy of his creditors and it was not until the eighteenth century that the slow build-up in ameliorating legislation which provided some sort of security began to take shape. As a result the London prisons, particularly the Fleet and the Kings Bench but also the large number of criminal and private institutions, were crowded with debtors trapped by the system and usually with little hope of release. In Newgate special accommodation for men and women debtors was provided on the common side in cells known as 'Tangier' and the 'Pigeon Hole'. Being placed under a Statute of Bankruptcy was particularly damaging before the legislation of 1706. As Defoe pointed out, it

> was like a man being taken by the Turks, he seldom recover'd liberty to try his fortune again, but frequently languish'd under the tyranny of the commissioners of bankrupt, or in the *Mint* or *Fryers*, or *rules of the Fleet*, till he wasted the whole estate, and at length his life, and so his debts were all paid at once.[65]

One damaging incidental to insolvency in the booktrade could be its impact on membership of the Stationers' Company. From the 1690s a growing number of individuals silently disappeared from the records after falling into difficulty while others, such as Samuel Heyrick and John Sims, were officially struck off the list of assistants as a result of indebtedness.[66] In Sims's case action was taken only after his release following a three-year spell of imprisonment in the Fleet.

It was against this background that Pitt embarked in the mid-1680s on the process of intended self-defence that was to lead directly to his ruin. His strategy, which was said to be common enough in London, involved the transfer of his assets and the creation of a structure of false debts.[67] The intention, which is fudged in the *Cry* but emerges starkly from the legal documents, was partly to encumber the estate to the extent that legal action against Pitt was hardly worth while and on the other hand to remove out of reach property which could otherwise be seized in an action and sold up, probably at half its value. His instrument in carrying out this dubious policy was Adiel Mill. This in itself seems to have been a terminal mistake. Pitt later accused Mill of stirring up his creditors in order to encourage the adoption of this line of action and there may have been some truth in this. Whatever the immediate cause Pitt, feeling himself under increasing pressure, began to sign over to Mill everything he possessed - in trust. This process began with a Statute Staple for £5,000 in the mid-1680s and continued through a sequence of documents by which stock, property and debts passed into the hands of Mill.[68] At the same time the accounts were deliberately falsified by the inclusion of unreal debts and the doctoring of others.

Given the fact that the whole policy was a suicidal mistake, Pitt made another series of fatal errors. In the first place he received nothing from Mill in writing, only his verbal agreement to the preparation of a deed of redemption by which everything would be handed back. Secondly he failed to examine any of the documents drawn up by Mill for his signature. It seems almost incredible that an experienced business man should take such a cavalier attitude to matters which were crucial to his well-being. However, as he himself stated in the instance of the Statute Staple he neither took advice nor 'soe much as read or perused the same'.[69] It also appears that he left the accounting procedure entirely to Mill and made few attempts at supervision. This sort of negligent approach to accounting was common enough among tradesmen in the late seventeenth century and while a growing number of books of commercial advice were published, members of the booktrade themselves continued to get into more or less serious difficulties through inadequate book-keeping. The surviving accounts of Henry Rhodes, for example, publishers of the _Exact Dealer_, are a model of confusion.[70] Dunton made a similar decision to Pitt, leaving everything to his wife who: 'commenced Bookseller, Cash-keeper, managed all my affairs for me and left me entirely to my own _rambling_ and _scribbling_ humour'.[71] The results in this case were entirely satisfactory but it was ironic that Dunton first got into difficulties with the confused, but possibly fraudulent, accounting of another member of the trade.[72]

The final crisis in Pitt's affairs has usually been put down to the failure of his building speculation. This was not the case, although he was certainly experiencing some difficulty in the late 1680s as one of his major enterprises became entangled with politics. Pitt had built a large house next to his own in Duke Street on land acquired from the arch-entrepreneur Nicholson Barbon. The property was subsequently let at £300 per annum to Chief Justice Jefferies who, finding that the space between the house and St James's Park was open ground, offered to obtain a crown grant for the entire strip of land on Pitt's behalf, providing he would build him a 'cause room' on it.[73] Urged on by Jefferies, Pitt added two substantial wings to the house at a cost, including the inside work, of some £4,000, in the process knocking down the park wall and building a raised terrace with a double flight of steps.[74] Pitt spent a good deal of time and money attempting to expedite the grant, but before it was ratified James II was bundled out of the country and Jefferies arrested. It was a cruel blow as Pitt found himself without a title to one of his major investments. Nonetheless he was not politically committed and while he succeeded in obtaining the contract for stabling for the retinue of William III he was also able to let the house itself to three Dutch ambassadors at the exorbitant rent of £720 per annum.[75]

The immediate cause of the crisis lay elsewhere and was apparently rooted in the commercial speculations of Adiel Mill. In 1687 Robert Scott, a major and long-term dealer in Continental publications, began to dispose of his stock and a large quantity of the books were acquired by Mill at a cost of £10,000. The transaction involved a down payment of £2,000, perhaps raised by Mill against Pitt's transferred assets, while the remaining £8,000 was added to Mill's rapidly rising debts. These were later said to amount in total to £30-40,000.[76] Whether the 'Glorious Revolution' interfered with Mill's plans or whether the books failed to sell at the series of

Detail from John Kip: 'A Prospect of the City of London, Westminster and St

auctions conducted by Benjamin Walford is not clear.[77] It appears, however, that Mill himself was coming under increasing financial pressure and this must have sharpened up the temptation of attempting to take permanent control of Pitt's property, an idea which may have been in Mill's mind for some time. In the Cry Mill's actions were presented as part of a long-term conspiracy involving his major creditor Sir Edward Wiseman, a mercer who was said to be owed £10,000 by Mill, and Nicholas Donning, part-scrivener and part-attorney, both from the neighbourhood of St Paul's. Pitt himself was becoming increasingly and belatedly aware of his vulnerable position and had been making strenuous efforts to get some agreement worked out with Mill for the return of his assets. Pitt's view of his own position was reasonably buoyant. He expected to raise £1,500 on the next volume of the Atlas which was almost ready for publication, while the sixth volume was 'a great part printed'.[78] By calling in his debts and selling off some of his property he expected to be in a position to meet the demands of his creditors and to consolidate his interest around the Westminster estate worth, according to his own estimate, about £1,500 per annum.[79]

In fact Nemesis was at his shoulder. After dinner on 18 April 1689 he was seized by five baillifs under a Statute of Bankruptcy obtained by Mill.[80] The cause cited was the Statute Staple for £5,000 and Pitt was hurried into a private prison before obtaining a transfer, under a writ of Habeas Corpus, to the Fleet. The suddennness of Pitt's arrest was clearly a precaution to avoid any chance of his absconding. Both Defoe and Dunton under similar circumstances left town and went on the run adopting various defensive devices, including - in Dunton's case - the unsuccessful use of women's clothes.[81] Others fled overseas or into one of the sanctuaries which offered security to debtors and which, in spite of legislation in 1697, lingered on as a feature of the commercial scene in London. Both of Thomas Gent's early employers, Francis Clifton and Edward Midwinter, removed to sanctuary taking up residence in the Rules of the Fleet and the Mint respectively and Pitt would have been well advised to follow the same course.[82]

His arrest and subsequent imprisonment were accompanied by the hardship suffered by any prisoner for debt whose access to funds was abruptly terminated by an unsympathetic creditor. The range and extent of such suffering was the subject of a large proportion of the Cry. In it Pitt combined detailed comment on his own case with an account of the personal experiences of debtors in the sixty-five county gaols, canvassed by post. The narratives were underscored by a series of harrowing copper plates. 'Debtors Lying Dead and Some starv'd, others Poison'd', 'Debtors brook out into Boyles Carbuncles and Botches', and so on. Those imprisoned for debt were thrown back either on the casual charity of strangers, solicited in various ways from the prison itself, or on the sympathetic intervention of friends, relations or business associates. In Pitt's case his head seems to have been kept more or less above water by his colleagues in the booktrade. Their help took various forms illustrating the cohesive nature of the trade in which mutual support was apparently strongly marked. The Stationers' Company charities and pensions were a more formal expression of the sort of engagement that appeared in the case of William Bowyer in 1713. Although he was reduced by fire from reasonable affluence to penury he was back in business within two months through the active and practical help of his colleagues who raised money, extended his credit and lent him premises.[83] The 'conger' itself, though a purely commercial device, may in some sense have emphasised the interconnections, charitable and otherwise, within the framework of the trade. Money for Pitt was raised by individual members of the Haberdashers Company as well as by his former neighbours in Pater-Noster-Row and Little Britain[84] but practical help was perhaps manifested most fully in support for the publication of the Cry. In his introductory comments Pitt thanked the booksellers:

> for their kindness in Subscribing for a very considerable Number of this small Book, without the Credit of which I, that have been concern'd in Printing of some Hundreds of Thousands of Books, in Folio, Quarto, Octavo etc. would

not have been able at this time to have Printed this small Narrative.

It may have been through the help of his ex-associates in the trade that he was able in 1690 to transfer to more comfortable premises in the rules of the Kings Bench prison.

Following his imprisonment Pitt became embroiled in a series of law suits of increasing complexity. His attempt to prove in Chancery that the transfer of assets to Mill had been a matter of trust failed completely and through a counter-suit at the end of 1689 all his property passed formally into the hands of Mill.[85] This led in the case of the Jefferies house to a pitched battle between Mill and his supporters and Pitt's son, brother-in-law and other friends who were all arrested and held briefly in the Fleet. The attempts by Pitt's other, and probably more sympathetic, creditors to get hold of his estate were blocked by Mill who, for reasons that are not entirely clear, was in turn declared bankrupt under a Statute raised by Robert Scott.[86] The confusion was endless. Mill himself after a period in the sanctuary of Grays Inn was arrested and the circle of ironies was completed when he himself 'was brought a Prisoner into the Fleet', in November 1690.[87]

While in gaol Pitt showed his usual energy in attempting to engineer his release. He was elected representative of the other prisoners in an attempt to obtain an 'Act for the Relief of Insolvent Debtors'. Two such Acts, which allowed for the release of those imprisoned for debt and held at a specified date, had been passed in 1671 and 1678 and Pitt launched himself into obtaining another. The material published in the Cry was accumulated as part of this process. In the event an Act was obtained and thousands of debtors released but, to Pitt's amazed disappointment, it specifically excluded those whose debts amounted to more than £100.[88] He was consequently thrown back on attempting to negotiate terms with Mill, sometimes through members of the trade including the bookseller Thomas Dring. Needless to say his recurrent hopes were in the end dashed and Mill declined to sign the note which could have obtained his release, or to contribute effectively to his subsistence.

Pitt's case was more or less hopeless and he was still in prison in 1696. His affairs were in too great confusion for any sort of reasonable settlement and it is hard to see how he could have made a commercial comeback. He seems to have resigned himself to his fate and in the mid-1690s engaged in the occasional publications of his own writings through Richard Cumberland the successor to Watts in the St Pauls Churchyard premises. His modest output consisted of a pamphlet in answer to George Hickes, and an odd item about his Cornish nurse, Anne Jeffries, 'who was fed for six months by a small sort of Airy People call'd _Fairies_'.[89] Both contained advertisements for the _Cry_ of which he must still have had a large stock remaining on his hands. However, much of Pitt's time in prison seems to have been devoted to charitable works on behalf of insolvent debtors, in collecting and deploying money raised for this purpose, and in taking up cases of particular hardship - such as that of the creditors of the notorious Benjamin Hinton.[90]

The story continued indeterminately. Mill, for example, went out in a blaze of ambiguity. He came to a friendly composition with his creditors who auctioned off his books in 1691 and he may have obtained his release on the strength of this.[91] It appears, however unlikely, that he died on board H.M.S. _Lancaster_, a man-of-war of the third rate, in 1695.[92] His will suggests some sort of royal grant in 1689 concerned with the navy but I have found no other trace of this. At the same time an Adiel Mill, the name is unusual enough, was appointed in 1700 to a commission, under John Pitt, to suppress pirates on the coast of Coromandel.[93] A father and son relationship may be involved here but the details are obscure. Pitt on the other hand died in 1697 in the parish of St Paul's Bennets Wharf, a low-key area in the City, which may indicate that he had finally obtained some degree of liberty.[94]

Insolvency in the booktrade, in all periods, is a subject which deserves a good deal of detailed investigation. Much of this needs to focus on the inner workings of the trade and be concerned with the identification of lines of weakness in economic relations and points of stress at which transactions assume a particularly dangerous aspect. Such studies will be based on an examination of the financial mechanisms which supported, or failed to support, individual businesses and of the intricate accounting process between, for example, paper merchants and booksellers or booksellers and printers. This paper has little to contribute in this area: I have been concerned more with the externals of insolvency and, in particular, with that tendency, even at the upper levels of the booktrade, for individuals to be wiped out by a combination of pressures not necessarily generated within the trade itself. This is close to the approach of Defoe in the Compleat English Tradesman where he was attempting to define the entire range of potential difficulties shared by all members of the trading community at different stages in a business life. In this context everything was grist. Dishonest apprentices, fraudulent partners, inadequate book-keeping, hostile customers, fire and self-indulgence, all figure as potential instruments of disaster. To Defoe the contingent nature of trade was everything. I have attempted in this short account of the rise and fall of Moses Pitt to suggest how such a view of the commercial world could be related to the circumstances of an individual tradesman.

To a great extent Pitt was the victim of his own personality: energetic but unworldly, active but careless he was an admirable bookseller but a flawed entrepreneur. Dunton's well-known account of Pitt reflects on this:

> He was an honest man every inch and thought of him,... he took as much delight in doing good, as if he had no other errand in the World. He had fathomed the vast body of learning, and in every several part of it was Master; ...nor did his conversation alone relish of his learning and piety...His wit and virtues were writ legibly in his face and he had a great deal of sweetness in his natural temper.[95]

However sympathetic, this is hardly the portrait of a commercial high-flier although, as Dunton also suggests, 'had his Atlas succeeded, or M[il]ls been a stranger to him, [he] had died worth Twenty Thousand Pounds'. At the same time Pitt was unlucky in his timing and any mistakes in judgement were compounded by the difficult circumstances of the period. By 1700 the commercial environment was beginning to undergo a radical change and Defoe often pointed up in his writing the more dangerous aspects of the immediate past. The gradual creation of a range of formal structures, including an effective banking organisation (in which members of the book trade became intimately involved), was providing an increasingly secure framework for economic activity. Pitt's death and the onset of what has been called the 'Financial Revolution' coincides with some precision providing, in a sense, the final irony in his story.

Notes

1 Pitt's age was stated to be fifty-two in his will dated 29 September 1691 (Public Record Office [hereafter PRO], Prob. II, 440). For a claim that Pitt was baptised in London in 1641 see Sarah Tyacke, London Map-Sellers 1660-1720 (Tring, 1978), p. 135. For other biographical information see the entry in the Dictionary of National Biography.

2 Royston's imprint address in 1668 was 'St. Bartholomews Hospital' and Chiswell's the 'Two Angels and Crown, Little Britain' (Edward Arber, ed., The Term Catalogues [hereafter TC], vol. i, 1903).

3 This was Sir William Noye, The Compleat Lawyer, 4th edn. (1667).

4 The correspondence between Pitt and Dr Pell is contained in British Library [hereafter BL], Add. Ms. 4279. See particularly Pitt to Pell, 19 April 1666, f. 201.

5 A.R. Hall and M.B. Hall, ed. and trans., The Correspondence of Henry Oldenburg, vol. vii, 1670-1 (Madison, 1970), p. 101.

6 Ibid, vol. xi, 1674-5 (1977), pp. 18-19.

7 TC, i, Michaelmas 1673, p. 153.

8 See illustration (p. 179 above) from John Ogilby and William Morgan, 'A New and Accurate Map of the City of London' (1676).

9 The material concerned with Pitt's shop is located in PRO, C.5, 538/15, 3 May 1680

10 [Moses Pitt], A Letter from Moses Pitt (1695), p. 15.

11 Paul G. Morrison, Index of Printers, Publishers and Booksellers in Donald Wing's Short-Title Catalogue (Charlottesville, 1955)

12 See James Sutherland, Defoe, 2nd edn. (1950).

13 Daniel Defoe, The Complete English Tradesman (1726 [for 1725]). The edition used for this paper is the third, published in two volumes in 1732. The spelling of 'Compleat' in the title was adopted in 1727. Hereafter Defoe, Tradesman.

14 ibid, vol. ii, p. 102.

15 ibid, p. 167.

16 The most useful studies of the Atlas project appear in E.G.R. Taylor, 'Robert Hooke and the cartographical projects of the late seventeenth century (1666-1696)', Geographical Journal, 90 (1937),

pp. 529-40, (hereafter Taylor, 'Robert Hooke'), and the same author's 'The English Atlas of Moses Pitt, 1680-83', Geographical Journal, 95 (1940), pp. 292-9. For the advertisements for the project in the London Gazette see Tyacke, London Map-Sellers, pp. 76-108.

17 For example Thomas Jefferys: see J.B. Harley, 'The bankruptcy of Thomas Jefferys, Imago Mundi, xx (1966), pp. 27-48.

18 For Scott see Harry Carter, A History of the Oxford University Press (Oxford, 1975), vol. i, pp.. 47-9 (hereafter Carter, Oxford Press), and for Owen, H.R. Plomer, A Dictionary of the Printers and Booksellers Who Were at Work in England Scotland and Ireland from 1668-1725, Oxford Bibliographical Society (1922).

19 Printed Proposals dated 3 May 1678 in BL, Add. MS. 4394, f. 405.

20 Carter, Oxford Press, p. 94.

21 ibid.

22 The agreement itself does not seem to have survived. However it is possible to reconstruct some of its content from the documents drawn up in 1685 for a case in Chancery between Guy and Parker on one side and Pitt on the other (Leake appears to have died prior to the case, perhaps as early as 1679), PRO, C.7, 260/8 (1685).

23 See, for example, his edition of Sir William Dugdale, A Short View of the Late Troubles (1681), 'Oxford at the Theater for Moses Pitt, London'. Most if not all copies contain a five-folio-page catalogue of books available from Pitt, including those printed at the Theatre. Pitt was in dispute with Richard Chiswell in 1686 over his share in a reprint of 'King Charles I's works with the Treaty of Uxbridge', the treaty figuring prominently in the Short View (PRO, SP, 44/71, p. 270).

24 Advertisements for volume I of the Atlas in the London Gazette between 7 July 1679 and 12 July 1680. Catalogus Variorum Librorum for the sale of Pitt's books on 24 February 1679 in BL, C 120 c. 2.

25 Moses Pitt, The Cry of the Oppressed (1691) (hereafter Pitt, The Cry), p. 101.

26 Peter Clark and Paul Slack, eds, Crisis and Order in English Towns 1500-1700 (1972), p. 336.

27 Norma Hodgson and Cyprian Blagden, The Notebook of Thomas Bennet and Henry Clements (hereafter Notebook), Oxford Bibliographical Society (1956), p. 5.

28 PRO, C.6, 243/71, 5 May 1681. A map of the area (reproduced above, p. 184) appears in J.T. Smith, Antiquities of Westminster (1807) as additional plate. See also M.H. Cox and P. Norman, eds, Survey of London, vol. x (1926) for information on the development of the estate but with no mention of Pitt.

29 These included properties in Shropshire and Portsmouth as well as in Shoe Lane in the City and between Chelsea and Parsons Green (PRO, C.9, 249/85, 2 May 1689).

30 The material on which the following section is based appears in PRO, C.5, 538/15, 3 May 1680. As well as Pitt's complaint, an answer by Dame Elizabeth Davies and Thomas Davies Esq., the widow and son of the original owner, is included.

31 The address given in Pitt's catalogue of 1681 is 'the Angel against the Great North-door of St. Pauls-Church'.

32 PRO, C.9, 249/85.

33 For the dispute with Hooke, see Taylor, 'Robert Hooke'.

34 The details of the apparently extended dispute with Guy and Parker are obscure and the timing difficult to establish; see Pitt, The Cry, pp. 113-15; PRO, C.7, 260/8; Carter, Oxford Press, p. 98.

35 PRO, C.7, 260/8.

36 For example PRO, C.6, 243/71, 5 May 1681; C.6, 249/71, 25 June 1684; C.6, 251/63, 1685.

37 Defoe, Tradesman, vol. i, p. 337.

38 ibid, vol. ii, p. vii.

39 John Dunton, The Life and Errors of John Dunton, ed. J.B. Nichols (1817), vol. i, p. 81 (hereafter Dunton, Life). Volume 2 contains additional works by Dunton.

40 Reference to Pitt's use of barter in a transaction with a Scottish bookseller in A Letter from Moses Pitt, p. 9.

41 Dunton, Life, vol. ii, pp. 445, 465.

42 ibid, vol. i, pp. 79-80.

43 A variety of other cases mentioned by Plomer and identified as for 'Trespass' or 'Assault' may have had a basis in actions for debt. A good example of individual financial collapse in 1685 appears in D.G. Vaisey, 'Anthony Stephens; the rise and fall of an Oxford bookseller', in Studies in the Book Trade, Oxford

Bibliographical Society (1975), pp. 91-117. The reintroduction of the licensing system created its own area of financial confusion; see Michael Treadwell, 'London trade publishers 1675-1750', The Library, 6, 4 (1982), p. 108.

44 Dunton, Life, vol. i, pp. 131, 214.

45 Pitt's relationship to Mill is specified in Pitt, The Cry, p. 116.

46 D.F. McKenzie, ed., Stationers Company Apprentices 1641-1700 (1974), 3032 (hereafter Apprentices)

47 Plomer, Dictionary (1922), entry for Hills.

48 A new edition of A Record of Auncient Histories and a Latin edition of the letters of Gerard Vossius. For the Vossius work see TC, vol. ii [Michaelmas 1689], p. 288 and Pitt, The Cry, p. 112.

49 Pitt, The Cry, p. 127. For material touching on Mill's Jamaican interest see Corporation of London Record Office (hereafter CLRO), Lord Mayors Court Depositions, Box 38, item dated 19 January 1683.

50 See the schedule of 'Moneys Received by Adiel Mill but not brought to Account' in PRO, C.9, 249/85.

51 A Catalogue for the sale on 30 November 1685, B.1. 821 i 4 (16). Pitt is identified in ms. only.

52 A Catalogue for the sale on 10 December 1685, ibid (18) and (19).

53 Pitt, The Cry, p. 116.

54 CLRO, Court of Aldermen, Repertory 90, f. 81v-82.

55 BL, Sloane Ms. 1674. The English multiples seem to be from the stock of John Martyn.

56 The auction of Mill's books took place on 9 February 1691.

57 PRO, C.9, 249/85.

58 Samuel Gellibrand; see McKenzie, Apprentices for 1672.

59 Hodgson and Blagden, Notebook, pp. 2-5.

60 PRO, C.9, 249/85, also Pitt, The Cry, p. 114, passim.

61 Stationers Company (hereafter SC), 'Bonds for Money Lent', 4 April 1671 to 30 January 1688.

62 Pitt, The Cry, pp. 135-7.

63 ibid, p. iii.

64 The best account of the legal process for debt, though concerned with a later period, is provided by Joanna Innes, 'The King's Bench Prison in the later eighteenth century', in John Brewer and John Styles, eds, An Ungovernable People (1980), pp. 250-98.

65 Defoe, Tradesman, vol. i, p. 166.

66 SC, 'Court Book G', f. 59, 5 May 1701 and f. 116, 5 March 1704. I am most grateful to Michael Treadwell for pointing out the bunching of insolvency cases reflected in the Stationers records of the 1690s. While the Company sometimes provided help for those in financial difficulty, it subsequently appeared that there was an almost formal process by which those who had compounded their debts were discharged from the Court; S.C. 'Court Book H', 7 November 1727.

67 Comment on London in a printed item on the legal process for debt (c. 1690) signed W.G. and apparently addressed to the House of Commons (BL, Add. Ms. 38, 856, f. 127).

68 These are described in PRO, C.9, 249/85.

69 ibid.

70 Cyprian Blagden, 'The memorandum book of Henry Rhodes, 1695-1720', The Book Collector, 3 (1954), p. 30.

71 Dunton, Life, vol. i, p. 79.

72 Sarah Malthus in ibid, vol. ii, p. 445.

73 Pitt, The Cry, p. 105.

74 A view of the house appears in John Kip, 'A prospect of the City of London, Westminster and St. James's Park' (c. 1710). Pitt claimed to have improved the adjacent park itself by draining and planting (The Cry, pp. 110-11). An official investigation into the tenure of the strip of land was made in 1690 (see PRO, Treasury Books, Warrants not Relating to Money, XIII, pp. 195-8).

75 Pitt, The Cry, pp. 111-12.

76 ibid, pp. 141, 153.

77 Walford as Scott's apprentice had been taken over by Mill with the books and appears in The Cry as his perjured supporter, pp. 138-41. Walford subsequently became the partner of Samuel Smith in the Pater-Noster-Row business.

78 Pitt, The Cry, p. 119.

79 ibid, p. 124.

80 ibid.

81 Sutherland, Defoe, pp. 43-4; Dunton, Life, vol. i, pp. 138-9.

82 The Life of Mr. Thomas Gent Printer, of York, Written by himself (1832), pp. 86, 137.

83 John Nichols, Literary Anecdotes of the Eighteenth Century, vol. i, (1812), pp. 50-67.

84 Pitt, The Cry, pp. 158-9.

85 ibid, pp. 144-5.

86 For obstruction by Mill see PRO, C.8, 547/12, 29 October 1691 and 12 November 1691.

87 Pitt, The Cry, pp. 153.

88 A mass of documents relating to the release of debtors from the London prisons under the Act of 1690 is preserved in the CLRO under the heading 'Insolvent Debtors'.

89 An Account of One Anne Jefferies (1696). At his death Pitt had almost completed 'A Catalogue of English Writers' which was never published (see Dunton, Life, vol. i, p. 234).

90 A Letter from Moses Pitt, pp. 13, 25-7. At the end of this work Pitt solicited the reader for money on behalf of the debtors through Lewis Prescot at Lincolns Inn, pp. 28-9.

91 Catalogus Variorum for the sale on 9 February 1691, BL, SC 1035 (I).

92 Will dated 8 March 1694 and proved 5 November 1695, PRO, Prob. II, 428.

93 PRO, SP 44/348, p. 186, 14 November 1700.

94 Will proved 8 October 1697, PRO, Prob. II, 440.

95 Dunton, Life, vol. i, pp. 233-4.

Depression and Innovation in the British and American Booktrade, 1819–1939

James Barnes

Trade depressions usually conjure up images of commercial contraction, unemployment, bankruptcy, and pessimism. For most booksellers and publishers in Great Britain and the United States, this has been all too true over the past two centuries. However, occasionally an individual or company has been able to weather the financial storm and turn the crisis to an advantage. These fortunate few comprise the subject of this chapter.

'Necessity is the mother of invention' could have been the motto for the book trade. For example, all three of the so-called 'paper-back revolutions' in American publishing history coincided with major crises in the economy.[1] Any number of other adverse conditions, both economic and social, can be cited for having either forced or enticed publishers and booksellers into new directions. Sometimes these turned into notable failures, but a surprising number resulted in spectacular successes.

In concentrating on economic impetuses to innovation, I do not mean to suggest that other kinds - political, social, legal, technological, and cultural - do not exist, for they clearly do. In this respect, one of my favourite passages, from James Lackington's memoirs, reflects the effects on the book trade of the turbulence of the French Revolution and the Napoleonic era.

> I have always found that bookselling is much affected by the political state of affairs. For as mankind are in search of amusements, they often embrace the first that offers; so that if there is anything in the newspapers of consequence, that draws many to the coffee house, where they chat away the evenings, instead of visiting the shops of booksellers - or reading at home. The best time for bookselling is when there is no kind of news stirring; then many of those

> who for months would have done nothing but talk of war or peace, revolutions and counterrevolutions, etc. etc., for want of other amusement will have recourse to books; so that I have often experienced that the report of war, or the trial of a great man, or indeed any subject that attracts the public attention, has been some hundreds of pounds out of my pocket in a few weeks.[2]

Lackington argued aptly that for every political crisis that diverted people from buying and reading books, there was probably a corresponding increase in the amount of time and money spent on newspapers, magazines, and casual conversation; or, to put it another way, while booksellers lost customers, the news vendors, coffeehouses, and pubs gained them.

Ever since I began to study the book trade I have been impressed by the impact that economic conditions have had upon it. Dibdin aptly characterised the typical middle-class penchant for bargains when he described the depressed London market in 1832: 'Men wished to get for five what they knew they could not formerly obtain for fifteen shillings.'[3] John Murray's comment to Gladstone in 1851 reveals the perennial predicament of many booksellers and publishers each time the economy turned downward:

> But it must be borne in mind that books are a luxury; when a time of distress comes the first expense to be curtailed is the purchase of books. That is done (without any outward display of economy) rather than laying down a carriage or dismissing servants.[4]

Others, like Murray's contemporary, G.R. Porter, viewed books in a quite different light and welcomed any lowering in their price: 'Books can no longer be considered, as they were in bygone times, a luxury, to be provided for the opulent, who alone as a class, could read and enjoy them. From year to year the circle is widening in which literature becomes almost a necessary of life...'[5] Since my early glimpses into these commercial vicissitudes, I have felt increasingly impelled to relate changes in economic conditions to corresponding ones in the publishing and marketing of books. I do not for a moment regard myself an economic determinist but rather an historian whose methods are eclectic. What follows is meant more by way of suggestion than proof.

During the nineteenth century especially, one finds no lack of trade-cycle depressions. They occurred with monotonous and, for those who lived through them, devastating regularity. Following the Napoleonic Wars, there were major panics in 1819, 1825-26, 1829-32, 1837-42, and 1847-48. Then the cycle lengthened considerably. Almost ten years separated the crises of 1857, 1863, 1873, and 1893, although there were lesser dips in between.[6] The fact that there were political and social crises concurrent with these severe fluctuations in the economy both simplifies and complicates our task. Let us consider the circumstances first in England, then in the United States, and conclude with a few observations appropriate to both.

Nowadays we so take for granted the nineteenth-century trend toward lower book prices that we often forget that the opposite occurred during the first quarter of that century. This earlier trend was due partly to the inflation that accompanied Britain's involvement in war from 1793 to 1815, and partly to the government's policy of discouraging the production and distribution of cheap printed matter by taxing manufactured paper, advertisements, and political newspapers. Whereas the average price of a new novel in the 1780s was 3s.6d., it rose to 10s.6d. by the 1820s.

Testifying before a Committee of the House of Commons in 1818, one printer observed: 'Books are a luxury, and the purchase of them has been confined to fewer people. In general, those who would be disposed to purchase books, have not the means of so doing, and are obliged to be frugal.'[7] If 10s.6d. was considered a luxury in 1818, it is clear that only middle- and upper-class readers could own a volume costing 31s.6d., and then only occasionally. More tempting bargains were offered in the form of non-copyrighted works in special reprinted editions and drastically reduced 'remainders'.

Following the panic of 1819, a few book entrepreneurs (most notably the firms of Whittingham and Limbird) reduced prices on new or recently published works, but it was not until 1825 that a major publisher like Constable greatly extended his markets by issuing works at

3s.6d. Unfortunately, before he could really launch his Miscellany he was forced into bankruptcy by the crisis of 1825-26. However, Constable reasoned that during times of economic hardship such a project made even more sense, so he continued planning for it, with the result that the first of these nonfiction volumes appeared in January 1827, followed by others in the series at three-week intervals

The scheme had to be abandoned shortly thereafter because Constable finances were beyond salvaging, but the experiment intrigued other leading firms in London and Edinburgh. In 1829, with trade still stagnant, John Murray launched his Family Library of new or nearly new nonfiction works and sold each volume for 5s. At about the same time Longman & Company began Lardner's Cabinet Cyclopaedia, Oliver & Boyd of Edinburgh came out with its Cabinet Library, and Colburn & Bentley inaugurated its National Library. In 1831 Colburn & Bentley even went so far as to take some of its backlist from five years or more, reissue the titles in attractive single volumes labelled Standard Novels, and sell them for 6s. each. Other lesser known publishers imitated the prestigious houses and claimed that their new series, like the others, were meant to offer the reading public a windfall of current literature at greatly reduced cost. In his book, <u>The English Common Reader</u>, Richard Altick nicely captures the mood of provisional optimism: 'Between 1827 and 1832, therefore, London and Edinburgh publishers behaved as if they stood on a peak in Darien, beholding for the first time a vast sea of common readers.'

Expectations of reaching a vast new readership were illusory for the very reasons that inspired them. In times of adversity middle-class book buyers were bound to retrench, and 5s. or 6s. a volume was still too dear. This held all the more true for artisans and clerks, whose salaries of two or three pounds a week could not possibl cover such purchases. Nonetheless, for every publisher like John Murr who had to give up his series after a few years, there was a Longman or a Bentley who carried on successfully, and their middle-class customers expected to be provided with new books at greatly reduced prices decade after decade.

For readers who were not willing to wait several years to sample the latest literary offerings, there was the option of subscribing to a circulating library. These libraries adjusted their fees depending upon the clientele, the class of books handled, and the frequency of borrowing, so that lower-class patrons might pay only a few shillings a year while middle-class borrowers were charged two guineas. There is little doubt that the number of circulating libraries grew steadily during the first half of the nineteenth century in response to high book prices, periodic trade slumps, and the recognition by the middle class that it was considered respectable to borrow in this fashion. The most successful of these lending libraries was begun by Charles Edward Mudie in the depression of 1842. His instincts directed him to offer new subscribers a tempting bargain in hard times, so he lowered his annual charge to one guinea instead of the usual two.

Hard-pressed middle-class readers also responded in increasing numbers to a form of instalment buying that Charles Dickens made popular in 1836-37 with Pickwick Papers. Publishing a work in weekly or monthly parts had been tried before by religious tract societies and producers of family bibles, but Pickwick Papers was different in that those who put down a shilling for each part knew they had secured the latest number. People with greater financial resources had no particular advantage over those of more modest means. Many more families felt that they could afford an occasional shilling for the latest part-issue, and they regarded it a marvel of thrift to be able to save one pound for the completed version.

Part-issues were among the many instances of an innovation that began in a year of relative prosperity and undoubtedly continued to be profitable during subsequent years of depression. From 1837 to 1842 many firms cut back and printed smaller impressions of books on their regular lists, yet they increased the printing of part-issues by Dickens and other novelists. One obvious advantage of part-issues was that they brought in a steady flow of cash from weekly or monthly sales and thus helped to meet paper and print expenses.

Travelling by train was another phenomenon in which a great many middle-class readers indulged and for which they required reading matter to help pass the time. A solution was found in the depressed year of 1848, when W.H. Smith launched his first railway bookstall in London's Euston Station. Although a publisher himself, Smith found it more advantageous to sell cheap editions of popular works produced by others. Soon a market developed in 'railway libraries' that stocked tried-and-true favourites and sold them for a few shillings each.

Throughout the first half of the nineteenth century one firm in particular prospered from the financial failures of others in the book trade: Thomas Tegg and Son. It dominated the remainder trade and acquired at vastly reduced prices the copyrights of works that had not sold well or whose proprietors had gone bankrupt. From 1825 to 1827 Tegg bought up some of Scott's copyrights in this way, and by 1834 he took over Murray's entire Family Library. By offering thousands of titles at only a few shillings per volume, Tegg created markets where none had existed before.

The aforementioned examples have illustrated ways in which publishe tried to lure middle- and upper-class readers into purchasing or borrowing books at significantly lower prices during times of economic distress. However, publishers and printers came increasingly to the realisation that lower-middle-class and working-class readers might also become bibliophiles if the contents were to their liking and the price low enough. At the end of the eighteenth century, there were cheap tracts produced by moralists who wished to inculcate upright behaviour and religion and were highly successful at publishin at the other end of the spectrum tales of romance and adventure were produced in the form of chapbooks and ballad broadsheets that sold for mere pennies. Literature designed for the mass market tended to fall into two broad categories: one that sought to improve, and another that was meant to pander. The pioneer efforts of Charles Knigh Henry Brougham, and other supporters of the Society for the Diffusion of Useful Knowledge produced literature of the first type. In the distressed conditions of the 1820s, they launched a Library of Useful Knowledge, each fortnightly issue of which cost 6d., and also a Library of Entertaining Knowledge, which sold for 2s. per part. Sales of some part-issues reached 20,000 copies, and as time went on it became evident that the purchasers came from the ranks of the lower middle class more often than from the working class. The society launched two other ventures aimed at its humblest patrons: the _Penny Cyclopaedia_ and the _Penny Magazine_, both of which were successful in spite of a general decline in the rest of the book trade. For more than a decade Charles Knight was able to sustain his vision of enlightening the masses through cheap and edifying publications, but eventually he was forced to concede defeat. A combination of government taxation and working-class indifference ultimately undermined his publishing enterprise.

A commercially more successful publisher who also provided 'wholesome' literature for the lower class was William Milner of Halifax. As a printer he found his business going from bad to worse, and so he decided to launch a clothbound series of cheap fiction reprints. Known as the Cottage Library, the series sold for 1s. per volume and soon attracted imitators. Milner extended the range of reprints to include such poets as Robert Burns, of whom he sold more than ten thousand copies in 1837 and more than thirty thousand by 1839.[9]

Books were not the only means publishers used to attract the pennies of the lower classes. Following the success of Charles Knight's _Penny Magazine_, others soon recognised the sales potential of cheap periodicals in times of economic distress. William and Robert Chambers began to sell their _Edinburgh Journal_ at three half-pence and, because they were not under any moral constraints, met with greater long-term success. As Richard Altick noted, 1832 was indeed the _annus mirabilis_ for cheap periodicals. 'Within a few months were born the _Half-Penny Magazine_, the _Christian's Penny Magazine_, the _London Penny Journal_, the _Girls' and Boys' Penny Magazine_, the _True Half-Penny Magazine_, _Dibdin's Penny Trumpet_, the _Penny Comic Magazine_, the _Penny Story_

Teller, and the Penny Novelist.'[10]

Preparing the way for cheap periodicals were the Sunday newspapers of the late eighteenth and early nineteenth centuries. Soon after the Battle of Waterloo, Robert Bell launched his Weekly Dispatch, which sold more than forty thousand copies by 1840. Later that year the Sunday Times became dissatisfied with its circulation of only about twelve thousand and began to serialise a novel by William Blanchard Rede entitled The History of a Royal Rake. This idea may well have been inspired by the depression-born weeklies published in America, Brother Jonathan and the New World. Serialisation caught on quickly in Britain. Edward Lloyd soon introduced stories into his Penny Sunday Times and Police Gazette and, by eschewing politics, avoided the Newspaper stamp duty.[11]

A Nottingham printer, Herbert Ingram, took the weekly publication one step further. He came to London in 1842 to start an illustrated weekly in which he could promote his own patent medicine. But the medicinal cure-all was rapidly eclipsed by the spectacular popularity of his new Illustrated London News, whose sales climbed steadily from twenty-five thousand to sixty thousand in its first year of publication. During the 1850s its circulation rose from 130,000 to two hundred thousand and a few years later to three hundred thousand. Although the weekly sold at the relatively high price of 6d., it provided so many illustrations that customers could not resist;[12] it also appealed primarily to the family. Recognising this, George Big started the Family Herald in 1842. Wholesome in tone, it combined cheapness with respectability and appealed to the lower middle class rather than to the working class.[13]

Almost every experiment calculated to lure middle-class readers into the market - remainders, library series, railway fiction, or cheap periodicals - had its counterpart in a cheaper version that sold for a penny or two and was aimed at the lower classes. Dickens's part-issues of Pickwick Papers were not only plagiarised in penny instalments but the idea of part-issues also was extended to a whole new genre of fiction known as 'penny bloods' or 'blood and thunder' tales or, later still, 'penny dreadfuls'. Edward Lloyd (1815-90) is generally acknowledged as the originator of 'penny bloods' in their familiar eight-page, double-column form, which was adorned by a lurid woodcut illustration on the cover. By 1836 he had spawned four part-issue series: Lives of the Most Notorious Highwaymen; The Gem or Romance, or Tales of Intense Interest; The History of Pirates of all Nations; and the Calendar of Horrors.[13] Lloyd's talent lay in exploiting and imitating the product of others, by creating his own cheap versions of Sunday newspapers or illustrated weeklies. His publishing career commenced in the calm of 1836, but it prospered especially during the chaotic years of 1837-42. While the British middle and upper classes fretted over the Corn Laws and Chartism, the lower classes sought escape in romance, gothic horror, highway robbery, and criminal intrigue.[15]

During the 1860s the authors of the 'penny dreadfuls' substituted youthful heroes in place of the standard adult villains in order to appeal to a younger audience. The dozen or so juvenile magazines that featured violence and crime provoked a strong middle-class reaction of distaste and condemnation. To counteract the pernicious influence of these publications, the Religious Tract Society began the year 1879 with a new, illustrated weekly, Boy's Own Paper. Within six months it reached an incredible circulation of five hundred thousand copies, and the following year witnessed the appearance of Girl's Own Paper. Together the two weeklies vanquished many of their competitors.

On the surface it may not be apparent that these two weeklies originated in a depressed economy. However, what made them unusual was that they were publications of a society and not a trade publisher. This had not been the Society's intention, but no commercial firm would undertake the project because it was presumed no one could produce a juvenile weekly that combined wholesomeness and adventure. Other reasons commercial publishers may have had for declining to issue the new periodicals included the altogether discouraging economic climate - business was slow and credit scarce - coupled with the recognition that existing publishing patterns would be difficult to change. The Society, on the other hand, had no choice but to attempt the impossible, and it was not long before it congratulated itself for being able to further its overseas activities with income derived from the sale of its magazines.[16]

Viewed from a different perspective, the Society succeeded largely because it had sufficient resources to experiment with a new product in a highly competitive field. The history of the British and American book trade abounds with stories of firms that either perished or survived depending on their ability to make timely acquisitions or sell literary property. Thus, the timely extension or withholding of credit (or property) was integral to successful publishing. We have seen how Archibald Constable went bankrupt in the 1820s in spite of owning such a valuable asset as the Encyclopaedia Britannica. Adam Black's ability to raise enough money to acquire this encyclopaedic work enabled him to reap its rewards for the rest of the century, which included the preparation and sale of the ninth edition during 1875-1888. An estimated half-million sets were sold in the British market, even though Black was unable to prevent at least twelve American piracies of part or all of the work. When the heirs of Adam and Charles Black decided to part with the Encyclopaedia at the end of the century, it was bought by the financially ailing London Times with help from an American, Horace E. Hooper. When Times subscribers were offered the whole set at half price, the sales that were realised immediately generated close to £500,000 in profit.[17]

Another example of the necessity of having adequate financial resources is the story behind Everyman's Library, which would have foundered had its owner, J.M. Dent, not been able to secure timely credit. Mindful of the risks of launching an extensive series of hardcover reprints, Dent set aside £10,000 to cover anticipated costs. From earlier years he had known all too well what it was like to be near bankruptcy; thus he was determined not to incur debt from financing the Everyman project. Ironically, the initial volumes sold so well that too much capital had to be tied up in reprinting new stock. Soon there were precious few funds left to publish additional volumes in the series. Furthermore, his bindery in London could not keep up with the demand due to a shortage of space, so Dent decided to move his plant as well as his work force thirty-four miles out of London to a new town in Hertfordshire. This was an added expense that had not been anticipated, but it was only the first of many such surprises. By moving the workers to the proposed site, he had hoped to improve their living conditions and enable them to go home for a midday meal. However, flats and houses in the new town were too small, so Dent was forced to build a number of cottages for his employees. It was then discovered that the land designated for the bindery was not level. The simplest solution was to dig a full basement under the building, a decision that then led Dent to install his printing works in the basement. Before he knew it, Dent had spent an additional £20,000. In his memoirs he mused:

> As paper was the cause of the large capital outlay, I resolved to lay the matter before my paper-makers, showing them what large sums I had owing to me and the necessity of keeping the books in print. They were very good and helped me by extended credit, and I was able to get on for twelve months without much difficulty.

Somewhat later he noted:

> My original £10,000 had long since disappeared, but money was beginning to come back, though of course it was inadequate for all of the undertakings which grew out of one another with such rapidity. In spite of myself I was forced to get money from the bank, and I also had to appeal to my good friends the paper-makers, who, becoming somewhat alarmed at the amount of my credit, refused to extend it.

Because Dent was a major customer he was able to take his business elsewhere and secure further credit, but his case reminds us that innovation depends upon solvency, whether the times are prosperous or hard.[18]

Let us now consider the great depression of the 1930s. Not surprisingly, this was a crucial formative period for booktrade development. Although the idea of book tokens had been suggested in the 1920s, it was not until 1932 that Harold Raymond of Chatto

& Windus acted on it. There was perhaps nothing inherently depression-related about such a scheme, and yet its growing success during the 1930s suggested several underlying connections. Because only members of the Associated Booksellers could acquire tokens, there was some incentive to maintain a strong trade association at a time when business was slow. As more and more bookshops sold and redeemed the tokens, customers grew eager to have them and usually bought more than the value of their gift tokens. Given the tight money supply at the time, the tokens could be redeemed only for books. Although book tokens continued to flourish in prosperous times, their origin seems to be distinctly related to belt-tightening and modest expenditures.[19]

Another phenomenon that began during the 1920s but came into its own in the 1930s was the literary book club. The first such organisation in Britain was called the Book Society, no doubt inspired by the Book-of-the-Month Club and the Literary Guild in America. It followed the American example and avoided underselling, offered new titles at reduced prices made possible by its large-volume purchases, and thus enabled subscribers to feel they were keeping up with the latest and best literature of the day. Among the most successful of the British clubs was the Left Book Club. Begun in 1936 by Victor Gollancz, it was initially conceived as a vehicle for distributing some of its founder's own avant-garde publications. At the end of its first month, six thousand subscribers had joined, and by 1939 there were sixty thousand members. Not only did the club provide a new title each month, it also fostered discussion groups, lectures, and even group tours. As one historian noted:

> It coincided with the triumph of the Popular Front in France and with the beginning of British interest in the Spanish Civil War. The economic climate in 1936 also contributed to the Club's rapid success. The depression had passed its worst stage, and a scheme based on monthly contributions was workable, while the constant danger of economic crisis kept the enthusiasm of Club members at a high pitch.[20]

Gollancz recognised the potential for a special-interest club sooner than the rest of the book trade. Eventually many publishers followed suit by establishing clubs devoted to history, gardening, antiques, and recorded music.

Probably the most famous example of an innovation born of the depression was the founding of Penguin Books by Allen Lane in 1935. As one of Lane's business associates later recalled, there was little doubt as to his motivation:

> Allen Lane's decision to try his luck with paperback reprints of successful novels and biographies was little more than a rather desperate last throw to save the fortunes of a small publishing house, The Bodley Head, which had become famous in the 1890s, had run into financial difficulties during the 1920s...and was on the verge of bankruptcy after the slump of 1929 and the great depression that followed.[21]

In stark contrast to Dent, who began his Everyman series with more than adequate equity but later found himself in debt, Lane started Penguin with a mere £100, and very soon began to see profits roll in.

What distinguished the early Penguin books was not their paper binding nor even their low selling price of 6d. Rather, they were remarkable in that they were reprints of other publishers' works that were still being sold in hardcover editions. Financially, the breakeven point fell somewhere between fifteen thousand and twenty thousand copies for each title. The early success of Penguin books can be attributed in part to the thirty-four-thousand-copy purchases of each of the first ten Penguin titles by the book buyer at F.W. Woolworth Company, whose wife happened to be present when Lane was trying to persuade him to stock the books. Because she was convinced that the average shopper at Woolworth would readily buy such book bargains, her husband agreed to carry them.

The shoestring operation that was Penguin books in its infancy had as its first business address the crypt of Holy Trinity Church on Euston Road. There the delivery vans would discharge their cargo in the church cemetery, from where it was conveyed by a drop chute to the office underground. As Ian Norrie described it, 'The petty cash was kept in one empty tomb, the invoices in another. The packers pinned up nudes above their benches and the management arranged for blinds which could be quickly pulled down to obscure them when the Vicar paid a call to 'see how the dear boys were getting on'.[22]

During its first year (1935), Penguin issued around twenty titles. Thereafter an average of fifty new titles appeared annually until the outbreak of the war. All were fiction reprints taken from the current lists of the leading publishers and, as a consequence, Lane was frequently put to the task of having to convince his professional colleagues that Penguin paperbacks would not jeopardize the hardcover market but rather would lure readers to buy what they had previously ignored or borrowed. In 1937 the Penguin editions were joined by twenty nonfiction titles that were called Pelicans, which were received equally well. Three years later a series of children's books, called Puffins, appeared. Penguin did make an occasional departure from strictly reprint publishing and would publish original material (usually dealing with a contemporary political or economic issue) as a so-called Penguin Special. World War II, far from hurting Penguin, opened up a vast market for cheap paperbacks among members of the armed forces.[23]

The situation in the United States during this period will be examined, somewhat briefly, as an existing work deals in considerable detail with the years 1837-43.[24] Our discussion will begin with the depression of 1857 and will use case studies in an effort to establish a pattern.

The 'dime novels' of Beadle & Adams first appeared in 1860 and seem to have been a by-product of the hard times immediately preceding their publication. Erastus Beadle began a publishing business with his brothers in Buffalo, New York, during the early 1850s, but it was not long before his brothers grew discouraged and left. Unable to carry on by himself, Erastus sold the printing plant in 1855 and headed west to speculate in land that was then being sold in the newly acquired Nebraska Territory. However, this venture failed and Beadle was forced to return to the printing trade in Buffalo. During the

1857 depression, he decided to risk moving to New York City, where he published miscellaneous cheap reprints until he finally hit upon the scheme that eventually made him famous. Beadle's Dime Novels often sold for a nickel and were roughly one hundred pages long; decked in bright yellow or orange wrappers, they quickly became the rage. The conditions created by the Civil War substantially helped the sales of these tales of mystery and adventure, which had reached four million copies by 1865.

Of the three paperback revolutions in American history referred to by Tebbel, the first occurred in 1837-43. The second started with the depression of 1873, and the firm generally credited with touching it off was R.R. Donnelley & Sons of Chicago.[25] Richard Robert Donnelley was one of several partners in a printing and publishing business that grew steadily from 1865 to 1870. Thus encouraged, they constructed a new plant and had already installed the presses when the great Chicago fire of 1871 destroyed everything. Two years later Donnelley tried again to expand his firm, but this time the depression struck. Printers had to be laid off and a skeleton crew of forty-two workers carried on until the firm finally landed a contract to produce the Chicago City Directory. While this project was underway, the company could justify increasing its work force to more than eighty, but upon completion of the directory Donnelley faced the problem of redundant employees. At this juncture Donnelley's partner, Alexander T. Loyd, proposed the now familiar solution of publishing cheap reprints, which would both keep the presses going and attract additional customers by their low prices. Typical of most American entrepreneurs, he appropriated noncopyrighted British and American works. Appearing first in January 1875, the opening numbers of the Lakeside Library had twenty-four three-column pages and appeared twice a month at a price of ten cents each. The prospectus promoted the series as follows:

> The great popular want of to-day is CHEAP, GOOD LITERATURE. There is enough and to spare of the CHEAP, and no lack of the GOOD, but a woeful poverty of both combined. Dime Novels are issued by the million and good books by the thousand, but to the mass of readers the one is as distasteful

> as the other is inaccessible. The favored few accumulate extensive and costly libraries, but the many must content themselves with literary Weeklies, cheap, and equally poor, Novels, and perhaps, the Magazines, with only occasional Books, which, after all, form not only the foundation but most of the superstructure of sound and desirable mental culture.
>
> Scarcely a week passes but the reader of this is reminded by a friend's praise of one book, or an extract in his local paper from another, that his library fails to keep even pace with his wants, and also, unfortunately, that the length of his purse forbids its desired extension.
>
> The aim of the present series of publications is to cure this evil - to make the BEST BOOKS as cheap as the literary trash now flooding the country, to offer GOOD LITERATURE at the price of the poor and pernicious. It takes possession of the vast middle-ground, with dime novels and 'blood and thunder' stories on the one hand, and costly, unattainable books on the other.
>
> In brief, the theory of the omnipresent, inexpensive daily and weekly Newspaper, is carried into the hitherto exclusive domain of literature, and its treasures popularized and made free to all.

The second issue further extolled the virtues of cheapness.

> Very few readers care for the expensive paper and elaborate binding that make the better class of novels, tales, travels, etc., so costly as to be beyond the means of the masses. What is wanted is simply the author's work, complete and unabridged as it leaves his pen, clearly printed on good paper, in a convenient form for perusal and preservation. This want the Library fully supplies.

By the end of its first year, the Lakeside Library showed distinct signs of having been accepted. A new instalment came out every ten days, each containing thirty-two pages. Soon forty pages appeared weekly, and efforts were made to persuade the post office that the issues could be classified as magazines and therefore qualify for reduced postal rates. Besides being sold by subscription, the instalments were distributed through a large network of newsstands where many readers of modest means could buy them.

For a while the Lakeside Library dominated the market for cheap but respectable reprints, but before long rival series emerged. Most formidable among them was George Munro's Seaside Library, which was published in New York. It had much larger financial resources and produced three time as many volumes as did the Chicago competition, so that by the late 1870s Seaside boasted a list of six hundred titles compared to Lakeside's two hundred. In the Lakeside Library's ninety-eighth number (1877) the following note of concern was issued:

> The various publishers of dime novels, sensational trashy weekly papers, etc., finding no market for their pernicious stuff since the inauguration of 'The Lakeside' cheap reprints of good reading, are now seeking by formidable imitations of the Lakeside editions to steal the benefits of our wide-spread advertising and the popularity ensuing, from the cheap publications of good literature.

By the time Lakeside issued number 192 (1878) this note of apprehension had become far more shrill:

> We would caution our readers against counterfeits and imitations of our popular The Lakeside Library put forth by certain unscrupulous New York publishers. These counterfeits are published in miserably small, poor type on poor paper with only one coarse illustration. The unreadable fine type of these counterfeits will soon dim or even utterly destroy the strongest eyesight. Beware of them!

Alas, Donnelley was forced to concede the contest in the spring of 1879 and sold his Lakeside Library, numbering 270 issues, to his arch rival Munro. As was so often the case, the creator of the new product did not enjoy his achievement very long before competition became fierce and the market glutted.

The 1880s saw a change in the size of the popular paperback. Quartos gave way increasingly to the more convenient duodecimos, while the number of major firms producing them increased: there were fourteen by the end of 1870, twenty-three by the end of the 1880s, and fifty on the eve of the 1893 depression. All the while that this tremendous expansion was taking place, one man, John Lovell, was trying to monopolise paperback production by buying the plates and stock of his competitors in the hope of controlling the market and putting a halt to the ruinous price-cutting. His failure, and the consequent bankruptcy of his United States Book Company in 1893, was the most spectacular of many similarly ambitious schemes.

By the twentieth century fewer than a half-dozen recognised paperback publishers remained, the largest being Street & Smith.

Its success can be attributed in part to the failure of John Lovell and in part to its authors, who included Gilbert Patten, Edward Stratemeyer, and Horatio Alger, the creators of heroes such as Nick Carter, Frank Merriwell, the Rover Boys, the Motor Boys, and Tom Swift. The 1893 depression disgorged an estimated seven to eight million paperbacks onto the market, many of which were bought by Street & Smith and enabled that firm to savour the commanding market position for which Lovell had so longed.[26]

Of the American book clubs, we will discuss briefly the most famous, the Book-of-the-Month Club (BOMC), because it raises some rather puzzling questions regarding factors that either promoted or impeded survival and growth in the depression years. Begun in 1924, the BOMC attracted forty-five thousand subscribers during its first year. An impartial jury of literary experts would select one of the best books of the year as a monthly selection that would then be offered to subscribers, who were expected to purchase it at the moderate price of $3. Later this requirement was reduced to four books per year. By 1927 membership was up to sixty thousand and two years later had risen to 110,000. With the 1929 crash, people cancelled subscriptions, and because the cost of securing new members kept rising, prospects for growth looked dim. A low point was reached in 1932, when several of the club's leading executives resigned. By 1935, however, things had turned around, and by 1940 over 350,000 people belonged to the club.

How does one account for such a reversal during the depths of the depression? Perhaps it can be explained better by the growing sense of confidence in the nation than by any specific policy changes made by BOMC. Yet planned purchasing was attractive in such times of retrenchment because it allowed people to avoid impulse buying and still commit themselves to a minimum of four worthwhile and popular books each year. The club itself also took measures to make its offerings more attractive and tempting. Opposed in principle to radical price-cutting, BOMC resorted to other incentives, such as offering a free book with every two purchases, allowing new subscribers to receive the current monthly selection free without obligation to join the club, or providing premiums in the form of especially costly and deluxe editions at cut-rate prices. The club also stopped buying its monthly selections directly from the publisher and began paying a royalty to acquire the printing plates from the original firm so that it could issue its own special club edition.[27]

In 1938 the U.S. post office gave a helping hand to book clubs by reducing their rates. While the charge had ranged previously from seven to fifteen cents per pound depending upon distance, the new regulations proclaimed a uniform one-cent postage. This change may have been largely in response to congressional and public pressure and contrasts markedly with the earlier policies of the post office that put cheap paperback reprints out of business in the 1840s and the 1870s.[28]

There was also an American version of the Penguin. Heedless of Allen Lane's success, most American booksellers and publishers were unenthusiastic about paperbacks in 1939, especially since the United States had comparatively few bookshops within easy reach of potential buyers. What did exist in every town and village, however, were news-stands, druggists, and cigar stores, and these became outlets for the new Pocket Book series. As with dime novels and Penguins, Pocket Books were bolstered enormously by the outbreak of war. Within six years over one hundred million copies were published, many of which were contracted by the U.S. government for distribution to the armed forces. The logo of Pocket Books was a kangaroo, and as one historian noted: 'They had highly attractive covers of the kind that appealed to readers of periodicals and comics.'[29]

Now that we have cited examples and set forth illustrations, it is perhaps appropriate to draw one or two conclusions. If necessity _is_ the mother of invention, as we suggested at the outset, it cannot be said to be the only stimulus to innovation. However, our purpose here has been to demonstrate that severe economic crises often encourage new directions and undertakings in spite of conditions of chaos and commercial devastation. Although lowering prices has been the usual response to economic depression and the hopeful strategy to attract the public's dwindling income, an alternative was found in raising prices for books aimed at a narrow but well-to-do clientèle. Circulating libraries were a case in point, as was vanity subscription publishing, which is not dealt with here.

Experiments that began in times of comparative prosperity often managed to survive a subsequent downturn in the economy. This was especially true for part-issues, which allowed customers to spread payments over a long period of time. The same applied to magazine subscribers, who found they could 'pay as they read', so to speak. Finally, we have noted instances in which individuals sought to improve their lot by launching bold undertakings that may or may not have been responses to trade depressions but that were innovations born of adverse circumstances. The ability to command credit and solicit customers simultaneously often made the difference between success and failure for many publishing ventures.

By emphasising the economic impetuses to innovation, I have tended to ignore other factors, such as technological change, individual genius, shifts in popular taste, and relevant legal decisions. Yet it must be remembered that members of the booktrade were first and foremost business people, and their decisions to act or to refrain from acting depended primarily on their perception of the economic climate.

Notes

Acknowledgement: Reprinted from Books and Society in History with permission of the R.R. Bowker Company, copyright © 1983 by Xerox Corporation.

1 The notion of three paperback revolutions figures prominently in John Tebbel's four-volume A History of Book Publishing in the United States (New York, 1972-81).

2 As quoted in J.J. Barnes, Free Trade in Books: A Study of the London Book Trade Since 1800 (Oxford, 1964), pp. 113-14.

3 As quoted in S. Bennett, 'John Murray's family library and the cheapening of books in early nineteenth-century Britain', Studies in Bibliography, 29 (1976), p. 158.

4 Murray to Gladstone, 3 September 1851, as quoted in Barnes, op. cit. p. 79.

5 ibid. p. 96.

6 For those who seek to correlate trade fluctuations with levels of political and social discontent, see W.W. Rostow, British Economy of the Nineteenth Century (Oxford, 1948), pp. 33, 124-125; and G. Rude, 'Protest and punishment in nineteenth-century Britain', Albion 5 (1973), pp. 1-23.

7 The subject of increasing book prices is dealt with briefly by Graham Pollard in his unpublished Sandars lectures of 1959; lecture No. 4, typescript p. 39. For the years 1800-24 and the printer's quotation of 1818, see R.D. Altick, The English Common Reader (Chicago, 1957), pp. 260-2.

8 ibid. p. 274. For Murray's Family Library series, see Bennett, op. cit. passim. See also Barnes, op. cit. p. 111.

9 V.E. Neuburg, Popular Literature (Harmondsworth, 1977), pp. 177-8 and 184.

10 Altick, op. cit. p. 338.

11 For a discussion of Sunday newspapers, see H. Hobson et al., The Pearl of Days: An Intimate Memoir of the Sunday Times, 1822-1972 (1972), pp. 3-25; and L. James, Fiction for the Working Man, 1830-50 (Harmondsworth, 1974), pp. 39-40.

12 C. Hibbert, The Illustrated London News (1975).

13 James, op. cit. p. 44.

14 P. Haining, ed., The Penny Dreadful (1976), pp. 14, 24, 30.

15 Concerning Edward Lloyd, see ibid. p. 30; Hobson, op. cit. p. 15; James, op. cit. pp. 29, 39-43, 51; and Neuburg, op. cit. pp. 170-1.

16 P. Dunae, 'Boys Own Paper: origins and editorial policies', Private Library, 9 (1976), pp. 123-58.

17 Barnes, op. cit. p. 147; F.A. Mumby and I. Norrie, Publishing and Bookselling (1974), pp. 221-2; P. Kruse, 'Piracy and Britannica', Library Quarterly 33 (1963), pp. 313-28.

18 J.M. Dent, The Memoirs of J.M. Dent, 1849-1923 (1928), pp. 124-31; E. Rhys, Everyman Remembers (New York, 1931), pp. 234-6.

19 Book tokens are discussed in Barnes, op. cit. p. 151; Mumby and Norrie, op. cit. p. 315; and T. Joy, The Truth about Bookselling (1964), pp. 96-9.

20 S. Samuels, 'The Left Book Club', Journal of Contemporary History, I (1966), pp. 65-86.

21 H. Schmoller, 'The Paperback Revolution', in Essays in the History of Publishing, ed. A. Briggs (1974), p. 297.

22 Mumby and Norrie, op. cit. p. 365.

23 For further information about Penguin Books, see Penguin's Progress, 1935-1960 (Harmondsworth, 1960); and W.E. Williams, The Penguin Story, 1935-1956 (Harmondsworth, 1956). I am indebted to Robin Myers for calling my attention to these and other sources used in the preparation of this article.

24 See J.J. Barnes, Authors, Publishers and Politicians: The Quest for an Anglo-American Copyright Agreement, 1815-54 (London and Columbus, 1974), especially chap. I.

25 I would like to acknowledge my gratitude to the Donnelley Company for permitting me to examine the extant archives in its memorial library. Although the evidence is fragmentary, a fairly clear picture emerges as to how and why Richard Robert Donnelley began to issue cheap reprints in the 1870s.

26 For background on John Lovell and on Street & Smith, see Tebbell, op. cit. vol. ii, pp. 487-507.

27 Book of the Month Club, 'Special 50th Anniversary Supplement, Book of the Month Club News, April 1976; Tebbel, op. cit. vol. 3, pp. 386-90, 493-8; C. Madison, Book Publishing in America (New York, 1966), pp. 393-4.

28 For some discussion of postal rates and how they have affected publishing ventures in the United States, see Barnes, Authors, Publishers and Politicians, pp. 18-23; Tebbel, op. cit. vol. ii, p. 496. For information about rates for mailing books in the 1930s, I am indebted to the director, Office of Rates, US Postal Service.

29 Madison, op. cit. p. 548.

Publishing Pathways Series

Maps and Prints: Aspects of the English Booktrade	Robin Myers and Michael Harris
Author/Publisher Relations during the Eighteenth and Nineteenth Centuries	Robin Myers and Michael Harris
Sale and Distribution of Books from 1700	Robin Myers and Michael Harris
Development of the English Book Trade	Robin Myers and Michael Harris (out of print)
Publishing East and West	Toyohiko Yoshizaki (out of print)
Out-house Publishing	Colin Ridler (out of print)

Now distributed by:

Chadwyck-Healey Ltd
Cambridge Place
Cambridge CB2 1NR
U.K.

Chadwyck-Healey Inc.
1021 Prince Street
Alexandria, VA 22314
U.S.A.